REPRESENTATIVE
PRACTICES

AMERICAN PHILOSOPHY SERIES
Douglas R. Anderson and Jude Jones, series editors

REPRESENTATIVE
PRACTICES

Peirce, Pragmatism, and
Feminist Epistemology

KORY SPENCER SORRELL

FORDHAM UNIVERSITY PRESS   NEW YORK   2004

American Philosophy Series No. 15
ISSN 1073-2764

Library of Congress Cataloging-in-Publication Data

Sorrell, Kory Spencer.
    Representative practices : Peirce, pragmatism, and feminist epistemology /
Kory Sorrell.—1ˢᵗ ed.
        p. cm. -- (American philosophy series ; no. 15)
    Includes bibliographical references and index.
    ISBN 0-8232-2354-X
    1. Peirce, Charles S. (Charles Sanders), 1839–1914—Contributions in
philosophy of representation. 2. Representation (Philosophy) 3. Feminist
theory. I. Title. II. Series.
    B945.P44S67 2004
    121'.68—dc22

                                                                    2004013166

Printed in the United States of America
08 07 06 05 04 5 4 3 2 1
First edition

Contents

Abbreviations

CP   *The Collected Papers of Charles Sanders Peirce* (1931)

EP1   *The Essential Peirce,* Vol. 1 (1992)

EP2   *The Essential Peirce,* Vol. 2 (1998)

PS   *Pierce on Signs* (1991)

PW   *Philosophical Writings of Peirce* (1955)

SW   *Charles S. Peirce: Selected Writings* (1958)

W1   *Writings of Charles S. Peirce* (1984)

Foreword

E dward W. Said insists, "authority can, indeed must, be analyzed" (1978, 19). Kory Spencer Sorrell fully agrees with this claim. In his attempt to explain epistemic authority, however, he refuses to explain it away. We need to come to terms with such authority, to come to more thickly descriptive and consistently critical terms than we have done thus far. This means not only confronting the actuality and indeed ineluctability of epistemic authority, but also acknowledging our commitments and appeals to those whose voices are, in *particular* circumstance and concerning *specific* issues, more authoritative than other voices. The question of who counts as an epistemic authority cannot be decided anywhere but on the ground, in the diverse local contexts in which the merits of conflicting claims are assessed.

Hence, we are offered in this work a rich, nuanced analysis of epistemic authority eschewing the widespread tendency to construe any exercise of authority as the arbitrary imposition of one party's private preferences on others. The wholesale debunking (or dissolution) of authority is no part of Sorrell's project; central to this work is the painstaking analysis of how authoritative persons might, often in the face of severe opposition, come to be recognized as such.

The inability to recognize such persons is intimately connected to the inability to allow for any preferences except for purely private ones. Conversely, the recognition of legitimate authority is inseparable from the acknowledgment of shared (or sharable) values on the part of those who constitute a community, no matter how inchoate or implicit. Indeed, Sorrell's critical analysis of epistemic authority is undertaken in the service of shared values, envisioned as integral

features of our shared practices. Although all human values are ultimately rooted in the consummatory experiences of the human
organism, deliberation regarding such experiences enables us (in the
words of John Dewey) to "steady, vitalize and expand judgments in
creation of new goods and conservation of old goods" (1988a, 311).

In the foreground of Sorrell's investigation is reliance upon Charles
S. Peirce's technical doctrine of categories and theory of signs, but in
the background is Dewey's pragmatic understanding of moral criticism.
"After the first dumb, formless experience of a thing as good, subsequent perception of the good contains," Dewey insists, "at least a germ
of critical reflection" (1988a, 300). That is, such reflection is immanent
in our experience of what we take to be inherently worthwhile or fulfilling. "Criticism is reasonable and to the point, in the degree in which
it extends and deepens these factors of intelligence found in immediate
taste and enjoyment" (1988a, 300). The unending work of moral criticism is performed for the sake of instituting and thereby securing
more enduring and encompassing values (see, e.g., 1988a, 302).

From the perspective of such criticism, the utterly haphazard enjoyment of purely episodic goods comes to be seen for what it is—a style
of living, encouraged by advertisers and others, in which sustaining
fulfillments are impossible and intense pleasures are all too fleeting,
precarious, and costly. A contrasting ideal takes hold of the moral
imagination, the ideal of a life in which integrated fulfillments of an
enduring, encompassing, and emancipatory character are deliberately
cultivated. Though idiosyncratic and episodic pleasures are not in the
least to be disparaged, widely shared and regularly recurrent ones need
to be nurtured, precisely because they demand so much in the way of
deference and sacrifice. Also the intensity of enjoyment is not necessarily reduced by the enjoyment being widely shared; indeed, extensively shared goods might be intensively felt ones, and their intensity
might be in part a function of their being communally shared.

The accent here falls not on those values we actually happen to share,
but on those we might come to share as the result of wider experience
and deeper deliberation as well as of more thoroughgoing identification with others. In our world, one in which globalization so often

intensifies ancient hatreds and generates new antipathies, the effective cultivation of shared values becomes a more urgent task than ever before (not least of all because global networks of communication and technological innovations in weaponry render vulnerable even those nations possessing the largest armies and best weapons). At the very least, such cultivation of these values requires enlarged sympathy, especially with those others whom we have been enculturated to degrade, despise, or even vilify. We are always already connected with those whom we are inclined to denounce or nullify. However inchoate and unacknowledged, these connections provide some bases for assisting in the growth of more extensive, stable, and stabilizing connections. That is, they provide the bases for wider realizations of the human community. The shared values actually in place are thus invaluable for those we might yet secure.

Peirce's conception of thirdness is, in Sorrell's work, given not only a pragmatic stamp but also a human face, for this conception is cashed out in terms of generality, and, in turn, generality is connected to processes of generalization (thus, the ideal of generalizability). These processes are themselves envisioned here as work needing to be done by humans in the various sites of their everyday lives. Accordingly, the given of actually shared values, practices, and narratives gives way to the work of *trying out* their locally inherited forms in novel locations and innovative ways. Determining the limits of generality—the extent to which a value or practice, mode of representation or genre of narration, might be extended beyond the site of its origination or current predominance—is an experimental question. Too much contemporary theorizing tries to determine these limits a priori, from on high. Sorrell offers multiple considerations, amounting to a compelling argument, of why the limits of generalizability can be worked out only experimentally, on the ground. On his insightful reading of the pragmatic tradition, the work of critical intelligence encompasses working out the experiential possibilities of shared human values beyond the narrow, arbitrary limits of our diverse yet overlapping histories.

Today we are sensitive, perhaps hypersensitive, to the possibility that an appeal to authority might provide a cover for privilege. Sorrell wants to maintain and, indeed, enhance this suspicion without debunking entirely the ideal of authority. So, too, in his endeavor to account for the mechanisms, processes, and evaluations by which representations of facts, situations, and preferences are generated, sustained, and contested, he is unwilling to jettison the ideal of objectivity. Some representations are more reliable and thus useful than others, and one of the main reasons (if not the main reason) why this is so is that these representations are more objective than are their rivals.

We might represent (as Richard Rorty tends to do) the task of representation as one involving or demanding a perspective beyond the pragmatic spiral of our experimentally warranted representations. If we do, only two options are apparently available to us: either we can argue for the possibility of such a perspective, or we can reject this possibility and, along with it, the notion of representation itself. If we take the first option, we rescue representation at the cost of an alliance with some form of transcendentalism. Only a transexperiential vantage point, a perspective above the pragmatic spiral of our inherently fallible representations, appears to allow us to draw in a principled manner the distinction between representation and reality. The incredibility of such a perspective, however, inclines many to reject representationalism along with what might be called (though somewhat misleadingly) transcendentalism. For the antirepresentalionalist, then, the distinction between representation and reality collapses. With insouciance, the antirepresentationalist bids good riddance to representation. Such a theorist urges us to shift our concern from accurate representations to novel vocabularies and especially to liberating metaphors (ones freeing us from constraining or debilitating facets of our linguistic or cultural inheritance).

Sorrell in effect deconstructs the dualism between an antipragmatic realism and an antirepresentational pragmatism. Though not in the least slighting the importance of such vocabularies and metaphors, he is no more willing to allow for precluding the possibility of accurate representations than he is for disallowing the possibility of reasonable authority, progressively shared values, or indefinitely applicable generalizations. He ingeniously deploys the resources of Peirce's pragmatism, in particular the doctrine of categories and theory of signs, to make a forceful case for community, continuity, generality, mediation, representation, and much else. There are more accurate and useful ways of representing the work of representation than those put forth by unpragmatic realists and the neopragmatist critics of such realists, just as there are more inclusive and thus democratic, more effective and thus authoritative ways of authorizing (or accrediting) human authorities.

Sorrell's nuanced defense of pragmatic realism is a truly constructive endeavor in a twofold sense. It incorporates within itself the most useful insights of what is commonly identified today as constructivism, but it does so on the basis of a constructive critique of social constructivism and other widely influential doctrines (e.g., feminist standpoint theory and Rortyean neopragmatism). That is, Sorrell carefully works through an array of theories bearing upon representation, mediation, and allied topics, theories ranging from Rorty's deconstructive neopragmatism to Donna Haraway's pragmatic constructivism, from Nancy Hartsock's feminist standpoint theory to the critiques of this theory offered by Kathleen Jones, Bat-Ami Bar On, and Helen Longino.

As already suggested, Rorty has characterized pragmatism as antirepresentationalism. To him, it also is a form of antiauthoritarianism. But Sorrell's treatment of authority is predicated on the necessity to maintain the distinction between the authoritarian and the authoritative. He, too, is an antiauthoritarian. Any critique of authority resulting in the annihilation of the very notion of authoritative persons or positions, however, would be self-defeating: in the name of critique, criticism would have destroyed its own possibility and usefulness. Indeed, such criticism would have rendered itself worse than useless, for it would have generated the illusion of being able to live and act without reliance upon authorities, thereby deflecting critical attention away from the ever urgent task of calibrating the concrete differences resulting from the differential procedures, policies, and perspectives of variably located actors.

Sorrell's treatment of representation is also predicated on the necessity (not the assumed, but the demonstrated necessity) of maintaining the distinction between the representative and the misrepresentative, as well as between what is and how we try to represent what is. The impossibility of completely eliminating from our representations every distortion does not touch our abiding practical need in countless situations to distinguish between more or less reliable representations. An abstract awareness of the imperfect character of virtually every humanly constructed representation fails to disclose (or even to help us reveal) the specific ways in which particular representations are, to the disadvantage of some and the advantage of others, misleading or unreliable. We can no more do without representations than we can do without authority. What we understand by *representation* might be, of course, quite different than the mode of depiction represented by those who call themselves (or whom others call) representationalists. Just as reality might be too multifarious, subtle, and complex to leave to doctrinaire realists, so representation might not be best left to its most doctrinaire defenders.

We might ask any number of questions concerning what are the most reliable or useful representations of the practices by which we try to represent facts, situations, and preferences, but at some point our reliance on representations under some description must be acknowledged. Part of Sorrell's effort here is to force us, especially those who claim an allegiance to pragmatism, to own up more fully—more consciously, conscientiously, and thus critically—to our commitments. Along with everyone else, pragmatists are committed to representations in some sense. The point is not to give the notion of representation to the representationalists and thereby to wash one's hands of having anything to do with the business of representing the myriad matters calling for dependable depiction (e.g., how many individuals were killed during this confrontation? Were they soldiers, as reported in the mainstream media, or were they mostly civilians, as reported elsewhere?). The point is rather to represent our practices of representing matters more accurately than most (perhaps all) traditional theories have done thus far and, beyond this, to show at least some of the most important ways in which the differences that practically make such a humanly significant difference (the differences that humanly matter) can be ascertained. For doing this, I know of no better work than the one to which I am adding my own words here.

Sorrell's pragmatic realism is thus a constructive and (in a sense) constructivist pragmatism according to which the calibrations of agents variably situated in multiple practices are the pivots around which everything turns. In other words, the pragmatic upshot of his critiques and proposals is a form of pragmatism in which critical attention is directed toward how to secure reasonable bases for comparative judgments (what I earlier called the calibrations of variably situated agents). The foci of his investigation help to clarify this point, and they do so by suggesting concrete situations in which conscientious agents are desirous to act well (i.e., better than they might act if, say, they are habitually inattentive or, worse, systematically blind to certain identifiable features of the situation in which they are implicated and active). Most prominently, these foci are authority, representation, practice, and privilege. Authority can be *more or less* reasonable (or more or less arbitrary). Representations can be more or less accurate. Practices can be more or less inclusive. The processes by which certain individuals or groups are privileged can be more or less transparent.

William James once suggested: "The whole originality of pragmatism, the whole point in it, is its use of the concrete way of seeing" (1975, 281–82). He immediately added that pragmatism "begins with concreteness, and returns and ends with it" (282). Many misguided criticisms of the pragmatic position are rooted in the failure of its critics to appreciate the extent to which it is committed to concrete ways of seeing the multifarious situations and multiple communities in which human agents are implicated. James made this point regarding a topic related to Sorrell's concerns. He asked, "when the pragmatist speaks of opinions, does he mean any such insulated and unmotivated abstractions as are here supposed [by the critics of pragmatism]?" (*310*). As though his rhetorical question required an answer, he interjected: "Of course not." The pragmatist intends "men's [and women's] opinions in the flesh, as they have really formed themselves, opinions surrounded by their grounds and the influences they obey and exert, and along with the whole environment of social communication of which they are a part and out of which they take their rise" (310–11). Opinions *abstracted from* the processes by which they have been formed, the grounds to which their advocates appeal in defense of their espousal of these opinions, and the other affairs mentioned by James are, indeed, "insular and unmotivated abstractions" (310). In contrast, the idea of opinions, or representations, highlighting their concrete embodiment in the ongoing affairs of human practitioners who are members of multiple communities is also an abstraction. But it is one designed to direct critical attention to the concrete circumstances in which human representations are crafted and circulated, accredited and challenged. It is, to this extent, more concrete than the abstraction wielded by the critics of pragmatism.

The concrete circumstances in which human opinions or representations possess their distinctively human forms, functions, and effects might be more or less abstractly acknowledged (more or less thickly described). One irony is that the classical pragmatists, in their strenuous insistence upon descriptive thickness (or greater concreteness), often rely on unduly thin descriptions. For example, James (that most loquacious and sociable of philosophers) hardly ever offers a truly thick description of "the whole environment of social communication" in which ideas and stories struggle against rivals to make a personally decisive or socially critical difference. The differences that make a difference do so ordinarily by making their way against entrenched alternatives and fierce opponents.

The originality of pragmatism is arguably connected to cultivating ever more concrete modes of critical attention, thus ever thicker descriptions of concrete affairs. Without question, Kory Sorrell's informed defense of pragmatic realism significantly contributes to the advance of pragmatism by showing, more concretely than the classical pragmatists tended to do themselves, how concreteness is attained— or, more accurately, is better approximated in some accounts or practices than in others.

Concreteness is approximated in various ways, not least of all by personally inflected narratives. Here, too, there is an irony, for James suggests, "biography is the concrete form in which all that is is given; the perceptual flux is the authentic stuff of each of our biographies, and yields a perfect effervescence of novelty all the time" (qtd. in Seigfried

1990, 395). But he leaves largely unthematized and hence unexplored experience in its irreducibly biographical form. For my purpose, this understandable but regrettable neglect of biographical and other forms of narration is less to the point than a fragment of Sorrell's biography. As an undergraduate, Kory Sorrell studied at Texas A&M University with John J. McDermott (though he met McDermott through one of McDermott's students even before going to A&M). John McDermott studied with Robert Pollock at Fordham University. And, while teaching at Fordham, Eugene Fontinell (who also studied with Pollock at Fordham), I, and indeed others in New York met Kory Sorrell through John McDermott. Complexly mediated relationships at the personal level suggest a metaphor for the complexly mediated relationships constitutive of a vital intellectual tradition. McDermott initially presented James to Sorrell in a manner capturing the spirit, passion, and élan of James himself, as I hope I presented Peirce to Sorrell in a manner faithful to Peirce's texts, aspirations, and achievements. A living tradition is an intergenerational argument involving complex mediations—personal, intellectual, and otherwise. Moreover, intellectual traditions are exceedingly complex and (to some extent) surprisingly fragile affairs involving multiple factors, not least of all chance encounters and resolute commitments to carrying on the unfinished work glimpsed so often only because of such chance meetings.

There is little question in my mind that Kory Sorrell's work bears testimony to the eloquent and unforgettable voice of a philosopher and teacher whose tone, cadence, and concerns are so distinctively pragmatic. For Kory Sorrell, as for so for so many others of us, John McDermott spoke about James and, more generally, about pragmatism with an unmistakably authoritative voice, but one unmarred by any trace of authoritarianism. He put us in touch with what might have remained (apart from his efforts and insights, interpretations and celebrations) distant from and foreign to us—with texts, thinkers, and indeed a tradition still all too widely neglected even in the United States. Here was someone to whom we felt we must listen, in large measure because he was someone from whom the intricacies and insights of others could be learned.

Kory Spencer Sorrell's *Representative Practices: Peirce, Pragmatism, and Feminist Epistemology* bears eloquent witness to his actual experience of having heard and indeed having been transformed by such an authoritative voice. Among other things, he learned that the persuasiveness and authority of McDermott's voice were in part a function of his teacher's self-critical insistence upon his own limitations, biases, and location, but also in part a function of this teacher's willingness to fall silent as a way of including others. Such, at least, is the way I am inclined to represent one of the most crucial experiences animating and underwriting this text.

Finally, it is impossible for me to imagine, especially among those of his generation, a better representative of an inclusively envisioned yet critically articulated version of pragmatic concreteness than the author of this book, for here is a version of pragmatism rooted in a painstaking engagement with Peirce's formidable texts, but also one informed by a critical encounter with contemporary feminism and other important movements. The way in which Sorrell engages in the delicate, multifaceted hermeneutical and critical mediations demanded of anyone striving to attain pragmatic concreteness offers the only kind of proof a pragmatist would ultimately find convincing. He exemplifies what he extols; he proves by example what he argues to establish in principle— the self-critical working out of open-ended inclusivity as a pragmatic ideal to be approximated, *more or less*. The delicate calibrations made on the ground by implicated agents—fallible actors implicated in evolving, shared practices—are the ones to which Sorrell directs our attention. The force and subtlety of his argument can be appreciated, of course, only by carefully working through the details and considerations of his text. My hope is simply to have highlighted some of the features of this argument so that its force and subtlety may be more readily and fully felt.

VINCENT COLAPIETRO
State College, Pennsylvania
December 2003

INTRODUCTION

Perhaps the immobility of the things that surround us is forced upon them by our conviction that they are themselves and not any thing else, by the immobility of our conception of them.

—Marcel Proust, *In Search of Lost Time*

Ralph Emerson once wrote that "[w]e have such exorbitant eyes, that on seeing the smallest arc, we complete the curve, and when the curtain is lifted from the diagram which it seemed to veil, we are vexed to find that no more was drawn, than just that fragment of an arc which we first beheld" (1951, 421). It seems that the most ephemeral flash of light, once having caught our passing notice, may be saved from oblivion; instead of fading from existence all together, it may be caught up, transformed, and reinscribed in real or imaginary contexts. No longer an arbitrary spark against a crepuscular void, it thereby becomes, as if by miracle, a harbinger of things coming or significant of realities present but not seen. Not a light, but a lightning bug perhaps; and not arbitrary, but the studied effort of an insect to find a mate. When this happens, when we as human agents perform this extraordinary act, something genuinely new is created in the universe. A representation is born, and, as Emerson trenchantly observed, it is an act of exorbitance. More than fact, representation entails reach, for by its very nature it is a sign of that which is not present to hand or open to the eye of the body. Stepping outside itself, it is a creation of mind, of a *desiring* mind, that seeks in the shadows for what it does not have, and it is this will that prompts the effort or act of representing. As Emerson also knew, the act is often a treacherous one. In going beyond, we inevitably go astray, often misstepping and "miss-taking" one thing for another, one event as prescient of others impending.

Moreover, in some of these instances, treachery becomes treason: in our desire to transmogrify events into representations, present realities are inevitably subjected to the will and preference of those performing the act, and so representation may well reflect more the purpose of the artisans than that which it purports to represent. This is more than vexatious; it is, at least potentially, a form of violence done to real events and to the persons involved in them on behalf of purposes that are often foreign to their lives and to their preferences. And so representation, in addition to being a form of revelation, is a common cause of frustration, of deep communal concern, and not infrequently of oppression and marginalization.

This book addresses the extraordinary and sometimes deeply problematic practice of representation and tackles a cluster of problems usually gathered under its name. What these problems are may be more clearly seen in the ways in which the term *representation* is commonly used. In one sense, a representation is an image, a picture, or perhaps an exhibition. It can be a result of the plastic arts but is more often the result of written or verbal narratives that in some way present a scene, an event, or even a history in a coherent way to interested persons.

The second sense of *representation,* closely related to the first, refers to a kind of act, something that someone or some group of persons actually do. Representations are not discovered whole cloth, but are constructed, woven together out of many strands, by fingers that care about how they are put together and submitted to—or imposed upon—other persons. In this sense, representation is a kind of authority or authorship.

Third, representation takes on the meaning of "being on behalf of." In this context, something stands in for something else in some respect or capacity. It performs the service of mediation, of working on behalf of that other toward some end. This is the sense in which an attorney stands for her client. Abused by another or perhaps accused by the state, a person is confronted by an extraordinarily complex legal system. In order to navigate its dangers and put it to work on her behalf, she entrusts her cause to one experienced in its channels and byways. She entrusts herself to an attorney, who (she hopes) will represent her interest and advance her case as far as law will allow. In so doing, the attorney, through her mediation, brings her client into direct (though mediated) relation with the law and the justice it has to offer.

Each of these characteristic meanings brings with it trying questions. The first involves an ancient controversy that turns on the relationship between representations and the realities they purport to represent. Here it is wondered how anything like representation can really happen, and even if it does, how we, as epistemic agents, can know that it does. What is the nature of reality such that it can be represented, or, conversely, what is the nature of conceptual categories such that they can be said truly to "map on" to the real? Supposing that representation of the real is possible, are there better and worse ways to go about it? This problem involves the question of whether or not the imposition of some sort of programmatic method may improve communal representation.

The second use of *representation* invokes a different set of questions. Given the fact that representations are human artifacts, what does this fact mean for representation generally? Does it entail that "real" representation, in the sense that an image or picture is said to "map on" to the real, is always beyond the grasp of the hands that make it? Because power is always present in the author's work, is not representation itself always a kind of violence perpetrated on that which is represented?

Finally, how is it that representations—and not just in the sense of an attorney, but in the sense of images, pictures, books, narratives, museum exhibitions, film—mediate our actions? What sorts of work do they do, and how might these forms of mediation themselves be subjected to normative constraint? In other words, how might mediation itself be more intelligently mediated? How we describe the real and the signs that advertise it is extraordinarily significant, for it goes a long way toward answering the cluster of questions identified previously. It is therefore not surprising that much of the debate occurs here. But description is not an end in itself, for the goal of such efforts is ultimately normative. Description is undertaken in order to find ways in which representation might be improved, improved not just in the sense of being more adequate to the real, but in the sense that better representations may ameliorate other aspects of our lives as well. This is one of several ways in which this book is overtly pragmatic: its focus is on the practice of representation, and one measure of its success is the degree to which it will assist in the improvement of this practice. As John Dewey would say, its value lies in its consequences.

Before saying more about what follows in the book, I should say something about the resources used. Above all, I am interested in a *problem,* and Peirce's role is pervasive because I think he offers tremendous resources for addressing the issues involved. But as Peirce himself insisted, the work of developing a theory of representation had still only begun at the end of his lifetime (1914), so I use a number of other writers to cast light on the difficulties that ensue. The other pragmatists, William James and John Dewey, have been a constant source of assistance. The differences among these thinkers were many and sometimes quite important. But without passing over these distinguishing characteristics, we can say it is surely also true that they agreed with and often furthered one another in many respects. When it is appropriate and helpful, I use these other pragmatists in supporting roles.

Beyond the pragmatists, I draw most significantly on work written in the recently developed tradition of feminist epistemology. I find in this tradition subtle discussion of problems surrounding the intersection of different kinds of power and representation that I think are both crucial to understanding practices of representation and useful for suggesting promising strategies for amelioration of those practices. So although I follow Peirce a great deal, I also go significantly beyond him in order to address novel features of the problem and even further his approach in ways that he did not (but of which he may have approved). The material in this book, therefore, is "Peircean" rather than Peirce's and must ultimately stand criticism on its own.

In chapter 1, the book begins with a discussion of "the real" as Peirce understood and divided it up. This discussion involves a look at what Peirce called phenomenology, which I briefly defend as a tenable study in light of possible reservations that contemporary readers may have. The "defense" is abbreviated, but so much has already been written on this topic that I take the liberty of standing on the shoulders of others more capable than I and refer the skeptical reader to those texts. After I introduce the results of this study, I explain how phenomenological conceptions take on for Peirce full ontological status. The chapter closes by placing Peirce in historical context in order to further refine the reader's understanding of his ontology.

Chapter 2 further discusses the real in light of Peirce but offers critical emendation. My criticism, far from novel, follows very closely Sandra Rosenthal's revision of Peirce and for similar reasons. But having done this, I then depart from Rosenthal's claim that Peirce's approach is a processive metaphysical approach. I argue that Peirce offers (or provides the means for offering) a pragmatic reformulation of the doctrine of substance along pragmatic lines. I then develop and defend this pragmatic view of substance in the light of six possible criticisms.

The purpose of doing this is twofold. On one hand, it is an intervention in Peirce studies. Peirce scholars remain divided on the issue of whether or not Peirce actually has a substance metaphysics, and I insist he does as a matter of textual evidence and logic. More important, I want to develop a conception that is ultimately independent of what Peirce did or did not think of the matter. Such a conception can be defended not by citation of Peirce, but only in the open marketplace of criticism. On the other hand, developing this view offers an opportunity to provide a thicker understanding of what reality—more specifically, the world—is supposed to be like in a Peircean formulation. The light of criticism makes it possible to cast further into relief how a pragmatist might regard the features of the world, and this provides a useful backdrop for subsequent discussion of representation.

The focus moves in the third chapter away from the real as such to discussion of the nature of representation itself. The bulk of this chapter is devoted to explaining Peirce's theory of signs, his triadic divisions, and how these divisions go toward explaining how signs may be said truly to represent the real in a pragmatic approach. I treat particular problems in semiotics, such as the possibilities of infinite regress and infinite progress, primarily as a means for further explication of Peirce's semeiotic. Much has also been written on this aspect of Peirce, and I rely on this first-rate scholarship. The purpose of the chapter, which is actually the culmination of the first three chapters, is to show how the real constrains representation not only in the sense of "brute resistance," but also in terms of its content. This assures realism and, more important for what follows, normative constraints on practices of representation. There is in a Peircean approach a real sense in which representation may be said to be better or worse, more or less adequate, to that which it purports to represent.

Chapter 4 continues the discussion of representation but takes it up from a different point of view. Having shown that representation is a collective and constructive effort, I now discuss how persons go about this practice as authors within a community. In other words, the focus shifts from the first to the second sense of representation as introduced earlier. Employing recent developments in feminist epistemology, I argue against prevailing conceptions of the role of authority in representation. Although going models see it as undermining the struggle for objectivity and so seek ways to eliminate its influence, I suggest that authority is not only ineluctable but also appropriate in many, if not all cases. By this, I mean that good representations are produced precisely when authority in representative practices is reasonable. Going practices, once adequately described, may be subjected to normative criticism with respect to authority, and I suggest how this subjection may be effectively done.

I then offer an actual example, provided by Nancy Scheper-Hughes's representation of *carnaval* in northeastern Brazil, to explain my meaning further. The idea is that there is more to the production of objectivity than just constraint by the real and that normative guidelines other than those that refer to external constraint are not only possible, but needful. These guidelines make representations more objective by being more inclusive about the conditions under which they are constructed. That is, not only are they created under these conditions, but those features are actually included in the representation itself.

In the last chapter, I again shift in order to address the problem of representation from the angle of the third sense in which this word is used. Along the way, I will have argued that representation is a form of mediation that really modifies the conduct of members of the community, that it goes toward the production of some realities but not others. In this chapter, I thematize this view of mediation, contrasting it with the conception preferred by Richard Rorty in order to set the stage for specifically ethical consideration of practices of representation. The argument is that if acts of representation truly go beyond the construction of signs that mirror reality, then these acts may themselves be subjected to criticism in light of the ends they tend to realize. I again draw on Peirce and the other pragmatists to suggest that a notion of inclusivity (different from the one used in chapter 4) is available for such normative constraints. The idea is that those representations that tend toward forms of existence that contribute to the growth of the individual and the community are to be preferred to those that do not. Again, this form of constraint on representation is relatively independent of and yet compatible with the normative suggestions given in previous chapters.

Although no one of these various normative strategies can in any simple sense give the "one best answer" even in its own area of application, my suggestion is that all three, taken together, provide useful guidelines for practices of representation once these practices are better understood. In any act of representation, all three types of constraint should come into play: representation should be accountable to the real it represents, should be produced under warranted and well-accounted-for authority, and should be done in light of the ends that it will tend to manifest. Just as Peirce envisioned a viable philosophical system to be made up of strands of belief that are each more or less resilient, but that taken together can be woven into a strong rope, so I think that these multiple forms of constraint, somewhat weak on their own, may together tack down from different directions representative practices in ways that will make them better, more adequate, more pragmatically useful. The project is, in short, a further development of that "pragmatic epistemology" discussed by John J. McDermott in his *Streams of Experience* (1986, 92).

In the spirit of Peircean fallibilism, I end this introduction with some lines from Michel Foucault. All along the way in the writing of this book, I had so very many authors to consider, so many problems to address, and so little time and limited ability to do it that although I have argued what I could, I have left far more undone, and more still probably escaped my notice altogether. I therefore cannot agree more with Foucault when he writes: "As to those for whom to work hard, to begin and begin again, to attempt and be mistaken, to go back and rework everything from top to bottom, and still find reason to hesitate from one step to the next—as to those, in short, for whom to work in the midst of uncertainty and apprehension is tantamount to failure, all I can say is that clearly we are not from the same planet" (1985, 7).

ONE

PEIRCE'S CATEGORIES

A First Glimpse at Representation

Metaphysics means nothing but an unusually obstinate effort to think clearly.

—William James, *The Principles of Psychology*

The purpose of this book is to provide a normative account of practices of representation, one that is sighted by Peirce's pragmatism, his general categories, and his semeiotic. In order to understand and then evaluate these practices, a great deal must also be said about that which is the intended object of representation: reality. Michel Foucault may well be right in claiming that, beginning with the sixteenth century, "[t]he profound kinship of language with the world was thus dissolved," and henceforth "[t]hings and words were to be separated from one another" (1970, 43). But a responsible assessment of this displacement, one that goes any reasonable distance toward grasping what sort of relation language or, more generally, representation has to the world involves a discussion of both *relata*. And although the nature of language seems constantly under review, it seems that in present discussions of representation, the nature of what is being represented, of the real as such, is all too often left out. Too metaphysical and traditional perhaps, it is left to the controlling assumptions of the discourse in which it takes place or is presumed to be out of the reach of discourse altogether. This approach is problematic because how we regard the real—that is, what sort of nature we think it has and what relation we suppose that nature has to discourse and representation generally—is of paramount importance in determining the status of representation itself or is at least important enough not to allow such questions to be decided by arbitrary choice or the prevailing wind within a given community of inquirers.

Peirce certainly thought that questions concerning the nature of the real were central to adequately understanding and responding to the cluster of difficulties surrounding the problem of representation, and in this chapter I begin by introducing Peirce's phenomenological categories and the logical considerations that lead to these categories' becoming an ontology. This discussion involves a detailed look at the nature of firstness, secondness, and thirdness (or orience, obsistence, and transuasion) as Peirce understands them and how these categories relate to one another. I also suggest some of the reasons why Peirce thinks that these categories are necessary and in what sense. As Vincent Colapietro points out, "The value of this doctrine [of categories] resides not so much in the abstract articulation of purely formal conceptions as in the concrete applications of these conceptions to virtually every context of investigation" (1995, 29). In chapter 2, I specifically apply these analytic categories to a fuller description of concrete existence and provide a view of substance reconstrued along pragmatic lines. This should provide a fairly thick description of what reality is like according to a Peircean approach. Only thereafter will I shift to a discussion of representation as such in the third chapter. There again the categories lead the way.

Producing an account of the nature of the real is, of course, tricky business because any discussion of the object of representation is always already itself a representation. One may reasonably question, given this fact, our capacity as epistemic agents to say anything about reality that is independent of our representations of it and so wonder about the wisdom of beginning in this way. Indeed, some have not only questioned this endeavor but also concluded that it is impossible or incoherent or just an unforgettable (if forgivable) desire that many of us share. Although it is reasonably certain that there is no such thing as unmediated access to the real apart from modes of representation, Peirce nevertheless claims that we may have (and indeed do in many cases have) knowledge of the nature of the real—as it is, independently of how we prefer to think of it. Notice that this is not the same as claiming that we can know things in themselves, in the sense of "as they are, *apart* from our experience (which is itself a form of mediation) of the real."

The difference between the two is that in Peirce's approach, knowledge of the real emerges from the mediation of the experience of members of the community with the real, whereas the other proposes that knowledge of the real, independently of forms of mediation, is possible. Peirce many times insisted that this latter idea must be surrendered in favor of the former. When this is done, the problem is no longer one of explaining how we can get back of mediation—of signs or representation or experience—to a pure reality that is unmodified by our having handled it, but instead becomes a question of how mediation may be a means of discovery and not just distortion. Discovering how this might be so and how we might tell the difference between the two and develop better practices that really tend more to the former than to the latter is the task not just of this chapter, but of the entire book.

Phenomenology and the Larger Generalities

Pierce claims, in his outline for what he someday hoped to write under the title "A Guess at the Riddle," that "[t]o erect a philosophical edifice that shall outlast the vicissitudes of time, my care must be, not so much to set each brick with the nicest accuracy, as to lay the foundations deep and massive" (EP1, 246). Although exceedingly broad and therefore necessarily vague in content, the initial conceptions are of paramount importance because they support further development by determining which divisions are the more inclusive and what sort of questions properly belong to which province. Accordingly, Peirce divided all philosophy into three grand parts: phenomenology, normative science, and metaphysics (EP2, 259). He claims that the middle division "distinguishes what ought to be from what ought not to be" and is in turn divided into the study of esthetics, ethics, and logic (EP2, 259–60). I directly address normative science in chapter 5 but focus now on both phenomenology and metaphysics.

Phenomenology must be first, according to Peirce, because it provides support for the middle division of normative science. Peirce writes that phenomenology is "the basis upon which normative science is to be erected, and accordingly must claim our first attention" (CP, 5.39). It is a study that reveals "the elements of appearance that present themselves to us every hour and every minute whether we are pursuing earnest investigations, or are undergoing the strangest vicissitudes of experience, or are dreamily listening to the tales of Scheherazade" (EP2, 147). Phenomenology requires no special study of its own but is an examination of what is present to each of us—not just to the scientist or philosopher—in experience of every kind.

For this reason, Peirce would surely agree with John Dewey's claim, in the essay "Experience and Philosophic Method," that the subject matter of philosophy must begin with experience of the everyday and not with data that have already been refined by some other method of inquiry. Dewey only underscores Peirce's view when he points out that what is commonly considered to be strictly empirical observations are themselves already a dialectical development of data taken from physiology or some other selective science. Although such data are surely useful for the purposes that emerge in their respective domains, difficulties inevitably accrue when these data are naively and mistakenly thought to be results of pure observation rather than the products of discriminating inquiry. This is why Dewey writes in the original version of chapter 1 of *Experience and Nature* that "I would rather take the behavior of the dog of Odysseus upon his master's return as an example of the sort of thing experience is for the philosopher than trust to such statements. A physiologist may for his special purpose reduce Othello's perception of a handkerchief to simple elements of color under certain angular conditions of vision. But the actual experience was charged with history and prophesy; full of love, jealousy and villainy, fulfilling past human relationships and moving fatally to tragic destiny" (1988a, 368).

Experience, as Dewey describes it here, belongs to the domain of phenomenology according to Peirce's conception of that general science; it is a study that does not, as the special sciences do, require objects not readily apparent to all. Nor does it take already refined data as its starting point. On the contrary, it is the *obvious* but often unattended to which Peirce seeks to turn our attention. Writing of the object of phenomenology, which he more technically identifies as "phanerons," he states, "There is nothing quite so directly open to observation as phanerons; and since I shall have no need of referring to any but those which (or the like of which) are perfectly familiar to everybody, every reader can control the accuracy of what I am going to say about them. Indeed, he must actually repeat my observations and experiments for himself, or else I shall more utterly fail to convey my meaning than if I were to discourse of effects of chromatic decoration to a man congenitally blind" (CP, 1.286). Persons must repeat these experiments, Peirce argues, if they are to understand his meaning and be persuaded by his phenomenological claims. The repetition of the study provides an account of what is in any way present to the mind in terms of both detail and ubiquity. It "endeavors to provide minute accuracy with the broadest possible generality" (CP, 1.287).

One reason Peirce insists that phenomenology is not a special science is that the special science must ultimately depend on phenomenology to ground its discourse and therefore cannot control or condition phenomenological study. This may be seen more clearly, for example, in the context of the question concerning the status of laws in scientific description and explanation. The "problem of induction," as formulated in the philosophy of science, rightly sees that appeal to science in the form of practical success simply cannot justify the claim that the laws of science are genuinely predictive. This sort of response utterly fails because it says nothing about what will happen in the future as opposed to what has happened. As Popper suggests, "it is impossible to justify a law by observation or experiment, since it 'transcends experience,'" and "in science only observation and experiment may decide upon the *acceptance or rejection* of scientific statements, including laws and theories" (1985, 101, italics his). In order to determine whether laws are really operative in nature or are only convenient and useful tools for describing what appears to be "lawlike" behavior, one would not appeal to the special sciences (this would be circular), according to Peirce's view, but to the more general branches of philosophy.

One must engage phenomenology and metaphysics, to be more specific, in the light of logic in order to ground induction by showing that laws really are operative in nature and that they are of a general order. Only in this way may the viciously tight circle of the "problem of induction" be avoided. But such a demonstration would never get started if phenomenology were not distinguished at the outset from all the special sciences that subsequently depend upon it. Consequently, phenomenology must be prior to and fully autonomous from the special sciences.

In order to engage in the study of phanerons (the object of phenomenology), the student simply contemplates that which is before him, abstaining from any judgment as to the kind of reality that the phaneron presents. He must surrender to direct perception and not be influenced by any external considerations: "The student's great effort is not to be influenced by any tradition, any authority, any reasons for supposing that such and such ought to be the facts, or any fancies of any kind, and to confine himself to honest, single minded observation of the appearances" (CP, 1.287). Peirce's injunction may well give post-Kuhnian readers pause.[1] One may wonder how it can naively be supposed that observation unmediated by authority or regnant practices of interpretation is possible considering that in postpositivist philosophy it is commonly accepted that observation is in at least some way "theory laden." A person sees the world in ways prescribed by the theories that she holds, and confirmation or falsification of what is observed cannot be determined independently of the theory. Rather, all observations are given content by the theory or set of theories in question. As Kuhn puts it, "Scientists do not see something *as* something else; instead, they simply see it" (1974, 85).[2] But in "simply seeing," the object is always already the result of various individual judgments and social mediation. Therefore, no direct, unmediated observation is possible, and this seems to show that Peirce's phenomenological method is at the very outset naive and antiquated.

This criticism is an important one because if it is true, then Peirce's entire philosophical "construction" rests on untenable foundations. It cannot possibly provide the basis of further study because it is unaware of features of experience we now recognize as central and pervasive. But Peirce is untouched by this critique for at least three reasons, and showing how this is so will not only clarify what Peirce means by phenomenology, but also show what sort of work it is intended to do. First, he does not think that there is any unmediated access to reality. He would thus surely agree with post-Kuhnian philosophy of science, or, more accurately, he stands as its forerunner.[3] In the first question of "Questions Concerning Certain Faculties Claimed for Man," Peirce claims that there is no evidence for believing that persons have immediate intuitions of transcendental objects beyond the fact that they feel that they have them (EP1, 12). All thinking is in signs, according to Peirce, and all thought of an external object is mediated (or determined) by prior cognition that is likewise of the nature of a sign (EP1, 26–27). As such, experience of reality is ineluctably mediated by linguistic forms of expression, grammatical structure, and going theoretical (and commonsense) understanding of how reality fits together. There is simply no getting back of these features to an unmediated reality, and Peirce thinks it a drastic mistake to believe otherwise.[4] Peirce was "Kuhnian" in this sense as early as 1868, and it is one way in which he may be distinguished from other pragmatists. He never defended a doctrine of immediate empiricism, as James did (and as Dewey at one point did).[5]

A second reason to think Peirce's phenomenological study immune to the criticism of Kuhnian wholism is that Peirce's inquiry is carried out at a level of greater generality than that of Kuhn. Peirce is pressing for the ultimate or most general features of reality ubiquitously present in experience, and this is neutral with respect to which paradigm or theory is at work in the observation of particular events. An example makes this significantly more clear. In *The Structure of Scientific Revolutions,* Kuhn argues that observers who operate with different sorts of background assumptions "see" different events and draw very different conclusions. He writes that

> To the Aristotelians, who believed that a heavy body is moved by its own nature from a higher position to a state of natural rest at a lower one, the swinging body was simply falling with difficulty. Constrained by the chain, it could achieve rest at its low point only after a tortuous motion and a considerable time. Galileo, on the other hand, looking at the swinging body, saw a pendulum, a body that almost succeeded in repeating the same motion over and over again ad infinitum. And having seen that much, Galileo observed other properties of the pendulum as well and constructed many of the most significant and original parts of his new dynamics around them. (1974, 118–19; see also Longino 1990, 53)

Although it may be true that the Aristotelian and the Galilean observed quite different phenomena owing to differences in their explanatory models, both saw a world of some kind or another; both experienced qualities, activities, resistance, and tendencies in the objects observed. The questions for them—and for the point Kuhn is making—are, which of these qualities, activities, and so on are observed, and how do they most reasonably go together?

But Peirce's investigation, given the level at which it is undertaken, is indifferent to these sorts of paradigmatic consideration. He is interested in what kinds of most general features are present in *all* experience, regardless of what in particular is observed or what canopy of explanation is being employed. The dispute between the Galilean and the Aristotelian casts no shadow of doubt on the presence of these more general features that are the subject of Peirce's phenomenological study, for both exhibit them. Consequently, rather than suggesting a criticism of Peirce's study, the argument between the Aristotelian and the Galilean provides further evidence in support of Peirce's findings. The pendulum, no more or less than the Aristotelian body "seeking rest," exhibits the phenomenological traits that are the objects of Peirce's study.

Finally, Peirce is quite specific about that to which the inquirer is asked to remain neutral, and this neutrality is not the sort that post-Kuhnian philosophers insist is impossible. They assert that the scientist cannot observe phenomena independently of the interpretive theories he holds either explicitly or as background assumptions. But Peirce claims that the scientist must abstain only from "supposing that such and such ought to be the *facts*" and "to confine himself to honest, single minded observation of the *appearances*" (CP, 1.287, italics his). An inquiry must remain neutral to the *ontological status* of what the scientist observes. He must not presume in advance what may or may not be counted or what grade of reality or actuality the observed should have. Peirce writes that "This must be a science that does not draw any distinction of good and bad in any sense whatever, but just contemplates phenomena as they are, simply opens its eyes and describes what it sees; not what it sees in the real as distinguished from figment—not regarding any such dichotomy—but simply describing the object, as a phenomenon, and stating what it finds in all phenomena alike" (CP, 5.37). It is to the dualistic conception of appearance and reality, or of what should be as opposed to what seems to be, that one must remain neutral. Peirce is not, at this point, interested either in which interpretive framework is in place or in the fact that experience of phenomena is theory laden. His concern is that the descriptive enterprise of phenomenology not be subjected to normative constraints concerning what aspect of reality is the more "real." As he would put it, phenomenology is a study of phanerons in their firstness, or as they appear, not in their secondness, or what ought to be the case. In other words, and this is Peirce's real interest, the questions of realism and nominalism cannot be addressed in this division of philosophy, nor should they influence one's account of what is observed at the outset.

It may be recalled that one of James's more aggressive criticisms of monistic idealism is that in producing a conception of the Absolute in order to render experience logically consistent and meaningful, it also denigrates the reality of personal experience. Concepts, because eternal, are taken to be more real than perceptual reality, and sensible experience is then regarded as deficient and illusory. James writes,

"Conceptual treatment of perceptual reality makes it seem paradoxical and incomprehensible; and when radically and consistently carried
out, it leads to the opinion that perceptual experience is not reality at
all but an appearance or illusion" (1977, 246). This distinction is what
Peirce seeks to avoid when he enjoins judgment of what is experienced. Such abstention is quite difficult, he thinks, especially given the
all-too-human tendency not to observe carefully what is directly
before one and the inveterate habit of modern subjects to presume a
nominalist view of the world (CP, 1.19, 1.560, 2.168, 5.42). But it is possible. One may develop, Peirce insists, the skill of the artist who
describes candidly what is before his eyes and not "his theory of what
ought to be seen" (CP, 5.42, italics his). The artist, not the scientific
inquirer, is, according to Peirce, the more practiced phenomenologist
and most fitting to be imitated in this study.

   Phenomenology provides a description from which general categories emerge. The third of the three divisions of philosophy, metaphysics, determines the ontological status of these categories: what
phenomenology naively proposes, metaphysics subsequently disposes.
Unlike phenomenology, whose object is experience, metaphysics, for
Peirce, has as its subject the objective world. The question it addresses
is whether nominalism or realism be the truer doctrine—that is,
whether the categories of phenomenology refer to experience merely
or to the world at large. Both the nominalist and the realist experience
qualities and regularities in their experience. The difference is that the
nominalist thinks that these are only names, attached to the phenomena of cognition. General concepts are extremely useful because, as
James often insisted, they help us get from one part of experience to
another. But, according to the nominalist, it is not proper to ascribe
them to anything beyond subjective experience, even if they are shared
subjectively in other persons' experience. The realist, in contrast, finds
it necessary to regard these general features found in experience as real
constituents of nature, or the objective world. Peirce writes, "Roughly
speaking, the nominalists conceived the *general* element of cognition
to be merely a convenience for understanding this and that fact and to
amount to nothing except for cognition, while the realists, still more

roughly speaking, looked upon the general, not only as the end and aim of knowledge, but also as the most important element of being" (CP, 4.1, italics his).

The essential difference between the two positions is that the nominalist restricts *all* generality to cognition only, which means that her system of representation is entirely contingent on the community that produces it. Choice depends primarily on the aesthetic or practical ends that members embrace, not on any constraint independent of the community. Conversely, the realist thinks that qualitative descriptions, laws, and logical forms do refer, at least in some cases, to something that both transcends and constrains the community. In this view, any adequate representation must in some way reflect the nature of the real as it is independently of how the community chances or prefers to think of it. The problem then becomes one of discerning those descriptions, forms, and so on that manage to constrain from those that are merely the constructs of human imagination.

Richard Rorty's view in *Philosophy and the Mirror of Nature* is telling in this regard. He claims that contact with reality (a causal relation) should not be confused with dealing with reality (which involves description, prediction, and modification of reality). "The sense in which physical reality is Peircean 'Secondness'—unmediated pressure—has nothing to do with the sense in which one among all our ways of describing, or of coping with, physical reality is 'the one right' way. Lack of mediation is here being confused with accuracy of mediation" (1979, 375). What Rorty ascribes to others as confusion, however, turns instead on a reasonable disagreement. Realists think that there is more to reality than just brute opposition and that whether or not a person deals successfully with the real turns fatefully on the adequacy of her representations of the real as it is independently of how she or any number of members of the community choose to think of it.

The question of realism and nominalism most properly belongs to metaphysics because metaphysics is the first of the sciences to investigate the nature of the objective world as it is, but resolving this issue turns on logical consideration. As Peirce states,

> You know what the question was. It was whether *laws* and general *types* are figments of the mind or are real. If this be understood to mean whether there are really any laws and types, it is strictly speaking a question of metaphysics and not of logic. But as a first step toward its solution, it is proper to ask whether, granting that our common-sense beliefs are true, the analysis of the meaning of those beliefs shows that, according to those beliefs, laws and types are objective or subjective. This is a question of logic rather than of metaphysics—and as soon as this is answered the reply to the other question immediately follows after. (CP, 1.16, italics his)

The true metaphysics emerges, according to Peirce, from the analysis of commonly shared beliefs. In lecturing on pragmatism in 1903, Peirce took as an example the falling of a stone. Everyone in the audience believed that, if released, the stone really would fall. No one doubted it, which is clear from the fact that none in the audience would bet against Peirce's prediction that the stone would fall—even at odds of a hundred to one. Peirce then inquired as to what also must be true if it is conceded that the stone would fall. He claimed that only the scholastic realist could with consistency say that the stone, given a specific set of conditions, would act in a specifiable way, so he concluded that scholastic realism is the truer doctrine (CP, 5.95).

This "demonstration" by Peirce was a part of a public lecture and so was necessarily conclusive; in the following discussion of Peirce's categories, I highlight more detailed logical considerations to support Peirce's view of metaphysics. It is only in the light of logic that Peirce's categories, which begin as purely phenomenological descriptions, accrue metaphysical standing in a realistic ontology. This ontology then provides the basis of everything that comes after.

Categories of the Real

Although Charles Peirce became an extreme realist in his mature years, it is significant that he began as a nominalist.[6] In "An Unpsychological View of Logic," dating from 1865, he wrote that "Qualities are *fictions;* for though it is true that roses are red, yet redness is nothing but a fiction framed for the purposes of philosophizing; yet harmless so long as we remember that the scholastic realism it implies is false" (W1, 307, italics mine). Later, in 1868, Peirce expressed a similar position with regard to generality. He claimed that general categories too corresponded to nothing outside of the mind and language. "The nominalistic element of my theory," he wrote, "is certainly an admission that nothing out of cognition and signification generally, has any generality" (MS, 931). This view indicates Peirce's early devotion to Kant as well as to Ockham and his razor.

Despite these predilections and early training, he eventually became a realist who advocated both a kind of immanent realism and a kind of transcendentalism. By *immanent realism,* I mean a view in which real generality is actually constitutive of the objects of everyday experience and not merely in the mind of the observer. Generality refers to the world, not just to experience, and through lawful mediation objects "conform" to some generals and not to others. Peirce thus far may be said to have sided with Aristotle and against his early mentor, Kant. By *transcendentalism,* I mean a view in which generality does not depend on existing things that happen to be conforming to or "instantiating" those generals for their reality or inclusion in the ontology. Generals are, for Peirce, real even were they never to be involved in the affairs of the existing world. In this respect, Peirce ultimately sides with Plato instead of with Aristotle both on the status of universals and on the priority of possibility to actuality. In short, it appears that Peirce traveled the entire philosophic spectrum, abandoning an extremely nominalistic metaphysics and eventually embracing the most realistic position available. Indeed, Peirce considered his most realistic of predecessors, Duns Scotus, to have barely escaped nominalism himself. My summary of Peirce's categories and of the logical arguments attached to them recounts Peirce's own narrative of his journey between the two extremes.

In his later writings, Peirce argues for both realism and transcendentalism and includes three distinct kinds of being in his ontology.[7] He describes these as "tones or tints upon conceptions" but thinks that each of the three can be distinguished and characterized as it is, in itself, and *as such* (CP, 1.353). "My view is that there are three modes of being. I hold that we can directly observe them in elements of whatever is at any time before the mind in any way. They are the being of positive qualitative possibility, the being of actual fact, and the being of law that will govern facts in the future" (CP, 1.23). In making this statement, Peirce is relying not only on phenomenological study, which suggested the modes in the first place, but also on logic and metaphysics. Consequently, in discussions of each mode, it is necessary to show how logic and metaphysics contribute to Peirce's conclusions.

Although abstract quality is in important respects prior, it is better to begin with facts, or with what Peirce called secondness or obsistence. Obsistence is distinguished from the other two categories in three principle respects. First, in addition to having being, which the members of the other categories also have, seconds are actual. They *exist* in the world to which everyone commonsensically refers. Second, unlike qualities and laws, secondness is determinate; it is always individual. "[W]hatever exists is individual, since existence (not reality) and individuality are essentially the same thing" (CP, 3.613). Third, obsistence is essentially diadic, which means that secondness is brute force or opposition, blind resistance against something other than itself (CP, 1.427). Individual things have properties, qualities made determinate in the here and now of an actual object. But "mere qualities do not resist. It is the matter that resists. Even in actual sensation there is a reaction" (CP, 1.419). Qualities, as such, cannot actually react if not materialized in some object. So "qualities are concerned in facts but they do not make up facts" (CP, 1.419) because, in addition to qualities, facts have actuality, are determinate, and actively resist definite others existing in the world. Peirce does not think that secondness exists in itself apart from qualities (that would be to suppose that an abstraction—secondness as such—is somewhere actual in the same manner that it is abstract). He only insists that existing objects (facts) have secondness that is not reducible to the qualities they also possess.

Moreover, Peirce underscores in his account of secondness that the diadic nature of actuality ensures that all actual individuals are intrinsically related to other actual individuals. There is for Peirce nothing that is absolutely individual. "[A]n isolated fact could hardly be real" (CP, 5.457). To be actual and not merely possible is, according to Peirce, to be actively engaged with others. It is this activity, this action of agency and enduring, that renders individual things determinate with respect to all forms of generality.

The category of firstness, according to Peirce, concerns qualitative possibility. Firsts are "the qualities of phenomena, such as red, bitter, tedious, hard, heartrending, noble" (CP, 1.418). Orience is the inexhaustibly lush and diverse aspect of reality. As John Dewey suggests in his discussion of Peirce, a first refers to "sheer totality and pervading unity of quality in *every*thing experienced, whether it be odor, the drama of King Lear, or philosophic or scientific systems" (1960, 200, italics his; cf. CP, 1.531). This category comprises those properties that Peirce called monadic. Each is a suchness, sui generis, not affected by comparison with anything else and so is absolutely free. It is just what it is and exceeds all articulation or description. Peirce writes, "Imagine me to make and in a slumberous condition to have a vague, unobjectified, still less unsubjectified, sense of redness, or of salt taste, or of an ache, or of grief or joy, or of a prolonged musical note. That would be, as nearly as possible, a purely monadic state of feeling" (CP, 1.303). Peirce drew his examples of firsts from psychological conceptions. "Feeling is the true psychical representative of the immediate as it is in its immediacy, of the present in its direct, positive presentness" (CP, 5.44). But he thought these firsts can be readily converted into phenomenological conceptions, and feeling then becomes "a pure nature, or quality, in itself without parts or features" (CP, 1.303).

Peirce repeatedly points out that qualities are, in themselves, mere possibilities. The following remarks are representative of his conception of firstness:

- For we have seen already that feeling is nothing but a quality, and quality is not conscious: it is a mere possibility.
- A quality is a mere abstract potentiality.
- Qualities are mere possibilities. As such, they have no existence and no individuality.

- But if we compare the monad [first] implicated in a genuine
  dyad [second], as red is in "this thing is red," with that dyad, we
  see that the latter is more than any mere explication of red. . . . It
  involves existence, while red or any mere explication of red is but
  a possibility. (CP, 1.310; CP, 1.422; CP, 1.475)

Firsts are mere abstract possibilities because they are, in themselves,
indeterminate. Red, as a possibility, may be actualized in many different things, and as such, as part of a second, it is distinct from all other
manifestations of red. This distinctive character is achieved by its
becoming part of an actual (and therefore determinate) individual.
"[T]he individual is determinate in regard to every possibility, or quality, either as possessing it or as not possessing it" (CP, 1.434). This is
firstness in relation to secondness, as described earlier. Prior to this
relation, however, a quality such as red is general or indeterminate. It
is not itself red, but merely the possibility of being red. For this reason,
red may be predicated of many distinct individuals: multiple individual things manifest a determinate quality that is an actualization of a
general possibility. But this determination, although unique, does not
transform the nature of the firstness as such, as redness or hardness.
"It is related to the matter accidentally; and this relation does not
change the quality at all, except that it imparts existence, that is to say,
this very relation of inherence, to it" (CP, 1.527).

   Peirce claims that qualities are both real and general regardless of
whether or not they inhere in some substance. This is the first indication of Peirce's realism and transcendentalism, and it separates
him from the conceptualists and the nominalists. According to
Peirce, both groups make gross errors. He writes that "It [a quality]
is not anything which is dependent, in its being, upon mind, whether
in the form of sense or in that of thought. Nor is it dependent, in its
being, upon the fact that some material thing possesses it. That quality is dependent on sense is the great error of the conceptualist. That
it is dependent on the subject in which it is realized is the great error
of all the nominalistic schools" (CP, 1.422). The conceptualist errs
because he thinks that in order for an object really to possess some

quality, such as red or hard, it must actually display that quality. In this case, the "realm" of qualitative possibility is restricted to what is actually perceived by some sentient being. Schopenhauer expressed this view when he claimed that "the existence of this whole world remains ever dependent upon the first eye that opened, even if it were that of an insect" (1928, 26). Peirce himself, in his early writings, tarried with this position (or rather, as he says, "wavered" over it). He claimed in his 1878 article "How to Make Our Ideas Clear" that "[t]here is absolutely no difference between a hard thing and a soft thing so long as they are not brought to the test" (SW, 124). So long as the diamond is not experienced or tested by some inquirer, Peirce insists that it is merely a question of nomenclature whether one describes it as hard or soft.

Later, in "Issues in Pragmaticism" (1905), Peirce corrected himself. He there says that the pragmatic maxim, even as stated in 1878, concerns the question of "not what did happen, but whether it would have been well to engage in any line of conduct whose successful issue depended upon whether that diamond would resist an attempt to scratch it" (CP, 5.457). The ascription of some quality to an object does not require its actual perception; it involves rather a subjective conditional that indicates what would be the case, which means that qualities are not, as the conceptualist thinks, dependent on sense. Peirce rhetorically asks, "[H]ow can the hardness of all other diamonds fail to bespeak some real relation among the diamonds without which a piece of carbon would not be a diamond? Is it not a monstrous perversion of the word and concept real to say that the accident of the non-arrival of the corundum [another resistant substance, the arrival of which would "test" the hardness] prevented the hardness of the diamond from having the reality which it otherwise, with little doubt, would have had?" (CP, 5.457). Objects have or may have qualities not perceived by any sentient creature. Under appropriate conditions, the entity *would* act in a definite way: it would be red, it would be hard. If a quality is embedded in an object, then it is possible for that object to actualize that quality in its reactions with other entities. It is not that the object *becomes* red or hard, for it is red or hard all along. The interaction provides an occasion for the object to make the quality in question manifest. It allows it to express a capacity it already has. In other words, even if a person were colorblind to red, the object, if it possessed this quality, would still be red.

This fact is independent of perception or mind. Peirce writes, "[T]hat the quality of red depends on anybody actually seeing it, so that red things are no longer red in the dark, is a denial of common sense. I ask the conceptualist, do you really mean to say that in the dark it is no longer true that red bodies are capable of transmitting light at the lower end of the spectrum?" (CP 1.422). If one espouses this conceptualist view, then one must intend that the entity necessarily becomes indeterminate when not beheld. But if the entity becomes indeterminate, then one cannot truly predicate properties of objects not seen or make true predictions. To say that X is red or hard is to say that X has a capacity: X *would* manifest red or hardness. Yet if the object is actually indeterminate, then one cannot truly predicate properties because, strictly speaking, properties are not yet had by the object. One therefore cannot say what X would do, but Peirce thinks that one simply cannot hold this view in the face of ordinary experience (much less in scientific inquiry). An object must have properties and tendencies even if no one is directly beholding the object manifesting those properties at the present moment. As Lesley Friedman points out, statements of mere regularity or uniformity are not able to support counterfactuals, whereas statements of natural law are: "Consequently, statements of uniformity cannot be understood as law-statements (nor can they explain law-like phenomena) as the antirealist would like us to believe" (1995, 383). This means that claims about how the future really would or will be are unsupportable. By banishing real generality, the future cannot but be indeterminate.

So far Peirce maintains that embodied qualities, even if not experienced, are real, which is a kind of immanent realism that separates him from the conceptualist school. But he is an "extreme" realist: he insists on the reality of transcendental possibilities, of qualities not *anywhere* embodied. "A quality of feeling can be imagined to be without any occurrence, as it seems to me. Its mere may-being gets along without any realization at all" (CP, 1.304). This insistence is what separates him from all nominalist schools. The nominalist thinks that qualities depend on actual entities for their being, but they are not because "[t]he mode of being a *redness,* before anything in the universe was yet red, was nevertheless a positive qualitative possibility. And redness in itself, even if it be embodied, is something positive and *sui generis*" (CP, 1.25, 1.527).

Qualities are real and general even if uninstantiated and are what they are apart from that which happens to embody them. "That mere quality, or suchness, is not in itself an occurrence, as seeing a red object is; it is a mere may-be. Its only being consists in the fact that there might be such a peculiar, positive, suchness in a phaneron" (CP, 1.304). As a mere may-be, such a quality remains indeterminate and general.[8] Peirce argues that it is impossible to hold that qualities are real only when they are embodied in facts. If that were the case, then only facts would exist, and laws would be fictions (CP, 1.422). But if only facts exist, then only the present state would be real, and the future would be "entirely indeterminate and so is general to the highest degree" (CP, 1.422). This is not the case, however; predictions, as Peirce emphasizes in his pragmatism lectures of 1903, can be readily made. Therefore, unembedded qualities must be real. Moreover, without unembedded qualities, it would be impossible to state counterfactuals. For example, even if there were no instances of red objects, one would want still to be able to say that if X could transmit light at the lower end of the spectrum, then X *would be* red. But if properties were not somewhere embedded, this would not be possible. Qualities, both embedded and not, must therefore have real being.

It is now possible to introduce Peirce's last category, thirdness or transuasion. Like firsts, thirds are indeterminate or general and are not actual. They have being that consists in mediation or continuity only.[9] Peirce characterizes thirds as laws that bring together firsts and seconds. By facilitating this relationship, thirds determine facts, whether actual or possible. "As *general,* the law, or general fact, concerns the potential world of quality, while as *fact,* it concerns the actual world of actuality" (CP, 1.420). In relation to firsts, thirds determine which properties are consistent with other specific properties or qualitative possibilities. They also determine what qualities higher-order properties may or may not have.[10] Regarding the actual world, thirds guide action. In itself, actuality, as secondness, is blind; it is a brute force. Thirdness represents the effect of mediation in the universe. For example (Peirce's own), the law of gravity mediates in definable ways—that is, it tends toward the manifestation of some possibilities and not others insofar as it guides the interaction of physical bodies with one another. Thirdness refers to what *would* occur under specifiable circumstances. With regard to what is actual, thirds provide direction or orientation and vaguely determine what *will* occur. I say vaguely because the activity of thirdness is not mechanistic, and a variety of outcomes will sufficiently answer to its form of mediation. Vagueness, however, does not preclude real effect, and it is real effect or the possibility thereof that ensures the reality of thirds.

Peirce's arguments for the reality of laws closely resemble those he gives for the reality of qualities and so may be attended more briefly. As already noted, to refuse generality entry into one's ontology amounts to claiming that only facts are real, which means both that the future is "general to the highest degree" or indeterminate and that predication is problematic. Mere facts simply cannot account for generality, according to Peirce. "No collection of facts can constitute a law; for the law goes beyond any accomplished facts and determines how facts that *may be*, but *all* of which never can have happened, shall be characterized" (CP, 1.420, italics his). Also, as in the case of firsts, Peirce insists not just on the reality of thirds that actually influence actual objects, but also on the reality of thirds that have never influenced existence and may never do so.

Peirce stipulates only that a general law, in order to be counted real, must at some time possibly have effect: "A true general cannot have any being unless there is to be some prospect of its sometime having occasion to be embodied in a fact, which is itself not a law or anything like a law" (CP, 1.304). A third may be real even if it *never* is realized in a fact. There need only be at some time a real chance of it being so realized. So long as possible, it does not have to be in any way actual to be real. For example, in a possible world in which there were no solid bodies, Peirce would hold that if there were to come into existence in the future a solid body, then this body would be subject to certain general laws in relation to other actual facts of that world.[11] The only generals that Peirce refuses are those that for some reason are impossible. They are mere fictions, having their being only in the mind of the individual who entertains them.

Peirce in Historical Context

However brief this survey, it provides an introduction to Peirce's ontology and to his commitment to the transcendental reality of qualities and to general laws. Both, broadly speaking, place him in the tradition of Plato and Kant, but his view is in important ways distinct both from the Platonic espousal of abstract entities and the later transcendentalism characteristic of *The Critique of Pure Reason.* Because these views have come under so much criticism, it is important to see more precisely how Peirce departs from them. Like the Platonist, Peirce is committed to abstract entities. Firsts and thirds are, as such, supersensible. One does not see laws, only their effects; one does not perceive a quality in itself (the mere possibility of being red, for instance), only the individuals that manifest it. Firsts and thirds are also independent of space and time in their mode of being. Peirce writes, for example, that "a quality is eternal, independent of time and of any realization" (CP, 1.420).

But unlike the Platonist, Peirce does not regard firsts or thirds as actual *things.* Only seconds are things because only they are determinate. Or rather, more accurately, only that which exhibits secondness may be considered an actual thing. Firsts and thirds are by nature indeterminate or vague. Red, as a first or mere possibility, is not a thing that is itself red: it is merely the real possibility of redness in the universe. Similarly, a third is but a "would-be" that itself has no properties. It only actualizes certain firsts when it mediates the activity of seconds.

Peirce identifies the great error of the nominalist to be his belief that only seconds, or facts, are real. It is similarly a "nominalistic" mistake to think that if one posits the reality of qualities or laws, then these qualities or laws are actual things. This mistake leads to insoluble problems such as: "If there is a thing existing called 'redness,' then doesn't it also have to be red? If so, then redness has something in common with a red thing, and this too must be accounted for." Thus begins the regress of the third-man argument. Peirce identifies the flaw as mistakenly thinking that redness is either actual or a thing. It is neither. The regress is forestalled because a first, such as redness, is not itself actual. It is not actual because it is indeterminate; and if it is indeterminate, then it surely is not a thing. Because it is not a thing, it is a mistake to ask what actual properties it has. Redness is itself the mere possibility of being red, which is what makes it predicable of many existing things. If, conversely, redness were a thing or were actual, then it would not be predicable of more than one. In the terms of the fourteenth-century debate over universals, positing redness as a thing would lead to attributing a nature such as "Socratesness," which is individual or individuating, to many individuals, an absurd attribution. Peirce avoids all of this by insisting on indeterminacy (or generality) for firsts and thirds. Beyond this description of them, he claims that there is nothing more to say. They are ultimate. "[T]o ask why a quality is as it is . . . would be lunacy" (CP, 1.420). To ask what firsts and thirds are like—that is, to demand characterizations of them other than "mere possibility" or "would-bes"—is similarly unreasonable.

For Peirce, there is but one actually existing world that is itself surrounded by real possibility of two kinds, both of which are general. As he writes, "A Fact . . . is, or may be Real, yet, in its Real existence it is inseparably combined with an infinite swarm of circumstances, which make no part of the fact itself" (MS, 647). In this respect, Peirce's view resembles less the "two-world" ontology of Platonism than the transcendentalism of Kant and Schopenhauer or of the early Wittgenstein. One achievement by these thinkers is the collapse of the "two-world ontology" into one world with two faces (phenomenal/noumenal and sign/symbol distinctions, respectively). One is visible in space and time, whereas the other is transcendent of all actual manifestations (Kant 1965, 274; Schopenhauer 1928, 9; Wittgenstein 1996, 3.11, 3.326, 3.327). Peirce's commitment to the transcendental reality of firsts and thirds seems analogous to the occluded face of the real.

But Peirce doggedly opposed the notion of a Kantian thing-in-itself. Even as early as 1868, although in some respects still nominalistic, he wrote, "that which is thought . . . is the real, as it really is. There is nothing, then, to prevent our knowing outward things as they really are" (CP, 5.311).[12] It is true that Peirce's ontology includes as real those possibilities and laws that do not exist as part of the actual world. There is an ontological distinction between being that exists and being that does not, and he includes both. But unlike other transcendental approaches (such as that of Kant or the early Wittgenstein), his does not impart any *epistemic* barriers. Those firsts and thirds are real that may in some way intrude on the actual. When they do so, they may be known through interaction with actual objects. This is to say that if they were actual, then they may come into diadic opposition to persons and be known by them. One might abstract those newly appearing qualities or infer these laws just like any other that is constitutive of the universe.

Moreover, Peirce claims that from the actual one may know the merely possible as such: "Rightly understood, it is correct to say that we immediately, that is, directly perceive matter. To say that we only infer matter from its qualities is to say that we only know the actual through the potential. It would be a little less erroneous to say that we only know the potential through the actual, and only infer qualities by generalization from what we perceive in matter" (CP, 1.429). Through experience of actual individuals' determinately having some qualities and not others, as well as being regulated by some laws and not others, one may infer to still other qualities and laws not instantiated or expressed by the actual world. Peirce's transcendentals are *knowable*, even if not known, both because their instantiation does not transform the nature of the general itself and because generality does not depend on instantiation for its reality. Thus, although Peirce is committed to an ontology of which at any given time much is unknown and a very large portion is not actualized, much may be further actualized in the future and be increasingly known. If the collapse of the two-world ontology into one world with two faces was Kant and Wittgenstein's achievement, then Peirce's accomplishment is greater still. He offers but one face, more or less known to those who through experience are pressed upon its features.

One must be quite cautious and explicit in describing Peirce as a transcendentalist, especially because it is all too easy to read him back into a tradition of which he is quite critical. Nevertheless, his view is a transcendental one, and it is important to see that this view is a reconstruction, a critical appropriation, of traditional resources rather than either a simple departure or (worse still) an uncritical defense of an ancient but out-of-favor doctrine.

TWO

THE SUBSTANCE OF
PEIRCE'S CATEGORIES

The World Phenomenologically Conceived

A Day, a livelong day, is not one thing but many. It changes not only in grow-
ing light toward zenith and decline again, but in texture and mood, in tone
and meaning, warped by a thousand factors of season, of heat or cold, of still
or multi winds, torqued by odors, tastes, and the fabrics of ice or grass, of bud
or leaf or black-drawn naked limbs. And as a day changes so do its subjects,
bugs and birds, cats, dogs, butterflies and people.

—John Steinbeck, *The Winter of Our Discontent*

The previous chapter provided an introductory account of Peirce's
most general categories and showed how these phenomenological
traits become for Peirce fully metaphysical conceptions. This chapter
first reconstrues one of the basic terms of Peirce's analysis, as suggested by Sandra Rosenthal in her monograph *Speculative Pragmatism*
(1986) and for the same reason: doing so facilitates better description
of everyday experience. But it then departs from her approach, which
she characterizes as a processively metaphysical one, by offering a
specifically pragmatic conception of substance. This definition of
substance follows and furthers previous suggestions made by Vincent
Potter in his essay "Peirce on 'Substance' and 'Foundations'" (1996)
and by Vincent Colapietro in his *Peirce's Approach to the Self* (1989). I
develop this view in the context of six criticisms in order to show not
only that a pragmatic formulation may responsibly meet these
charges, but also what sort of work this formulation is capable of performing. Demonstrating the former should quiet some legitimate

concerns about reinvoking this ancient but troubled concept; suggesting the latter is intended to make a Peircean understanding of substance attractive to those who are critical of the tradition, but who see no plausible alternatives in the field. The doctrine of substance, as here developed, emerges from Peirce's categories and provides a conception of the real that, in conjunction with a semeiotic approach to representation, shows how a pragmatist may claim that representation really does coincide with the reality it takes as its object.

Above all, it is important to note that a doctrine of substance is *itself* a representative claim about the real. It represents the real as being intrinsically representable by virtue of its substantial nature. Only if there are substances to be represented may going representations more or less represent them, and this assertion—that there are such existing entities—must be recognized as a prior representative claim. Whether or not this claim is persuasive turns on considerations such as whether the doctrine is descriptively adequate to experience, whether it is logically consistent, whether it may be tested through the further hypotheses that it produces, and, finally, whether it proves useful in solving problems more or less conceptually remote from the context that initially produced it. In what follows, I lend support to a view of substance conceived in light of Peirce's categories by suggesting that this claim is indeed descriptively adequate (perhaps necessary even), self-consistent, testable in various ways, and practically useful.

Categoreal Reconstruction

According to Peirce, the discrimination of three modes of being is the result of acute study of the everyday. It marks the pervasive features of all experience had by anyone and at any time. But the purpose of these concepts is to grasp not merely what is commonly present at any one moment, but what Steinbeck called in the opening epigraph "A Day, a *livelong* day" (italics mine). They are intended to capture the process of change, of rhythm, and of growth and decay. But as Sandra Rosenthal points out, Peirce does not have an ontological category of process. There is quality, brute actuality, and continuity or lawful behavior, but not process *as such*. Yet, for Peirce, this set of categories does not signify the irrelevance of process, but rather its absolute centrality. The categories, as conceptions, are static, but they are not intended to replace that which they represent. As Rosenthal rightly insists, "process is the ontological characteristic that accounts for the features grasped by the categories of metaphysics. Process is not itself a categorial feature for Peirce, but is implicitly that which is understood through categorial delineations of its features" (1986, 113). The general features that emerge from Peirce's phenomenology and later become his metaphysical categories (because approved by logic) are intended to provide better understanding of the world experienced in all its variability.

For this reason, I follow Rosenthal's distinction between an *event,* or "an actuality," and *existence,* or what exists. The former refers explicitly to the category of secondness. Secondness, it should be remembered, is brute resistance, and it is that which is determinate, occupying some here and now. It positively has or does not have specific qualities (firsts) and is or is not regulated by specific forms of mediation (thirds). But a certain confusion is liable to take hold if Peirce is not properly understood here, and an equivocation of the meaning of *actuality* or *existence* promotes this confusion. As a category, secondness is (as such) blind, brute, and privative. Actual things in the world are characterized by secondness insofar as they are determinate and they resist other objects and act upon them in specifiable ways.

But actual things are not reducible to secondness. As Peirce claims, the absolutely individual "cannot exist, properly speaking. For what ever lasts for any time, however short . . . will undergo some change in its relations" (CP, 3.93n; cf. Rosenthal 1986, 128). Because existing things not only engage in relations with their environments but also change in those relations, they are not reducible to secondness. Were that the case, they would be absolutely static and absolutely unrelated to anything else. Existing things, however, are always characterized by all three categories, not just by firstness and secondness, precisely because they are neither static nor unrelated. Thirdness, in short, is ineluctable.

This suggests that the term *actual* has two distinguishable meanings and does too much work in Peirce's ontology. In one context, it is one of three abstract phenomenological conceptions; in the other, it represents the fullness of the real being described by all three categories. In order to mark this difference, I follow Rosenthal's distinction between existence and actuality. The latter strictly corresponds to what Peirce refers to in the abstract category of secondness. The former refers to the world at large in all its concreteness and diversity. This distinction is necessary because although the latter includes the former, it includes far more as well. As Rosenthal points out, in experience of the world "[w]e encounter possibilities and potentialities as well as actualities . . . and these former, as well as the latter, have a brute facticity and natural resistance that our knowledge must incorporate if it is to be successful. Thus, what exists, what is spatio-temporally real, is processive concreteness in all of its ontological activity modes, in all of its ways or manners of behaving. Existence and spatio-temporal reality are coextensive" (1986, 129; see also Rosenthal 1995, 98, for substantially the same claim). In this reconfiguration, actuality is restricted to a component of the world and existence refers to that which Peirce's metaphysical categories are intended to describe and explain. It is the fullness of the day—with all its transactions, possibilities, likelihoods, moods, and qualities—that exists. The actual, as a categorial component, is part of this reality and crucial to it, making it *this* day, even if it does not exhaust the day's reality. As Rosenthal claims, the possibilities and potentialities of a particular morning also have a facticity about them that must be taken into account. It advances along a continuous course, lights on some possibilities and potentialities but not on others, and achieves a qualitative whole not reducible to its parts.

But Rosenthal's view remains incomplete, I suggest, because she claims that this reconstruction suffices to account for what she calls *processive concreteness,* a term that coincides with the real as such. Firstness, secondness, and thirdness, understood as categories of concrete process, may adequately account for the fullness of what is experienced. She argues that Peirce's phenomenology not only has no place for what is traditionally called substance, but also must be intrinsically opposed to it. The shift to a metaphysics of process undermines entirely the struggle to articulate a doctrine of substance to account for continuity and thereby renders the concept superfluous. Moreover, it must be carefully avoided if one is to escape being drawn back into its unsolvable problems. She writes,

> Though process must be a metaphysical category, opposed, for example, to the metaphysical category of substance, yet the development of the metaphysical categories will be seen to be categories of process, modes of its activity. *The term* mode *as here used must of course be severed from its link with substance philosophy.* Modes of activity are manners or ways of behaving constitutive of the nature of processive concreteness; the ontological activity modes are ways or manners in which process functions. (1986, 113–15, italics mine)

Process metaphysics, which Rosenthal identifies as a shared approach among pragmatists such as James, Dewey, and C. I. Lewis (in addition to Peirce), is fundamentally opposed to substance because substance is ineluctably tied to a metaphysics of stasis, or that which remains unaltered in the midst of temporal change, but *nothing* remains unchanged in the concrete process of everyday experience.

Citing Lewis, Rosenthal herself claims that "Qualities and surd existence, then, are not sufficient; objects require either unalterable substance or lawful alteration" (1986, 118). Lewis chose the latter, as did Peirce, according to Rosenthal's account, but both of these thinkers failed, again according to Rosenthal, to grasp the significance of their decision. Each in his own way struggled to articulate his new position in terms of the still available but in that period outdated choices between realism and idealism. According to her, "Lewis, in his search for a metaphysical label, is trapped, like Peirce, in the historical alternatives that present themselves, failing to recognize the full significance of his switch from substance to process" (1986, 118). Rosenthal claims that Peirce's continued discussion of idealism and realism signaled both his narrow understanding of his own position and his failure to escape the alternatives proffered by the very metaphysics that he repudiated, that of substance. She also claims that Peirce would have done better to take James's advice and turn a deaf ear to the questions posed by this metaphysical tradition of long standing (1986, 119).

Whereas Rosenthal seems to take this criticism of Peirce and Lewis as her point of departure for developing her own pragmatic and processive approach, I suggest that there are good reasons for retaining a notion of substance. Rather than the dilemma of *either* an unalterable view of substance *or* merely lawful alteration, this is the third possibility of a concept of substance reconstructed by pragmatic insight. In this view of substance, the categories are intended to explain rather than explain away. It is a notion that performs a specific kind of work while avoiding the criticisms commonly brought to bear against the idea of substance. Before turning to this reconstruction, however, I first suggest some reasons why a view of substance is still desirable. Next I briefly point to the ways in which Peirce himself continually uses the term *substance* as a general conception of a thing. Then I turn to criticism of substance and show, at least in outline, that Peirce's conception escapes these charges. I argue that Peirce, rather than being bemused by the questions and framework of a substance metaphysics from which he somehow could not see his way clear, both recognizes the difficulty with substance as traditionally conceived and reconstructs (or provides means for reconstructing) this notion in a sustainable and useful way.

The Practical Uses of Substance

Peirce developed the general categories of firstness, secondness, and thirdness as means for grasping the pervasive features of all experience. Experience, as Dewey writes, "is *of* as well as *in* nature. It is not experience which is experienced, but nature—stones, plants, animals, diseases, health, temperature, electricity, and so on" (1988b, 12, italics his). Experience is of things transacting with other things, engaged in activities that transform the participants in multiple, complex, and sometimes (at least apparently) contradictory or conflicting ways. As a descriptive term, *experience* is relevant in both of its meanings here. On one hand, it denotes acting and suffering, agency on others as well as patience or enduring of those others. Sometimes such transactions are relatively trivial and passing. Casually saying hello to another person, feeling an afternoon rain, or seeing a falling star over the Southern Hemisphere may have little effect on those experiencing this event. The very same events or other ones, such as the loss of a beloved or the unpredictable touching down of a twister in a small town, may have immense consequences for those who suffer them. The difference between the two is one of degree of effect, not of kind—of the agent on the patient and vice versa.

But experience also denotes history; it is the storied past that informs the present, provides a context for its explanation, and directs future development along some lines and not others. In colloquial terms, the "experienced" man or woman is the one who has seen, done, and been subjected to much over the course of a lifetime. The source of his or her wisdom lies in the *protracted* suffering and doing that informs his or her ongoing experience. Writ large, experience refers to the career of any existing thing, a career in which the thing develops in response to and in conjunction with other things.

When both senses of the term are operative, experience is seen to be of things that are in the process of development or change, sometimes radically so, but continuous with their respective pasts. To invoke Steinbeck, it is not just bugs, birds, and butterflies in general, or "lawful alteration" as such, but *this* bug, *that* flock of migrating birds, and *those* beautiful orange-tinged butterflies. The drama and significance that unfold in experience, to say nothing of the complexly related causal factors, demand attention to particular objects unfolding over time, which in turn requires some notion of continuity or sameness in existence if justice is to be done to the world experienced or to persons' experience of it. The death of the butterfly, for example, would not be tragic were it not the same butterfly that a child had followed on its flitting course and that had potential for continued intercourse with the environment. Nor can one come to understand why this butterfly did not survive without attention to the concrete details of its particular history in light of general laws.

The point here is that something *more* must be taken into account than just general lawfulness or just particularity, something that includes both and is not reducible to either, but is something to which lawfulness and particularity refer. For this "something," I suggest that a notion of substance is required.[1] A substance is that *to which* firstness, secondness, and thirdness refer as an individual constituent of nature and experience, as something participant in the continuum or flow of being. It is for these acts of existence that the categories are constructed in order to gain some understanding of what is experienced.

Unlike the earlier distinction between actuality and existence, in which I followed Rosenthal's criticism of Peirce, I take this view of substance to be Peirce's own. Even though his writings on the subject are few, he nonetheless uses the term *substance* quite freely. He refers to the substance of a law, of a dream, of an argument, or to substance in the specific context of chemistry—protoplasm such as "nerve-slime" or "lion-slime" (CP 1.595, 5.65, 6.256, 6.250, 6.553). As Colapietro points out, Peirce also accepts the notion of substance in the Aristotelian sense of a thing (1989, 86). In "A Guess at the Riddle," where Peirce directly addresses the emergence, formation, and growth of substance, he distinguishes between the modern conception of substance and a conception that he considers more inclusive. In a footnote, he writes, "I use substance, here, in the old sense of a *thing*, not in the modern chemical sense" (CP, 1.515, italics mine). Peirce conjectures that the development of a substance in the sense of a thing occurs as follows: "Pairs of states will also begin to take habits, and thus each state having different habits with reference to the different other states will give rise to bundles of habits, which will be *substances*. Some of these states will chance to take habits of persistency, and will get to be less and less liable to disappear; while those that fail to take such habits will fall out of existence. Thus, substances will get to be permanent" (CP, 1.515, italics mine; see also Colapietro 1989, 82, and Potter 1996, 106).

Substance is defined here, at least implicitly, as bundles of habits. Habits denote the regularity of behavior exhibited by individually existing things in their interactions with other things. Peirce defines *habit,* in its broad sense, as "a specialization, original or acquired, of the nature of a man, or an animal, or a vine, or a crystallizable chemical substance, or anything else, that he or it will behave, or always tend to behave, in a way describable in general terms upon every occasion (or upon a considerable proportion of the occasions) that may present itself of a generally describable character" (CP, 5.538). Peirce insists that "[t]he existence of things consists in their regular behaviour" because otherwise objects are "liable to disappear" (CP, 1.515). This is the effect of continuity or thirdness in the career of existing objects. Otherwise, an object would be merely actual and would be a pure individuality that could not but fall promptly out of existence. But existence still involves secondness because obsistence is what makes it individual. As Vincent Colapietro points out, "existence [or actuality, as I define it in this chapter] (because it is an instance of opposition) designates the aspect of secondness exhibited by any individual substance, while persistence (because it is a case of continuity) designates one of the ways in which it manifests thirdness" (1989, 83). Both actuality and persistence are characteristic of phenomena. They *refer* to features that are everywhere present to the inquirer; the three categories, however, require a notion of substance in order to denote that to which persistence and existence are attributed.

When a concept of substance is included in the ontology, it may be seen that the bundle of habits that impart continuity, although general in themselves as habits, become distinctive in some particular substance in their mode of interpenetration. A substance is not just a "bucket" filled with so many isolated dispositions to act (thirdness), but is rather particular in the way the habits that mark it as continuous mesh, reinforce, or support one another (secondness) and in such a way as to achieve a distinct quality of its own (firstness). This interpenetration is, as Peirce points out, volatile. Habits develop in pairs with reference to other states, and to the extent that these habits achieve a continuity, they may be denoted substantial. But only some of these habits develop persistency, modes of interaction that sustain and reinforce other habits or dispositions to behave. When this reinforcement occurs, substance becomes permanent.

It should be emphasized that *substance* is here a relative term: it marks *degrees* of endurance, not unalterability as such. The word *permanent* is not to be taken as meaning "strictly unalterable," but rather in its etymological sense of remaining over some period of time. That a substance does so remain does not preclude alteration, either in some respects or ultimately in all of them over a protracted history of interactions. The history of a substance may well be an account of how a thing became transformed into something quite different from and in many respects opposite to its original nature. The continuity it displays is itself a history of successive transformations.

Substance so understood does two very important sorts of work in a pragmatic approach. On the one hand, it identifies existing objects that are in important ways distinct from other objects—that is, are individuals. This is not just substance in general, but substances bearing distinct histories and propensities (Aristotle's primary substance). On the other hand, substance also includes the aspect of thirdness. Self-referentially, this is persistence. It is a notion that captures the sense of "sameness" of a thing, of whatever sort, over time. Even after dramatic change, such as the transformation from larva to butterfly, something can be said to be still the same thing. This point is crucial if our representation of experience is to hang together as our experience itself surely does. In reference to other things, this persistence is another form of continuity. It shows that there is no such thing as a strictly isolated fact or object in the world. An object is what it is; it is the substance it has become, only in relation to its environment. Without those surroundings, the thing becomes a mere abstraction and, if taken to be what it is apart from that from which it is abstracted, becomes inexplicable as an existing thing.

That a concept of substance does considerable work, as it did for Aristotle, should not surprise anyone. The question is, What shape is substance to take in light of the powerful criticisms that have been brought to bear on it—and in such a way that it is not a mere shadow of what was promised? How does one respond to charges of essentialism, ahistoricism, acontextualism, unwarranted foundationalism, and even mysticism in defending a substance metaphysics? Is it possible to have a view that survives such criticism and remains useful? Certainly I can address only some of this criticism and not in the detail deserved. In the next section, I try to represent fairly the objections to a substance metaphysics, but with the explicit purpose of further developing a Peircean approach to the problem. I consider briefly six arguments against a substance approach, and in the context of each I discuss what a pragmatist may profitably say in response. I lifted these arguments from a range of historical and contemporary texts; I should point out, however, that criticism of substance is not always fully articulated by those who eschew it, and some of the very best criticism comes from the pragmatist tradition. James in particular is quite critical, so I draw on him extensively here.

Constructive Criticism

One argument against substance is that the term is itself inexplicable. It is an ultimate datum, a *non plus ultra* that, because not susceptible to further explanation, constitutes something of a mystery. Why this may be so can be gathered from a brief look at Aristotle's definition of substance. In the *Categories,* he claims that "primary substances are most properly called substances in virtue of the fact that they are the entities which underlie everything else, and that everything else is either predicated of them or present in them" (1941, 2b[15]). It is the individual, such as a particular horse or man, that Aristotle has in mind for a primary substance. In *Metaphysics* 5, he further distinguishes two senses of the term *substance.* One is the ultimate substratum, which cannot be predicated of anything else, and the other is "that which, being a 'this,' is also separable—and of this nature is the shape or form of each thing" (1941, 1017b[23]). Which, form or matter, is more properly said to be the substance of a thing is a controversy of long standing.

But regardless of which is privileged, both have become increasingly suspect as intelligible conceptions. John Locke suggested that we cannot avoid supposing the idea of substance. "The idea that we have, to which we give the *general* name substance, being nothing but the supposed, but unknown support of those qualities we find existing, which we imagine cannot subsist *sine re substante*, without something to support them, we call that support *substantia*" (1975, 296, italics his). Under closer scrutiny, however, Locke found the notion of substance not only *unknown* but also intrinsically *unclear*. He claimed that "We have no such *clear Idea* at all, and therefore signify nothing by the word *Substance*, but only an uncertain supposition of we know not what" (1975, 95, italics his). Locke's view marks the beginning both of a decidedly modern suspicion of substance in general and of a shift in the understanding of substance from form (as favored by Aristotle and neoplatonists such as Plotinus) to matter. Locke thought of substance as an idea "which we take to be the *substratum*, or support of those *Ideas* we do know" (1975, 296, italics his).

This idea of substance as substrate was further criticized by Berkeley, under the guise of Philonous, as philosophically unintelligible and superfluous and as a precursor of both skepticism and atheism (1979, 33–35, 63, 88). More recently, Morris Cohen suggested that a recovery of substance would entail getting rid of the Lockean confusion between matter and substance and recovering Aristotle's view (1964, 161). This would be a view of substance as principle or concept. But it isn't clear that only matter is under fire by the modern empiricists. David Hume, for example, claimed that matter *and* the concept of substance are fictive productions of a beleaguered mind. He wrote that

> Whenever it [the mind] views the object in another light, it finds that all these qualities are different, and distinguishable, and separable from each other; which view of things being destructive of its primary and more natural motions, obliges the imagination to feign an unknown something, or *original* substance and matter, as a *principle* of union or cohesion among these qualities, and as what may give the compound object a title to be call'd one thing, notwithstanding its diversity and composition. (Hume 1989, 221, italics his)

That Hume identified these concepts as a principle of union, which is reminiscent of Aristotle's claim that substance is in a sense a formula, suggests that his mentioning both matter and substance is not merely rhetorical apposition; rather, he thought that substance, either conceived as a merely material "something I know not what" or as something more abstract, is a fiction of mind. It is something that cannot be immediately known but is imagined to constitute the things experienced, underlying all their qualities. Because it cannot be known, it cannot be any further understood or explained than merely being supposed to exist, which is why it is regarded as mysterious. And if it is mysterious, why posit it at all? Doing so, as Peirce would say, merely blocks the road to further inquiry that might well present a more plausible solution.

This view of substance as something not susceptible to further explanation is a conception that Peirce likewise thoroughly rejects. In his Harvard lectures on pragmatism, he begins in the following vein:

> The doctrine then was, as it remains in nineteen out of every score of logical treatises that are appearing in these days, that there is no way of defining a term except by enumerating all its universal predicates, each of which is more abstracted and general than the term defined. So unless this process can go on endlessly, which was a doctrine little followed, the explication of a concept must stop at such ideas as Pure Being, Agency, *Substance* and the like, which were held to be ideas so perfectly simple that no explanation whatever could be given of them. (CP, 5.207, italics mine)

Terms such as *substance* are thought to be so general as not to be susceptible of further predication. But these terms were also thought to be perfectly simple by those who initially posited them, and so not only was no further explanation possible, none was needed (a happy coincidence). Positing substance is in this view both reasonable and useful because it forestalls a potentially infinite regress. Peirce then continues, however: "This grotesque doctrine was shattered by the logic of relations, which showed that the simplest conceptions, such as Quality, Relation, Self-consciousness could be defined and that such definitions would be of the greatest service in dealing with them" (CP, 5.207).

Conceptions such as substance cannot be considered perfectly simple, according to Peirce, because they are indeed susceptible to further
explanation. That they may be further understood has three important
implications. First, substances are not, as was previously suggested,
ultimate because more may be said of them. Second, they are indeed
intelligible, not mysterious, notions. And third, because they are intelligible, they may possibly correspond or represent something in nature
that is independent of whether some person or persons suppose it to
exist. In short, they may not, as Hume suggested, be mere fictions of a
confused mind.

But what is this further logical explanation to which Peirce alludes?
In "The Architecture of Theories," which precedes by twelve years
Peirce's attack on substance as a simple conception, he writes, "Among
the many principles of Logic which find their application in
Philosophy, I can here only mention one. Three conceptions are perpetually turning up at every point in every theory of logic, and in the
most rounded systems they occur in connection with one another.
They are conceptions so very broad and consequently indefinite that
they are hard to seize and may be easily overlooked. I call them the
conceptions of First, Second, Third" (EP1, 296). These conceptions are
of course the general categories to which the reader was introduced in
chapter 1 of this book. There the nature of each category was discussed, which in itself indicates that these further terms of logic may
themselves be properly defined. It was also noted why Peirce concludes
that these three modes of being are real and active in the universe. So
far from fictions of mind, the categories constitute the real as well as
what exists, independently of what persons happen to think of either.

A substance, within a Peircean approach, is thus a thing characterized
by these categories. As it is actual, it determinately has some properties and not others, which means that it has the potential to act on
other things in definite ways and be acted upon by them and that it
displays tendencies or is regulated by laws that mediate its interactions
with others. Because regulated by law, it is continuous with at least
some parts of its environment but is sufficiently discontinuous to warrant being marked as a distinct thing. It is also persistent, retaining

features over time that make it continuous with its own past. Substance, so conceived, is a far cry from the "something, I know not what" posited by Locke and subjected to withering criticism by Berkeley; it is a concept that is both continuous with everyday experience and something that points the way to further explanation. It is the *what* that must be further explained by inquiry that is itself guided by the general categories of firstness, secondness, and thirdness. Identifying something as a substance is the prelude to further inquiry concerning the qualities and relations that make it what it is and no other.

This conclusion brings up a closely related second criticism of substance: that it does not itself do any explanatory work. It is of course one thing to be unexplainable and quite another to explain nothing. William James, citing Shadworth Hodgson, suggests that it is common for philosophers to follow the rule of "Whatever you are totally ignorant of, assert to be the explanation of everything else" (1950, 223). This practice occurs in the context of a discussion of substance in which one inference drawn is that substance, because inexplicable, cannot possibly be said to explain. The previous discussion argued that substance is not inexplicable. Given Peirce's further discussion of the categories, however, is not the concept of substance itself rendered superfluous? John Boler (1963), for example, claims precisely this. It might well appear so, but there is good reason to think that it is not.

In "How to Make Our Ideas Clear," Peirce argues that in addition to the two grades of clarity that treatises on logic commonly discuss, there is a third. The first two he identifies as *clarity* and *distinctness* because these terms are inherited from the Cartesian tradition. Clarity concerns acquaintance or familiarity; to say that a term is clear, according to Peirce, is but to say that we "have lost all hesitancy in recognizing it in ordinary cases" (EP1, 125). The second grade, distinctness, has to do with abstract definition. An idea is distinctly apprehended when a precise definition may be given in abstract terms. The third grade, which Peirce introduces, is the pragmatic maxim. It famously goes as follows: "Consider what effects, which might conceivably have practical bearings, we conceive the object of our conception to have. Then, our conception of these effects is the whole of our conception of the object" (EP1, 132). The third grade surpasses the second because it indicates what some object *would* do under specifiable circumstances—that is, what qualities it would display and how it would act on or be affected by others. The entirety of these grades taken together exhausts the meaning of any idea one might have of some thing.

This further clarification is itself guided by the general categories of firstness, secondness, and thirdness, but it does not render the prior two grades of clarity superfluous. Acquaintance and definition do provide important information. Moreover, I suggest that the term *substance* initially falls under the second grade of clarity. Substances are objects or things that are susceptible to definition by abstract terms. Such definitions are limited but significant. Even in the most infamous of cases, in which opium is said to cause sleep because it has a "dormitive power," the information may turn out to be crucial and sufficient unto the needs of that particular day and its problematic situation. If a patient's condition calls for her to be put to sleep and the question "What will do that?" is posed, then he who knows that opium possesses this dormitive power will know to employ it instead of something else.

Perhaps more important, the higher grade of clarity does not replace but rather refines our understanding of substances so defined on the second level. We may more precisely say what is meant by such a power, what may be expected from it, how it may be tested, or (of greater import still) to what other contexts it may be profitably applied in the future. Seen from this point of view, substance does important work. On one hand, it does the everyday duty of rough-and-ready knowledge; it tells us what we need to know under ordinary circumstances. On the other, it provides a starting point for what Dewey calls more intricate triangulations. It directs further inquiry, which is always an important service in scientific inquiry as well as in other kinds of practices.

My interpretation and elucidation of Peirce on substance differs considerably from John Boler's, who argues that Peirce discards the notion of substance and then criticizes him for having done so. He says, "For Peirce, however, the predominance of continuity tends to eliminate the concept of substance, and the supposit (Socrates, for example) comes to be treated as a process. What we call 'things' are not strictly individuals but generals" (1963, 151). He then states in his conclusion that "[t]he trouble I have with Peirce's position [the elimination of substance as a category] is that, while the interpretation of things as thirds serves to distinguish things and individuals, it becomes difficult to dissociate things from laws and types, which are the paradigms of thirdness; and, of course, 'no great realist' wants to hold that laws and types are things" (1963, 151). Boler is surely right that a realist would not hold that a law is a thing (a second), but it is not at all clear that Peirce has identified *thing* strictly with thirdness. As Colapietro points out, a thing is characterized by all three categories. Usually the context in which these categories are discussed is within an argument against nominalism, and so thirdness is emphasized. In response to Boler, however, the emphasis must shift to the irreducible presence of secondness (which includes firsts) to any existent thing. It is a mistake to identify substance with thirdness alone, just as it is (I argue) an error to think that substance has been discarded. Substance is that which is subjected to further clarification in light of the most general categories. When these two errors are avoided, one may both distinguish things from the (purely) individual (or existence from actuality as we have done) and distinguish between things and the laws that guide them as Boler wishes to do. There is, in short, no need to choose between them if Peirce is understood as maintaining, rather than jettisoning, a notion of substance.

A third criticism of substance is that it has historically been a strategy for privileging one portion or kind of reality over all others. In both *A Pluralistic Universe* (1912) and *Pragmatism* (1914), James informs his audience that the history of Western metaphysics has been a history of selective emphasis and metaphysical reduction.[2] Philosophers find experience too cluttered, so they introduce principles that reduce the many to a few or to a one. The instrument of choice is, according to James, the concept: perceptual reality is handled in conceptual terms that replace the much-at-onceness of reality with abstract relations that possess the virtues of being relatively few in number and eternal in nature (1912, 235; 1914, 128). James sees this replacement as a practically useful way of harnessing the particulars of reality on behalf of human purposes, but the practice becomes invidious when concepts are employed "privatively as well as positively, using them not merely to assign properties to things, but to deny the very properties with which the things sensibly present themselves" (1912, 218). Concepts or substantives, because eternal, are taken to be more real than perceptual reality; sensible experience is then regarded as deficient, illusory, or mere "appearance."

The result of this treatment is that the real becomes hierarchized, and a dividing line is drawn. One of James's more aggressive criticisms of monistic idealism is that it generates precisely this sort of privileging. He writes that "[c]onceptual treatment of perceptual reality makes it seem paradoxical and incomprehensible; and when radically and consistently carried out, it leads to the opinion that perceptual experience is not reality at all but an appearance or illusion" (1977, 256). Hegelians produce a conception of the Absolute in order to render experience logically consistent and meaningful, but in doing so they denigrate the reality of individual persons' experience because, in relation to the Absolute, experience is reduced to mere appearance and logical inconsistency. Of this reduction James is extremely impatient: "But while Professors Royce and Bradley and a whole host of guileless thoroughfed thinkers are unveiling Reality and the Absolute and explaining away evil and pain, this is the condition of the only beings known to us anywhere in the universe with a developed consciousness of what the universe is. What these people experience *is* Reality. . . . It is the personal experience of those best qualified in our circle of knowledge to *have* experience, to tell us *what is*" (1914, 30, italics his). Nor is it difficult to find others in the tradition who have sifted out some portion of reality as more real than another; the practice began, James informs us, with the pre-Socratics. For this reason, he urges his audience to leave off pursuit of metaphysics altogether and to get on with the work of empirical description.

Peirce's response to James is complex on this issue. One point of contention, with considerable implications, is the question of realism and nominalism. James, because he is a nominalist, thinks that concepts are "introduced" by interested agents for pragmatic purposes. He does not believe that there is anything in nature that may meaningfully be said to correspond to the concept, a notion that greatly informs his other claims. Peirce, because a scholastic realist, does so believe. He thinks that there are generals at work in nature and that general concepts of the mind may really correspond to them. But the issue at hand, narrowly considered, is whether or not Peirce's approach is tantamount to the privileging that James and others find everywhere in the discourse of metaphysics. I suggest it is not.

For Peirce, there are three modes of being, only one of which may be said to be actual, but each of these modes is equally *real,* each manifesting itself in the phenomena of everyday experience in its own way. In marking the differences in categorial terms, Peirce is not suggesting that one is more or less real than another; he is only further discriminating what the nature of the real is. It should be remembered that in the first chapter I showed how phenomenology was indifferent to distinctions of appearance and reality; subsequent considerations suggested that thirdness was indeed really operative in nature, which makes Peirce a realist. But the notion that thirdness is operative in nature does not denigrate, displace, suspend, or overcome the reality of the other two categories. Any appearance of thirdness includes secondness but is not reducible thereto. Conversely, secondness loses none of its reality by being mediated by thirdness. The particularity of the world, which James himself was so intent on privileging in his writings (as compensation to the historical preference for the abstract), remains intact and has its due in Peirce's representation of the real. The categories are conceptions that grasp the nature of the real, of the things encountered in experience—however they may manifest themselves. A substance becomes better understood when the inquirer employs these categories by allowing them to direct his study of the world and the things that dwell within it.

So far from committing the crime to which James objects, Peirce's approach *furthers* the empirical discourse James favors. It not only gives a place to the particularity of experience, but also demands that such particularity be brought into real relation with the other features of the reality persons experience. One might argue that whereas James reinscribes the duality between particularity and the general extant in the history of philosophy (metaphysics especially) by privileging the particular over the general, Peirce bridges this gulf through his triadic division of the real. Existing things have particular qualities and are distinct from other things, but because they are mediated by real generality, they are brought into existential relation with those other things. In Peirce's approach, there is, in brief, no need to choose between the particular and the general. Both are present, each has its own kind of work to perform, and neither is reducible to the other.

More specifically, the Peircean formulation of substance is not merely a concept useful for determining what something or some kind of thing most properly is. Substance surely is a tool for classification, for building out empirical descriptions of both the development and family relations of specific kinds of things. In biology, for example, it is useful in the articulation of historical evolution of kinds over time as well as of how closely related a given species is to other species. Insofar as substance is used in an empirical fashion, and provided that the notion of substance and classification is properly understood (see the fifth criticism of substance later for the details of this notion), a Peircean approach readily embraces this use. But this portion of the inquiry is only the initial phase and should not be mistaken for the entire inquiry. For the purpose of such classification, beyond mere curiosity or knowledge for its own sake, discovery must be made of not just what *is* and what is likely to be, but also of what *may be.*

Learning the nature of the things around us and experimenting with them generate new conditions of possibility, of growth or transformation that not only alter the relations entered into by the participants, but promise (at least potentially) alteration of the nature of the things themselves in an ongoing way. As George Santayana writes of substance,

> When these habits of nature are taken (as they should be taken) as the true principle of explanation, the belief in substance does become a great means of understanding events. It helps me to

explain their place, date, quality, and quantity, so that I am able to expect *or even to produce them*, when the right substances are at hand. If they were detached facts, not forms regularly taken on by enduring and pervasive substances, there would be no knowing when, where, of what sort, or in what numbers they would not assault me; and my life would not seem life in a tractable world, but an inexplicable nightmare. (1955, 209, italics mine)

Rather than a kind of descriptive quietism that implicitly privileges present realities regardless of what those may be (which is problematic for a number of reasons), a substance metaphysics as here conceived is part of a diagnosis that paves the way for potentially radical transformation.

To this extent, one may say of a Peircean approach what Michel Foucault claimed to be the task of all philosophy: "any diagnosis concerning the nature of the present," he replied in an interview, "does not consist in a simple characterization of what we are but, instead—by following lines of fragility in the present—in managing to grasp why and how that-which-is might no longer be that-which-is" (1988, 36). Discovering the specific nature of things provides information that may direct both future scientific inquiry as well as our conduct in our interactions with the environment and other persons. Bringing substances together in new ways unleashes potentialities that were not previously in present sight, and the world may be remade in light of ideal conception. In short, the claim that substances are immutable in the sense that the definition of the thing is eternal should be discarded from a pragmatic view of substance. When this is done, a conception of things that may guide both empirical description and practical transformation is intellectually secured.

A fourth objection to substance emerges from the way in which it has been regarded as *entirely* independent of its surroundings. Some argue that a substance does not depend on its environment for what it is because it is as it is, independently of aught else. Descartes claims, for example, that "Really the notion of *Substance* is just this—that which can exist by itself, without the aid of any other substance" (1988, 156, italics his). Spinoza says that "By substance, I understand that which is in itself and is conceived through itself" (1981, 355). Nor is a substance dependent on time or history because essences, or the natures of substances, are themselves eternal. As Aristotle points out, although a particular substance may perish, "there is no destruction of the formula [which is most properly substance] in the sense that it is ever in course of being destroyed" (*Metaphysics*, 1941, 1039b[20–25]).

It is not only the formula, or abstract definition, however, that is for Aristotle autonomous. It is sometimes said that the view of substance as completely independent is owing to rationalist excesses, but in the *Categories* Aristotle argues, "With regard to primary substances, it is quite true that there is no such possibility, for neither wholes nor parts of primary substance, are relative. The individual man or ox is not defined with reference to something external" (*Categories*, 1941, 8a[35]–b[25]). There is not even a *possibility*, in the philosopher's opinion, of primary substances being essentially dependent on their surroundings. This aspect of substance has of course become viewed with increasing skepticism. Few believe that anything is so independent, and some argue that the carving out of substances is itself essentially arbitrary. James is well known for this sort of response, but John Locke said it better and earlier. He claimed that

> the great parts and wheels, as I may so say, of this stupendous structure of the universe, may for aught we know, have such a connexion and dependence in their influences and operations one upon another, that perhaps things in this our mansion would put on quite another face, and cease to be what they are, if some one of the stars or great bodies incomprehensibly remote from us, should cease to be or move as it does. This is certain – things, however absolute and entire they seem in themselves, are but retainers to other parts of nature, for that which they are most taken notice of by us. Their observable qualities, actions, and powers are owing to something without them; and there is not so complete and perfect a part that we know of nature, which does not owe the being it has, and the excellences of it, to its neighbors. (1975, 587)

Locke's claim is that the substantial character of things is apparent only because every seemingly autonomous object is in reality intrinsically related to its environment in the sense that it is radically dependent upon other actual things for its own nature. Substance is therefore merely rendered nominal; it does not refer to anything actually independent, but only to what is of most interest to us. This is, of course, James's view when he claims that things are nothing "but special groups of sensible qualities, which happen practically or aesthetically to interest us, to which we therefore give substantive names, and which we exalt to this exclusive status of independence and dignity" (1977, 71). Such names, or essences, become purely teleological weapons of the mind according to James (1977, 321).

The account of substance as I have here reconstructed it should make one thing abundantly clear: the debate over substance is a polemical one. The choice seems to be a strict and drastic either/or. Either substance is understood as entirely autonomous of both diachronic and synchronic influence, being just what it is in and through itself, or there is no such thing as substance at all, it being little or no more than a name for human practical interests. The fact that James, Dewey, and Peirce all take relations and process quite seriously would suggest that, in response to the dilemma as it is here posed, each would align himself against substance (as Rosenthal claims). But the fact that pragmatists emphasize contingency and process does not entail, as Richard Rorty suggests, that they assert "the universality and necessity of the individual and contingent" (1989, 83). Rather, to come down on this side of the dilemma is but to impose a new form of absolutism. As Richard Shusterman points out, "Of course, in the sense of logical necessity, everything may be contingent. But some things are clearly more contingent than others, and failure to distinguish between these differing sorts of contingencies simply reflects our bad philosophical habit of absolutist thinking" (1992, 83). In other words, the problem as it is here represented lies not so much in the response as in how the problem is posed. Rather than an either/or response to substance, the view of what substance means needs to be reconstructed in such a way that both extremes are avoided. When the problem is reformulated in this way, we can readily see that it is the sort of problem to which pragmatism may be profitably applied, for this is precisely the sort of work pragmatism was intended to do: its function is to provide a clearer conception of what is meant by difficult words such as *substance.*

A Peircean response, then, is to reconstruct the term *substance* in light of the general categories. One finds that *every* primary substance, characterized by firstness, has qualitatively unique features. This blue, as it occurs on this sea shell today and on this beach, has its own distinct presence. Marked by secondness—that is, being *this* shell—the shell also persists or endures. It remains for some period of time and tomorrow; were this shell to be retrieved again, it would be this very shell. This is thirdness operative with respect to the thing itself. The thing is also regulated by thirds insofar as it is continuous with its environment. How it is continuous—that is, on which features of the environment it depends for its existence, from which it tends to suffer, and upon which it tends to act—is what makes it the sort of thing that it is. These features also determine—or rather, greatly constrain—what it is to become in the future.

That a thing is continuous with its surroundings is not, according to a pragmatist conception, tantamount to saying that it is connected to *everything* or to different things *equally;* such an assertion would not likely be true and would also reduce the conception of substance to a useless one because the conception would become devoid of any power of discrimination. Rather, a given thing is really continuous with some elements (to various degrees) and discontinuous with others (again, to greater or lesser extent). Pragmatism recognizes multiple connections but emphasizes also the reality of disconnection. Every real thing enters into intimate relations with other beings but also has a genuinely external environment. To be related to some things is not to be thereby related (immediately) to all things. As James suggests, "Things are 'with' one another in many ways, but nothing includes everything or dominates over everything" (1912, 322). A being is continuous with parts of its environment, but this connection is only part of the whole of the universe, and the being is merely "with" the rest of the universe. With these portions, it is not actively concerned, although it could become so. Actual continuity finds itself in a wider field of possible continuity. James claims that "Our 'multiverse' still makes a 'universe';

for every part, tho' it may not be in actual or immediate connexion, is nevertheless in some possible or mediated connexion, with every other part however remote, through the fact that each part hangs together with its very next neighbors in inextricable interfusion" (1912, 325). For example, one might think of an oil well and a typewriter. The two terms may be joined in thought or a public exhibition without having anything further to do with one another. "And" is the most that can be said of their relationship with one another. This relationship differs considerably from the kind of relation that holds, for instance, between a mother and child. These two beings are bound to one another in a vast complex of ways through their entwined histories. The question of which relations are extant—that is, what kinds of relations (immediate or external), to what degree, with which other beings, and to what effect—is what determines their respective natures.

Moreover, the fact that a thing engages in a wide range of relations with other parts of its environment indicates that, depending on the position from which it is experienced, it displays different and sometimes quite contrary forms of behavior that produce quite different qualitative results. One may indeed go further and argue that in many cases such contradiction is *necessary*, not only for the persistence of the object in question, but also for others around it that depend upon it for support. This is one reason why it is so difficult to identify, in definitional terms, precisely *what* something is, and this fact points to the need for a pragmatic explication that provides the third grade of clarity. Consider an example suggested by James: "That what in itself is one and the same entity should be able to function thus differently in different contexts is a natural consequence of the extremely complex reticulations in which our experiences come. To her offspring a tigress is tender, but cruel to every other living thing—both cruel and tender, therefore, at once" (1977, 272). Attributing multiple and contradictory properties to a thing is only to notice that the thing is capable of entering into further relations with other beings in which those tendencies and properties are revealed. A tigress is both cruel and not cruel because she manifests both tendencies, although not simultaneously to the same other being. Her infant depends on this complexity;

it is crucial to the infant's survival that the tigress nurture it and defend it against others. This is essential to the infant's being, and part of what it means to be this kind of thing is to participate in this sort of behavior in relation to a parent.

The parent is of course in one sense external to the young tiger, but in another it is intrinsic to the infant's survival. What is disconcerting about this description is that what is "natural" to something may in certain respects lie outside of the features that make the thing relatively discrete from its environment. In a sense, the infant is really separate from its mother, and yet tendencies essential to it lie "outside" of it and "in" its mother. As Dewey points out, "The epidermis is only in the most superficial way an indication of where an organism ends and its environment begins. There are things inside the body that are foreign to it, and there are things outside of it that belong to it *de jure*, if not *de facto*; that must, that is, be taken possession of if life is to continue" (1989, 65). This notion violates a commonsense (and often philosophical) belief that things are really discrete. But if continuity is taken seriously, then this cannot be so. What is intrinsic in one may in a significant sense be said to live or exist in another and so be essential to it.

Traditional conceptions of being have been, as James rightly asserts, either entirely too thin or positively false. They have failed to see that substances as they are, as they exist, manifest a potentially unlimited number of ways of being, depending on the ongoing relations into which they enter. Conceptions are too thin when they fail to account for the range of extant possibilities; they become positively false when they exclude some of those real relationships while privileging others in some hierarchical fashion. They become increasingly adequate, however, as these multiple tendencies and relations are detected and included in their pragmatic formulation.

In this pragmatic view, the positing of substance falls on neither horn of the dilemma described earlier: of having to choose between absolute independence and arbitrary choice. A thing is surely not radically autonomous. It depends on others, and these relations may change, sometimes drastically, over time. But neither is it a mere name, something ascribed by knowers interested in manipulating the abruptly shifting cosmic weather in which they find themselves. Rather, to say that some X is a kind of substance is to mark a cluster of qualities that some thing does exhibit and *will continue* to exhibit; to use that term is to forecast *tendencies* or habits of a thing to act with its surroundings in particular ways during its career or period of growth. These features of things in the world (features corresponding to the three categories) may become matters of practical interest, but independently of these sorts of considerations they really refer to the world regardless of how we choose (or prefer) to think of them. Peirce writes, for example, that although we make use of the animals about us for food and wood for warmth, "we are barbarians to treat the deer and the forest trees in that fashion. They have ends of their own, not related to my individual stomach or skin" (EP2, 39). A pragmatic view of substance seeks out these ends, looking beyond the inquirer's sub-jective interests to the forms of generality that govern the things she encounters. This makes the features ascribed to the substance independent of how she wishes to think them, however partial or perspectival the grasp of those features turns out to be. Substance is not just a matter of making experience convenient; it is convenient, or useful, because it really refers to things in the world.

The fifth criticism of substance to be considered here is the charge of essentialism. Rather than thinking of essence as eternal, as in the third criticism discussed earlier, this critique argues that a substance view turns on the claim that there is something (or some number of features) that all things of a given kind have in common. This is to say that some X is a member of a group because it has some identifiable property that all other members of the group have, and this property is the necessary and sufficient condition of their inclusion. It usually is not one property, but some set of properties that does the work.

This is the view C. I. Lewis found problematic and so important to avoid that he eschewed substance metaphysics altogether. In *Mind and the World Order*, he writes, "Such specific qualia and repeatable com-plexes of them are nowadays sometimes designated as 'essences.' This term, with such a meaning, will here be avoided; the liability to con-fuse such qualia with universal concepts makes this imperative. It is at once the plausibility and the fatal error of 'critical realism' that it commits this confusion of the logical universal with given qualia of sense by denominating both of these 'essences' " (1929, 60). The question of essentialism has historically taken the form of the question of whether nominalism or realism is the truer doctrine. For example, Georges Buffon, in preparing his scheme, criticized Linnaeus's analytic classifications of plant life for being excessively realistic in the identification of plants as independent substances. He accused Linnaeus of selecting qualities of plants for the purpose of providing real, and not merely nominal, definitions. These selections, according to Buffon, were arbitrary ones; they reflect our (or rather, Linnaeus's) purposes only, not anything "really" in the plants (Cassirer 1951, 78). Buffon claimed that Linnaeus had confused the substantive terms used to signify objects for the objects themselves. Buffon argued, however, that nature does not fit into the discrete categories of language; rather, it proceeds from species to species and even genus to genus imperceptibly. Traits or stages of development belong in part to one, in part to another, and the transitions are too subtle to be captured by the analytic categories Linnaeus employed. So Buffon argued, and he concluded that there were only individuals in nature and no real species or genera (Cassirer 1951, 78–79).

This view of nature and of its relationship to language is precisely the nominalism that Peirce opposed in modern philosophy. He insisted that, in addition to actual individuals and the concrete qualities they embody, "general principles are really operative in nature" (EP2, 183). These principles are the laws, natural or conventional, that guide the activities of existing individuals. They determine how events *would* happen, how actual things *will* likely behave. But these laws are not "in" things because they are not themselves actual or particular. They are not actual because they are not definite and lie in the future. As Peirce writes, "A law of nature, then, will be regarded . . . as having a sort of *esse in futuro*. That is to say that they will have a present reality which consists in the fact that events *will* happen according to the formulation of those laws" (EP2, 153). These laws are not particular because, as forms of mediation, they are vague, or continuous, and therefore admit of a potentially unlimited number of actual variations. In the pragmatism lectures of 1903, Peirce states, "Take any two possible objects that might be called *suns* and however much alike they may be, any multitude whatsoever of intermediate suns are alternatively possible and therefore, as before, these intermediate possible suns transcend all multitude. In short, the idea of a general involves the idea of possible variations which no multitude of existent things could exhaust" (EP2, 183). A general is a kind of being that is real, but because it is indeterminate, it may be predicated of many different existing individuals.

This means that to ascribe a general or a category to some group of individuals is not to take some one actual quality that a sample has in common and define the group in terms of this quality. It is to ascribe a *tendency* to actual individuals to conform to some more or less complex form of mediation in their future encounters. So long as some general mediates activity, this particular kind of conformation regularly produces some qualities and not others. There will be exceptions, but exceptions do not undermine the general because it is not of the general's nature to preclude variations from the norm. To think otherwise is to treat a category as turning on some particular property. But this again is the nominalism Peirce refutes. When one says that some X is a substance of some kind, as in "this creature is a deer," one is ascribing a set of tendencies to the thing that it has in common with other deer. Variation is possible, and emphasis may shift from individual to individual. But this variation does not undermine the ascription of kind, or the saying that some X is this sort of substance. It merely recognizes a fact that is rarely noted and less often remembered—namely, that generals are by nature vague and indeterminate.

Whereas the experience of actual variation and difference undermines traditional forms of essentialism, Peirce's conception of substance is not threatened. His view of generality not only expects broad variation in actual occurrences but includes differences that have never been or ever will be realized under some general form of mediation. *Rather than a world too messy or subtle for categoreal description (as Buffon insisted), Peirce's view of generality anticipates unlimited possibilities—not just those that happen to be.* All the variation that has been manifested—for example, by the things that go by the name *deer*—does not match the possible variation that the thing might manifest given sufficient time.

Yet the vagueness of generals does not mean that they are merely nominal definitions; on the contrary, they are causally efficacious. Actual individuals conforming to specific forms of generality interact causally with other individuals. It is through this action that generals are definitely effective in the world of existing things. For this reason, general categories provide explanations and not merely descriptions. Identifying the generals at play in particular events makes prediction possible. Peirce actually defined a law in 1901 as a "prognostic generalization of observations" (EP2, 68). From some group of observations, a person is able to detect generals at work that will guide the future, and thereby he or she can anticipate outcomes still in the making.

This Peircean formulation offers the means for better understanding the error Buffon detected in Linnaeus. According to Buffon, the problems were mistaking substantive terms for their objects and considering the former more real. But the oversight is not in mistaking one for the other; rather, it lies in the assumption that an object can be a member of a kind only if it has something—or rather, some quality—in common with other objects of that kind. But, again, this view turns on nominalist assumptions. One of these assumptions is that generals refer to particular properties—that is, are definite. The other is that the only things that are real are existing individuals. This means that it is misleading to say that Buffon *shifted from* a realistic to a nominalist account; the discourse to which he was responding was *already* nominalistic. He was committing the error that Lewis thought it so important to avoid: confusing a universal or general with a particular sense *qualia*. Buffon was only carrying an already extant nominalism to a further, radicalized conclusion. Peirce's response, however, is to criticize the earlier nominalist assumptions. Generals are vague, but they are really operative in nature as a form of being not reducible to existing individuals. This definition provides a robustly realistic conception of generality that justifies the ascription of substance to particular things. As general tendencies, generals are not universal ascriptions of *anything in particular,* which means that they need not falsify the nature of individual things.

This representation of Peirce's view also allows a critical eye to be cast on some recent interpretations of Peirce. As Menno Hulswit points out, Peirce scholars do not agree in their understanding of Peirce on the issue of ascribing natural kinds to nature (1997, 101). According to Susan Haack (1995), Peirce's scholastic realism includes the claims that events are governed by natural laws and that things do indeed come in kinds. Scientific inquiry, if pursued long enough, will reveal what these laws are, independent of how we choose to think of (or classify) them (Hulswit 1997, 101). At the other extreme is Christopher Hookway, who characterizes Peirce as an antirealist. Focusing on the continuous nature of thirdness (as the earlier quote on suns emphasizes), Hookway suggests that although for Peirce generality is real, which makes him a realist of sorts, "dividing things into classes reflects our interests and conventional decisions" (1985, 251). This analysis places Peirce close to James's view that conception is a purely teleological weapon of the mind, close to the nominalism James defended and Peirce abhorred in metaphysics and science. The *media tertia* is provided by Rosenthal, who suggests that the "cuts" provided by classificatory schemes reflect *both* persons' interests in knowing the world *and* in at least some measure the nature of the world known. The latter is sustained, it appears, because the world is made up of facts, whereas the former is owing to the reality of continuity. "A world," she writes, "is delineated by a system of facts, but facts are not independent of the selective knowledge process, for facts are abstracted portions of a continuum of events" (1994, 8). Which portion is abstracted reflects the interests of those doing the knowing, and, provided the interests were different, a different portion may well be abstracted. This means that the facts that come to the fore, that show up the "things" of the world, would be different also. Hence, the middle way: the "what" of the world is constrained by the world itself, and the "which" depends at least in part on the community.

My own view of the matter, in light of the foregoing, lies closest to Haack's. Both Hookway and Rosenthal are right to emphasize continuity in Peirce's account, but each seems to compromise Peirce's commitment to scholastic realism, although in different ways. Continuity, as I have already suggested, is a manifest character of all existing things, and its reality is in no way reducible to the categories of secondness and firstness. Yet this view does not entail the further claim that a thing, or a kind of thing, is equally closely allied with every other thing, and this is, in part, what conception is intended to capture. The fact that near the "edges" of a conception there is overlap with other general descriptions need not undermine the legitimacy of the concept so long as one recognizes that conception is by nature general. The fact that conceptions look arbitrary to us comes from the long accustomed but poor philosophical habit of thinking that conceptions, to be legitimate, must be determinate and that things, to be real, must be discrete. But this, of course, is the mistake of nominalism (yet again) that Peirce seeks to expose. That Hookway's interpretation leaves Peirce so close to nominalism is a sure sign that something is awry, that his representation of Peirce is too one-sided.

Rosenthal's view differs from Hookway's in the sense that although Hookway claims that cutting (through classificatory schemes) per se is arbitrary, Rosenthal argues that although cuts really refer to the real, the choice of which system of cuts may vary. This view seems to be in part a recognition of the finite character of inquiry, of the rootedness in time and place of inquirers, and of the ways in which our interest places emphasis on some portions of the real and not on others. All of these arguments seem to me (and to Haack, so far as I know) legitimate and should be included as relevant considerations. But there seems to be the further claim that the world of existing things (not just the continuum of possibility) is equally susceptible to multiple frameworks of interpretation. The world is sufficiently indeterminate that it may be captured by alternative conceptions chosen in light of subjective interests and is indifferent to which are applied. Although it is true that differing conceptions may each, to some partial extent, gain purchase on the real, Haack's (and my) fundamental claim is that inquiry may discern in time which of these (or some other) conceptions *better* captures the object in question—as it is, independently of how one chooses to think of it. Interest is certainly involved, but in this case it is the interest in knowing the object apart from subjective preference. Peirce surely thought that the community, given time, could do this, which is what makes him a scholastic realist about things and our knowledge of them. Denoting some portion of the real, a substance of a specific kind is not arbitrary because it is really more continuous with some portions of the real than with some others. Nor is this ascription an intrinsically tangled one—a composite of constraining reality and selective interest—that cannot ever be unraveled. Rather, it is a representation of the real that increasingly corresponds to the nature of that which is represented as it becomes freed over time from the bias of the community of inquiry. Indeed, a sign that a representation has become more objective than a preceding one is that the successor has been untangled from a bias now known to have infected the representation it successfully replaces.

The last criticism of substance to be considered here focuses on the distinction between nature and culture. From the previous discussion, it is clear that a Peircean approach to substance provides conceptions of things that are in some sense independent of what persons think of them. This means that however much experience of the world is mediated by social practices, especially linguistic ones, the nature of the world may be known by inquirers, and it may be known as it is independently of those limitations. This is surely not to say that knowledge is not perspectival in the sense that all inquiry takes place in a particular place and time and under conceptual constraints. But it is to claim that the knowledge generated by inquirers, although limited, does not directly depend on the community for being what it is. It is independent because what is grasped by the community refers (in at least some cases) not to the community's own practices but to the nature of what is under scrutiny.

A metaphysics that secures this sort of knowledge is especially attractive to those who wish to appeal to nature, in particular that of the human body, for moral criticism. Some feminists, for example, object to recent developments in poststructuralism because they perceive there the disappearance of the material/maternal body. Language is so pervasive in the approaches of feminists such as Judith Butler (1990, 1993) that it seems that nothing falls outside of what it posits. This view leads feminists to charge poststructuralism with a kind of linguistic monism. The issue is a concern for some feminists because they have often drawn on the specificity of sex to provide arguments for a specifically feminist ethics or epistemology.[3] There is *something* about the nature of sex, prior to discourse and various other kinds of cultural constructive activity, that has definite and identifiable consequences for the experience of women—or so they wish to argue. According to Carol Bigwood, for example, the body must be understood both as "culturally and historically contextualized" and as an "embodied givenness" for the specific experience of women. Sex may not lie entirely outside of discourse, but nor is it exhausted by it; and it is this *more* that needs to be retained against what is taken to be the sort of linguisticism Butler represents (1991, 57). Those of this frame of mind would presumably welcome Peirce's formulation because it offers access to something more than merely a cultural and historical representation. It offers mediated access to a world that is in some ways genuinely external (given) and constraining on our actions, including our representations of it.

But Butler's response to this criticism is interesting here because she argues against an articulation of "nature" that is in any significant sense independent of language and culture, such as the articulation provided by a Peircean approach. She thinks that feminists should be suspicious of appeals to the material as something in any way outside of discourse. In what remains of this chapter, I look at Butler's criticism in order to suggest that a Peircean pragmatic account of substance may indeed assuage her concerns.

Butler begins her linguistic argument with an understanding of nature as that which is prior to signification. "The body posited as prior to the sign, is always *posited* or *signified* as *prior*" (1993, 30, italics hers). The sign, "body," which is itself in some measure material, also represents that which is somehow outside of language. This something is determinate or determining independently of cultural or other discursive practices. It is the embodied given to which Bigwood appeals. But according to Butler, the act of signification produces as its own effect that which it supposedly finds as prior to discourse. The body, as signified, as it produces a representation for interpreters, is not antecedent to the act. It is an effect thereof because it is *posited* through language in accord with its systematic differentiations (such as gender or race). Because the "body" is an effect of discourse, it signifies nothing outside itself. Although the sign of the body is purported to represent or be mimetic of something that is decidedly other than the sign, what is this representation if not a further sign, a signified as produced by the linguistic community in which it circulates? According to Butler, it isn't mimetic at all: "If the body signified as prior to signification is an effect of signification, then the mimetic or representational status of language, which claims that signs follow bodies as their necessary mirrors, is not mimetic at all. On the contrary, it is productive, constitutive, one might even argue *performative,* inasmuch as this signifying act delimits and contours the body that it then claims to find prior to any and all signification" (1993, 30, italics hers). Butler's resorting to the image of *boundary* both here and elsewhere may be misleading. It gives the idea that only borders are patrolled, as if the edges are fuzzy and negotiable, but the interior is somehow just given as an unviolated core. It is better to take the sexed body as an example: certain features—organs, functions, capacities—are grouped together to *make* a coherent unity with a discernable end that is caught up in specific ways in a culture in order to constitute a gender with all its incumbent responsibilities and privileges. This unity, once produced, takes on a life of its own in the sense that it appears to be natural, not produced in time according to cultural exigency.

For this reason, the classical view of representation, as Butler sees it, is mistaken in its claim concerning the mimetic relationship between sign and object because the sign *conceals* its own activity by claiming to find or discover that which it imposes or posits. Constructions that actually put into play power relations in their mode of representations are themselves represented—indeed, represent themselves—as being nothing of the sort. By claiming to find a nature outside of itself in a mimetic relationship, representation becomes an instrument of power insofar as it hides its forceful and often insidious work. By concealing the effects of power, mimetic understandings of representation undermine the possibility of subjecting those operative forms of power to criticism and transformation. It is this further consequence that Butler finds most objectionable because she is above all interested in developing strategies for improving existing social formations (by way of performativity, for example).

Butler herself asks in a different context (a commentary on Freud and Lacan) if there is not indeed something that escapes this process that might be called the body and to which appeal might effectively be made in the context of a struggle on behalf of social transformation. Her response is that to say yes would be to reinstate a classically Kantian formulation. It would posit the body as an in-itself, that which is ontologically independent of the psyche, but which makes its appearance when the psyche constitutes it as an epistemic object. Butler finds this proposition untenable because it treats the psyche as a mere grid through which an antecedently given body appears (1993, 66). But bodies are not pregiven. Rather, the very contouring of the body, which provides or confers unity to that body, is itself a contested site of interaction. Bodies are "sites that vacillate between the psychic and the material. Bodily contours and morphology are not merely implicated in an irreducible tension between the psychic and the material but *are* that tension" (Butler 1993, 66, italics hers). One cannot refer to a body outside of this site because any body represented would already be a precipitate of this struggle between the psychic and the material.[4]

Butler is surely correct that bodies are posited within language and within a range of historical and social practices of a given community, including gender. Bodies are represented as having qualities and specific tendencies, and it is only *as represented* that they can have any being for us. Contact with reality, as Peirce himself points out, is always mediated. But a Peircean approach to how it is that objects are posited as being some specific kind of substance suggests strongly that at least some of these qualities and tendencies are constrained by the object in ways that are independent of our positing them. Peirce's own favorite example is hardness in the context of scientific inquiry, but for our purposes "sex" is indeed a more telling example. That we define sexuality in terms of particular external organs and chromosomal arrangements surely reflects particular preferences of the historical community and forms of power circulating therein. Even more revealing of that specificity is that we demand a two-party sexual system. We find, however, that whatever we wish or insist upon, our bodies do not live up to these demands. As Ann Fausto-Sterling suggests, there are a variety of possible combinations, and as many as 5 percent of births fall outside of this binary arrangement (1993, 21). This fact reveals that the binary system is itself not a natural fact but a social norm. And we know that it is a norm precisely because the body, as it is posited or represented, is resisted by that which it represents. More important, this representation is resisted in identifiable ways. Not all bodies are produced in accord with the desired matrix, and this difference is determinate both in how they fail to measure up and how often. That the body *tends* to fall into a binary system 96 percent of the time, according to recent studies, is a fact about our kind of organism, just as it is a tendential fact that it falls outside of this system approximately 5 percent of the time. These natural tendencies may be identified through scientific inquiry. To understand an object is, according to Peirce, to recognize the tendencies—and they are multiple—that define or regulate that object. It is also the case that objects are often created in conformity with the forms of regulation extant within a community. This means that in one sense those norms do depend on the community, and not just on nature, for their reality. But this dependence does not render them merely linguistic. On the contrary, these norms have real effects because existing things, including persons, conform to them. And they also may be known to the community independently of how we wish to think of them, even if they are parasitic upon the community for their reality. Moreover, there is always also mediation by natural laws, by generals that not only do not depend on the community for what they are but also are not parasitic on it for their reality. These generals, too, may be known by inquirers.

With these considerations in mind, I may be able to offer a more direct response to Butler's concern. Although she is correct to deny the possibility of positing a nature "outside of" and independent of the community, a move that imposes a Kantian dualism in both epistemic and ontological terms, her criticism does not really touch the Peircean formulation. Identifying substances and their natures need not impose a dualism at all. Rather, developing adequate conceptions requires that both sorts of generality, the natural as well as the specifically cultural, be taken into account. Many of the things of everyday experience are the products of long interaction not only with natural laws, but also with the specifically cultural practices that have conspired to produce them. The computer chip, a bomb, products of genetic engineering, cosmetic products, and so many others furnishing the content of experience are of this sort. They require consideration both of natural laws and of those norms that depend on—or are intrinsic to—the community if they are to be understood. The latter, those norms that are parasitic on the community, are, for example, the extraordinarily complex political, economic, religious, and aesthetic practices (to name only a few obvious ones) that inform the community by mediating interactions among persons and with the environment at large.

As Donna Haraway so capably shows, understanding the origins, the nature, and the potential consequences (i.e., the meaning) of some particular object such as the oncomouse (a genetically engineered animal patented by Harvard) requires the tracing out of a thick weave of interacting forces, some of which are quite independent of the community and some are not. Calling the oncomouse a "stem cell" in the technoscientific body, Haraway convincingly shows it to be the result of "a knot of knowledge-making practices, industry and commerce, popular culture, social struggles, psychoanalytic formations, bodily histories, human and non-human actions, local and global flows, inherited narratives, new stories, syncretic technical/cultural processes and more" (1997, 129). Things are not just the authors or results of these practices, identifiable and separable in fact, but are, as Butler insists, the tensions or intersections of these powerful interactions.

The fact that the production of artifacts such as the oncomouse and of the reality that goes by the name of gender is the result of so many different practices dovetailing together makes it useful and imperative to distinguish between those acts that are human (or better, the acts of encultured agents) and those that are not. Knowing the difference guides not only further inquiry but directs persons immersed in problematic or threatening situations toward manners and methods of response that may help ameliorate the conditions of their existence.

The point of the distinction, I must emphasize, is not somehow to "factor out" the influence of culture on nature (in this case the sexed body) in order to get hold of the purely natural. To regard the relation between nature and culture in this way is, as Clifford Geertz aptly describes it, a "stratigraphic" conception of the relations between biological, psychological, social, and cultural factors in human life" (1973, 37). However desirable this conception might be, there is no possibility of success. First, the relation between the two, as Geertz and others (including Dewey) point out, is a nonadditive one. In the anthropological conception of humans, for example, there is no "nature" of humans lurking behind their cultural expressions because they are essentially incomplete without the developing influence of culture. Such humans without culture "would be unworkable monstrosities with very few useful instincts, fewer recognizable sentiments, and no intellect: mental basket cases" (Geertz 1973, 59). The idea that we can somehow know what the body or other artifacts are like "before" culture sets in is incoherent because those myriad practices collected under the name of culture are intrinsic to the objects of study. The objects are themselves the products of these interacting cultural forces. To ignore them would be analogous to ignore arbitrarily some geological conditions while privileging others when trying to explain a particular physical formation: the resultant representation can *only* be a distortion or perverse representation of the object of inquiry. Only by including all the relevant conditions, which in many cases now includes the tendencies intrinsic to cultural formations, may the world around us be adequately understood and represented. Indeed, the case where such cultural formations are not relevant is becoming a rara avis indeed.

Another reason for not regarding nature as distinct from culture may well be understood as a corollary of the first reason. The image of a dualism between nature and culture is misleading because culture is always already inclusive of the natural. As John Dewey points out with regard to humans, cultural acts such as speaking, reading, and representing "are instances of modification wrought *within* the biological organism by the cultural environment" (1991, 59, italics his). Culture is here regarded as a *specific difference* within the natural order; it marks some portion of natural processes that have been redirected, transformed, and thereby invested with being and meaning by the community in which individual persons participate. If it is true that there is no getting at nature behind culture, there is surely no isolation of culture apart from nature, which means that however much some practice is dependent on the practices of a given human community, it is further dependent on a nature that is independent of whether or not it is known to that community and indifferent to how that community prefers to think of it. Nature of course may be modified or has already been modified through a history of transactions of the community with its environment, but it remains independent in the relevant senses.

The question, of course, is how to distinguish the natural and the cultural without either falling into the hard and fast dualism typical of classical formulations or reinscribing undesirable but contingent cultural practices by positing them as natural. Although features of the real will no doubt be sometimes mistakenly thought of as one (culture) rather than as the other (nature)—which can go either way, mistaking the natural for the specifically cultural or vice versa—the task is to show that this mistake need not be a systemic problem. That is to say, this sort of error may occur contingently within the history of a given practice of representation, but it is in no particular instance necessary because error may be discovered through subsequent inquiry. The difference is between, on the one hand, an epistemic view in which representation genuinely approximates the real and may become increasingly adequate to the object and, on the other, a view in which distortion is constitutive and ineluctable. The former is the approach upon which Peirce insists. This makes it important to note, at the outset, that there is no question of positing an "outside" to culture by way of positing an external nature (in the form of an independent substance or "body"), but of identifying and tracing out the myriad forms of mediation that constitute the everyday objects we encounter and collectively produce. The latter is done in order to discern contingencies and continuities, ways in which objects, as products of specific histories, may be transformed or preserved through further conduct with the environment (or as Butler suggests, through performativity). Rather than imposing an inside and an outside, a natural and an artificial or cultural, a Peircean approach recognizes that forms of mediation may be of two sorts (natural and cultural), both of which have real effects. This approach does not claim to know things as they are "in themselves" or apart from our interactions with them because it does not recognize, as pointed out earlier, any existence "in itself" for anything whatsoever. It insists only that objects may be known pragmatically (by way of categorial explanation) independently of what we *think* of them. Things may be known, as they are, independently of the community and its preferences, even if what things are is itself the result of ongoing interaction with the thing known. The operative and crucial distinction here is between independence of experience or interaction and independence of preference. As pointed out in chapter 1, Peirce repeatedly insists that the former is strictly out of our reach, whereas the latter is (at least fallibly) within our purview.

So long as we retain a pragmatic formulation of the distinction between culture and nature, it seems to me that those theorists such as Bigwood may have access to the body without committing the mistakes that worry Butler. One may, for example, study the liver, learn its natural functions in relation to the whole body, *and* discern the transformative impact of cultural practices on it (such as a culture of overconsumption of alcohol). Recognizing the difference between nature and culture recommends different sorts of responses. One may be to introduce a chemical into the liver that reduces the effects of alcohol, but another would be to struggle for social change on behalf of healthier lifestyles. Each is a plausible route, although different in terms of what sorts of general tendencies it is addressing on behalf of particular results. Other cases are no doubt trickier, and gender is surely one of these cases because it is so much more caught up in relations of power, but there is no systemic reason why it cannot be treated similarly. Indeed, one of the most far-reaching aspects of Butler's work is the way in which she has shown both the cultural contingency (and thereby the fragility) of gender and how difficult it is to transform these cultural practices. Peirce's approach is helpful precisely because it shows how one may speak of nature, of that which is independent of the community, without falling into the Kantian formulation that Butler wishes to avoid. In other words, one may have the body without being complicit, and one can both identify the pervasive/transformative effects of culture and try to transform culture without falling into linguistic idealism.

Although each response to the criticisms discussed in this chapter merits further development, all of the responses taken together, along with the preceding chapter, should provide a sufficient representation of what sort of world, in its most general features, persons encounter. This account is independent of what persons prefer to believe, is more general than the specific interpretive frameworks that various communities or subcommunities employ, and yet constrains what may subsequently be said about the world. If I am correct in my presentation in this chapter, then indeed substances there are. These substances, however, are existing entities engaging in complex interactions of many kinds; they are mediated by natural and cultural forms of thirdness; they develop in history and have truly contingent futures that are dependent on how we and others interact with them. A substance metaphysics, rather than intrinsically guilty of the offenses outlined previously, may be reconstrued in such a way that it sets two important tasks. One is that it demands far better descriptive practices from the community for our natural and social world to be truly known by us. The other is that it obliges us to see modes of contingency, ways in which what is encountered is truly precarious, so that these present realities may be sustained or transformed intelligently. In other words, epistemic agents may no longer claim merely to find the world and so thereby shirk responsibility not only for what they find, but also for the nature of what is found. These objects, these substances of the world, are so often not just epistemic constructions but rather ontological artifacts of our own making and doing, so that responsibility for the world and for the representations that bring it to life must be borne by the community of inquiry.

As we have seen, practices of representation are peculiarly situated in this process, for representation is itself a mode of intervention. Representation, itself a form of mediation between agents and the world, also mediates—reinscribes, modifies, transforms—these agents' subsequent *activities*. In short, practices of representation not only determine the quality of representation but also configure the nature of what is subsequently represented. The focus of the next chapter shifts to an account of representation as such. It advances a fuller account of how persons construct knowledge of social and natural reality, preparing the way for discussion of ways in which these practices may be improved.

THREE

MAPPING THE PROVINCE

From the Mirror of Nature to Constructive Representation

As knowledge advances, my conception of substance becomes a map in which my body is one of the islets charted: the relations of myself to everything else may be expressed there in their true proportions, and I shall cease to be an egotist. In the symbolic terms which my map affords, I can then plan and test my actions (which otherwise I should perform without knowing it) and trace the course of other events; but I am myself a substance, moving in the plane of universal substance, not on the plane of my map; for neither I nor the rest of substance belong to the realm of pictures, nor exist on that scale and in that flat dimension.

—George Santayana, *Scepticism and Animal Faith*

The previous chapter offered a distinctively pragmatic formulation of substance, of the things of the world, in light of a number of important historical and contemporary criticisms. Its aim was to provide a more robust sense of what things are like, how they relate to one another, how they come to be as they are, and what they are likely to become. That discussion provides the starting point for this chapter, which focuses on Peirce's view of representation. Having looked closely at what it is that must be represented (a look that was itself a representation of a somewhat different order), I now turn to the nature of representation itself and to precisely in what sense a Peircean pragmatist may claim that his or her representations truly represent the real. This subject requires at the outset an extensive discussion of Peirce's semeiotic, so the bulk of this chapter is devoted to the introduction of central concepts, to some of Peirce's trichotomies, and to explanation of what sort of work these divisions are supposed to perform. From this introduction emerges a preliminary understanding of what representation is supposed to be like, a topic further developed in chapter 4, where I locate representation in epistemic practices sustained by members of particular communities.

Any discussion of representation must engage in some general way the science of sign activity or semiosis. Peirce defined *semeiotic* as "the doctrine of the essential nature and fundamental varieties of possible semiosis" (CP, 5.488). The difference between semiosis and other forms of action in the universe is that semeiotic activity is essentially triadic, whereas other forms are essentially diadic. As Vincent Colapietro points out, "when Peirce explains what he means by sign-activity he characteristically distinguishes it from dynamical action" (1989, 1). This triadic form of activity is of such a nature that it cannot be reduced to multiple diadic relationships. According to Peirce, "All dynamical action, or action of brute force, physical or psychical, either takes place between two subjects [whether they react equally upon each other, or one is agent and the other patient, entirely or partially] or at any rate is a resultant of such actions between pairs. But by 'semiosis' I mean, on the contrary, an action, or influence, which is, or involves, a cooperation of three subjects, this tri-relative influence not being in any way resolvable into actions between pairs" (CP, 5.484). A transaction between two individuals, which in itself would be blind, is mediated by a third element directing or constraining that activity. When this mediation occurs, the action is raised from the brute or mechanical level to that of semiosis. This distinction should be quite clear from previous discussions of firstness, secondness, and thirdness. Mechanistic action is characterized by secondness, semiosis by thirdness, and it is the latter type of phenomenon that the science of semeiotic takes as its object. But as Max Fisch points out, Peirce is not suggesting a dualistic ontology in which there are two kinds of things, one that consists of signs and another that does not, as if semeiotic were the study of only one-half of the universe: "The fundamental distinction is not between things that are signs and things that are not, but between triadic or sign-*action* and dyadic or dynamical *action*" (1986, 330, italics his). This means that whatever else some thing may be, it is, at least potentially, also a sign because it is capable of participating in the sort of triadic relations that produce genuinely semeiotic activity. As Colapietro writes, "the being of anything is not exhausted in its being a sign; in fact, in order for anything to be a sign, it must be something other than a sign" (1989, 2). Semiosis always *includes* the diadic or mechanical relations from which it is distinguished, without being reducible thereto, which ensures that Peirce's distinction implies no ontological dualism.

Semeiotic proceeds by developing a general theory of signs that includes all possible varieties of semiosis. The question concerns not how we typically use the term *sign* in everyday usage, but how, given all the different forms semiosis may take, signs *ought* to be understood. Peirce claims that "If the question were simply what we *do* mean by a sign, it might soon be resolved. But that is not the point. We are in the situation of a zoölogist who wants to know what ought to be the meaning of 'fish' in order to make fishes one of the great classes of vertebrates" (CP, 8.332, italics his). The point is that Peirce offers, as T. L. Short points out, "a concept of sign that would, like the zoölogists' concept of fish, represent a real and not a merely conventional grouping of phenomena" (1981, 197). Accordingly, Peirce begins by examining ordinary conceptions of what is commonly understood as a sign or sign action and broadens them in order to develop a completely general theory of the nature of signs and their possible relations.

It may help to contrast briefly the method of this approach to that taken by the other founder of semeiotic, Ferdinand de Saussure. In the *Course in General Linguistics,* Saussure argues in his first principle of semiology that language is the "master pattern for understanding every kind of semiological process. The reason is that the relationship which constitutes the sign, that between signifier and signified, is wholly arbitrary" (1972, 67). For example, the idea of "sister" is not linked by any inner relationship to the succession of sounds *s-o-r,* which serves as its signifier in French (1972, 67). That this bond is arbitrary in linguistics is indisputable, according to Saussure; the real question is what its proper place is in the science of semiology, and he insists that its importance is primordial. He writes, "signs which are entirely arbitrary convey better than others the ideal semiological process. That is why the most complex and the most widespread of all systems of expression, which is the one we find in human languages, is also the most characteristic of all. In this sense, linguistics serves as a model for the whole of semiology, even though languages represent only one type of semiological system" (1972, 68). Language is not just an example of semiosis in Saussure's definition of semiology, but is its paradigm also. It showcases the characteristic that is to be sought in all branches of semiology. Saussure admits, as the previous quotation attests, that there are other forms of expression, such as pantomime, and he raises the question of whether or not such forms should be included in the study. He does not indicate the answer to this question but states that even if included, "the main object of study in semiology will nonetheless be the class of systems based upon the arbitrary nature of the sign" (1972, 68). That there are other forms of expression less arbitrary than the linguistic one in no way disturbs the method of semiology, so far as Saussure in concerned.

Peirce's approach is quite different. Whereas Saussure privileges one characteristic as the defining feature of semiosis, a method that in chapter 2 was closely associated with "essentialist" thinking, Peirce drives toward a more general conception that is inclusive of all types of sign activity. The difference, and it is a crucial one, is that Peirce's approach leaves open the possibility of forms of sign action that are significant without being *primarily* arbitrary in nature. Indeed, his approach tends toward a conception in which even arbitrary forms of signification depend on other sign action that is significantly nonarbitrary. Where Saussure underscores the arbitrary relation of semiosis as sign activity at its most sophisticated, Peirce sees this type of activity as but one kind among several and actually dependent on other kinds not arbitrary in nature. Much of the difference in their conclusions, as well as in the discourses that follow or develop Saussure and Peirce respectively, may be traced to this fundamental disagreement.

The Trichotomies

This section focuses not on the development of the science of semeiotic, a science Peirce thought still largely inchoate, but on the fruits of

Peirce's inquiry.[1] I trace Peirce's articulation of sign activity as it relates to a person who interprets it. This presentation involves a common methodological concession when introducing Peirce's semeiotic: it represents the fully general conception by way of a slightly more limited one. Peirce himself provided this limited conception because he thought his broader conception too difficult to convey to the reader (EP2, 478). The broader conception does not necessarily involve a person; it requires only a "Quasi-utterer" and a "Quasi-interpreter" in order to perform the act of semiosis, and neither of them must be (although either or both may be) a person in order for semiosis to occur (CP, 4.551). I begin with the more limited conception both because it is easier to convey and because it better sets the stage for the specific problems to be considered in this chapter and in chapters 4 and 5.

Like writers of the seventeenth century, such as Locke and Berkeley, Peirce held that all thought occurred in signs. He writes, "what we think of cannot possibly be of a different nature from thought itself. For the thought thinking and the immediate thought-object are the very same thing regarded from different points of view. Therefore, Berkeley was, so far, entirely in the right" (CP, 6.339, cf. 8.26). Thought takes place in an irreducibly triadic relationship that cannot be reduced to familiar dyadic relations such as that between knower and known or signified and signifier. Thought involves a sign as well as both an object that it somehow represents and an "interpretant" that it subsequently determines. In a manuscript on pragmatism, Peirce more precisely defines a sign as "anything, of whatsoever mode of being, which mediates between an object and an interpretant; since it is both determined by the object *relatively to the interpretant,* and determines the interpretant *in reference to the object,* in such wise as to cause the interpretant to be determined by the object through the mediation of this 'sign'" (EP2, 410, italics his). The word *interpretant* is one of Peirce's own contributions to the terminology of the discourse on signs. It suffices here to know that this term is intended to distinguish between a sign in the mind and the person in whom the sign occurs. The former is the interpretant, whereas the latter is an interpreter. The sign is itself defined by its structural relationship to both the object and the interpretant. "A sign or *representamen,* is something which stands to somebody for something in some respect or capacity" (CP, 2.228).[2] It addresses someone, creating in his or her mind a sign or representation that is in some respect equivalent or more developed than the sign that determines it.

A sign is something that by knowing it, one knows something more also—namely, something about the object that the sign in some way represents to the interpreting mind. The object is that which is related to the sign in such a way that the sign may truly represent it. This is to say that the object truly determines the sign. "The sign stands for something, its *object.* It stands for that object, not in all respects, but in reference to a sort of idea, which I have sometimes called the *ground* of the representamen" (CP, 2.228, italics his). Peirce, in later writings, dropped this conception of ground, developing instead a division of relations to an object in terms of the icon, index, and symbol (Colapietro 1996a, 132–33). He nevertheless retained the idea that ground so aptly communicates: signs have the capacity to signify by virtue of their real (loosely speaking, *grounded*) relation to some object. The object of the sign may or may not be a thing or substance as defined in chapter 2: although a sign may refer to an actual thing, it may also refer to a merely possible one or to some quality or to no thing at all, just to an idea or a law.

That which is created in the mind, the interpretant, is likewise of the nature of a sign and is so determined by the sign that it is brought into relation with the object. This created sign (the interpretant) may then take the place of the object in subsequent triadic relations even though the original object is not, strictly speaking, displaced. As Peirce writes,

> A *Sign,* or *Representamen,* is a First which stands in such a genuine triadic relation to a Second, called its *Object,* as to be capable of determining a Third, called its *Interpretant,* to assume the same triadic relation to its Object in which it stands itself to the same Object. . . . The Third must indeed stand in such a relation, and thus must be capable of determining a Third of its own; but

besides that, it must have a second triadic relation in which the
Representamen, or rather the relation thereof to its Object, shall be
its own (the Third's) Object, and must be capable of determining
a Third to this relation. All this must equally be true of the Third's
Thirds and so on endlessly. (CP, 2.274)

The function of the sign is to bring a mind into relation with some
object. It does so by producing in the interpeter's mind an interpretant
(a sign in the mind) that brings the interpreter into the very relation to
the object that the sign itself has. In the ongoing process of semiosis,
the created sign (the interpretant) then becomes the object of subsequent triadic relations just as the previous object was itself the product
of an irreducibly triadic relationship.

It is in this context that the question of semiotic idealism arises. It
is clear that for Peirce all experience of the world is mediated by signs.
All thought is in signs, and signs come between the object represented
and the object as it is had in the mind (again, in the form of a sign).
Moreover, this process is a potentially unlimited one. The progression
of objects determining interpretants that in turn become objects for
the determination of subsequent interpretants suggests a process that is
without end. At one point, Peirce himself defines a sign as "Anything
which determines something else (its *interpretant*) to refer to an object
to which itself refers (its *object*) in the same way, the interpretant
becoming in turn a sign, and so on *ad infinitum*. No doubt, intelligent
consciousness must enter into the series. If the series of successive
interpretants comes to an end, the sign is thereby rendered imperfect,
at least" (CP, 2.303, italics his). Both because the process is always
mediated and because it seems that semiosis must continue without
limit if it is to be fully adequate, apparently the finite interpreter never
achieves the reality represented. For this reason, Jacques Derrida suggests that Peirce "goes very far in the direction of what I have called the
deconstruction of the transcendental signified, which, at one time or
another, would place a reassuring end to the reference from sign to
sign" (1974, 49). On the one hand, it appears that, according to Peirce's
conception, every interpretant is a sign for something that follows it;
an interpretant must become an object for further determination

within the web of signs if the sign is not to be rendered imperfect. T. L. Short accurately describes this process as an infinite *progressus* of sign action (1986, 103). On the other hand, it also appears that every sign is also always already an interpretant. As David Savan writes, "Every interpretant is related to its object *through* the sign it interprets. If the sign itself is in the same relation to its object, it too must be related to that object through some sign which it interprets. In other words, for every sign there is an antecedent sign to which it is interpretant, and a consequent sign which is its interpretant" (1976, 43). The mediation of signs considered from this angle suggests an infinite *regress*. The interpreter does not have access to a world transcendent of signs because she may approach that reality only through a series of significations that, by virtue of its very structure, never actually reaches the object it purports to represent.

If so, this is a form of semiotic idealism. Semiosis no longer appears to represent something outside of itself; rather, signs perform a mimetic activity without any original within its reach. This view is similar to Derrida's notion of mimesis as he characterizes it in "The Double Session." According to Christopher Norris, "What we are forced to entertain, so Derrida argues, is the notion of an endless series of inscriptions, a perpetual redoubling of text upon text, such that the 'original' act of *mimesis* will always be lost beyond recall" (1987, 50, italics his; cf. Derrida 1991, 188). Because there is no retracing one's steps back to the original that set semiosis in motion (which is itself a series of traces), the world, as a transcendental object in itself and apart from the signification process, is out of reach. The interpreter is in the position of Tantalus, ever grasping for that which recedes as he advances, but unable to resist the clutch in his heart for what he cannot have. This is also the externally real and constraining world that Richard Rorty describes as a "world well lost." Rorty claims that "The sense in which physical reality is Peircean 'Secondness'—unmediated pressure—has nothing to do with the sense in which one among all our ways of describing, or of coping with, physical reality is 'the one right' way. Lack of mediation is here being confused with accuracy of mediation" (1979, 375).[3] Which of our representations of the world wins out does not, in this view, turn on external constraint because that constraint, to the extent that it is there at all, is not informing. It is mere brute resistance or Peircean secondness.

Rorty, who also champions Derrida's approach, suggests that it would be better to come to terms with our linguistic situation and resist the temptation of seeing our representations as corresponding to a "real world" independent of our descriptions. Rorty argues that the sciences are not—or should not be regarded as—efforts at correspondence. They are instead attempts "to modify our beliefs and desires in ways that will bring us greater happiness than we now have" (1982, 16). Peirce's semeiotic, understood as a form of semeiotic idealism (owing either to infinite progress or to regress), would lend ample support to Rorty's pragmatist project and to Derrida's formulation of unlimited semiosis. It would suggest that the play and development of signs are *all there ever is* and that any hope of transcending or getting back of this to an unmediated but informing world is genuinely hopeless. There is, in short, no way out of the house that language makes for us.

One difficulty with this interpretation of Peirce's semeiotic, however, is that it diverges widely, if not *wildly*, from how Peirce understood his own view. Even if we limit consideration to the manuscripts included in the *Collected Papers* they show show that Peirce championed realism, usually of a scholastic sort, no less than fourteen times. Typical is his characterization of pragmaticism's "strenuous insistence upon the truth of scholastic realism" (CP, 5.423). He represented himself as a "critical common-sensist," insisting on the claim that "that which is thought . . . is the real, as it really is. There is nothing, then, to prevent our knowing outward things as they really are" (CP, 5.311). Moreover, in a letter to Lady Victoria Welby dated 1908, he identified himself as "a convinced Pragmaticist *in semeiotic*" (SW, 401, italics his). If Peirce thought semeiotic supported pragmaticism and that one of the doctrines entailed by pragmaticism was scholastic realism, then it is sure that Peirce did not understand his own theory of signs as a form of semeiotic idealism.

In what remains of this chapter, I introduce and develop distinctions made by Peirce to show that an idealistic interpretation of Peirce is indeed a mistaken one. I use Peirce's categories, as described earlier, to illuminate the various divisions. As David Savan points out, the categories are central to correctly interpreting Peirce's view. "Semeiotic in all its definitions, divisions, trichotomies, branchings, and combinations is entirely governed, according to Peirce, by categorial theory" (1976, 15). Having shown this, I then turn to a discussion of just how it is that representation is thought to represent the real. This discussion involves a look at the notion of *constructivism* as that term is understood by Joseph Margolis.

A sign, it has been emphasized, is defined by Peirce in its relation to two other elements. Consequently, signs may be considered in three ways. They may be considered in themselves, as firsts; they may be considered by virtue of their relation to objects, as seconds; and they may be considered in relation to interpretants, as thirds. In considering signs as such, Peirce introduces the terms *qualisign, sinsign,* and *legisign.* A qualisign is a quality that is a sign. It is not actual and cannot act as a sign unless it is embodied in an actual object or event. But as a possibility, it is what it is, and whenever it occurs, it is just that quality. As Dewey writes in *Experience and Nature,* "*Any* quality as such is final; it is at once initial and terminal; just what it is as it exists" (1988a, 82, italics his). A quality belongs, in short, to firstness. It requires a second in which to inhere if it is to become actual; when this happens, a qualisign becomes a sinsign. A sinsign is an actual event, occurring as such only once, that acts as a sign. But it acts as a sign only by embodying qualities, so it involves qualisigns but is not reducible to them.

In addition to qualities, a sinsign has actuality or an indexical character. It takes place in some here and now, and this is why it happens only once as that particular sinsign. A sign that acts in conformity with a law or some set of laws, laws that may be either natural or conventional, is a legisign. Legisigns occur only through actual events or things, so they involve sinsigns. But the fact that the sinsign occurs in conformity with a law or laws means that the sign cannot be reduced to the nature of legisigns alone. The actual occasion, which itself can happen only once, is an instantiation or what Peirce calls a *replica.*

Replicas exist and embody qualities in accord with the rule or rules that determine them. They are sinsigns that recur. Peirce claims that as laws they are generally determined by convention, such as the word *the* signifying what it does in the English language (PW, 102). As a categorial determination of thirdness, it is a second that, in its conforming to a third, embodies some particular firsts and not others.

The significance of this triad lies, at least in part, in the fact that it broadens the conception of what a sign may be. It is of course common to think of entities such as words as signs; they are linguistic creatures that live only by virtue of their conventionally representative character. As Saussure emphasizes, they are arbitrarily fixed linguistically as being a representation of some other, such as the word *puppy* or *perrito* signifying the concept of a dog. But they are not the only sorts of signs by far. For Peirce, a quality, as either actually appearing or as merely possible, may perform the work of a sign. A shape existing only as a figment of imagination may signify no less than one actually present.

Moreover, an actual thing, by virtue of its many qualities and extant relations to other things that are themselves multiply related, may serve as a sign of a truly vast number of other things. This may happen by virtue of its having qualities or relations, but also by its coming to be associated by some interpreter with some other thing through a personal history in such a way that it produces distinctive and new interpretants. The possibilities for varied sign relations are in this regard potentially unlimited even if every actual sign is always limited in the relations that it actually sustains through a particular history.

The second tricotomy further develops the nature of sign activity by describing the possible relations between the sign and its object. In itself, a sign may be of three sorts. But this is independent of its relation to an object and may again be of three kinds. Peirce describes these kinds as the icon, index, and symbol. An icon is a sign insofar as it itself possesses a quality by which it really resembles some object; that is, the two indeed have something in common. "Anything whatever, be it quality, existent individual, or law, is an Icon of anything, in so far as it is like that thing and used as a sign of it" (PW, 102). In the context of firstness, it denotes an object that is only a possibility; it matters not at all to this sort of representation whether or not the object actually exists.

Moreover, an icon has no real relation to the object beyond the fact that it really resembles it. It is not "connected" to it in any existential way, and the fact that it resembles the object may be pure happenstance. The sense of déjà vu when a person sees a particular street corner, for example, may arise because it resembles another corner she saw sometime in the past, and they are really alike in some of their features. But the likeness is incidental, one having no direct influence on the other. That one operates as sign of the other depends on the interpreter taking it as such, and in this sense practically anything may be used as a sign of some other thing because any two things are bound to have one feature or another in common. In this way, iconic relations, through associations on the part of the interpreter, actually comprise a large and significant portion of possible representations. Most important here, however, is the sense in which these relations are *both* real *and* coincidental or dependent on the interpreter. That they are real ensures that a "realistic" view of representation is possible; that they are coincidental secures the freedom necessary for the ongoing play of signs.

Unlike an icon, an indexical sign is one that is really affected by an existent object. The sign cannot of itself be a mere qualisign, or possible sign, because a qualisign is what it is, regardless of anything else— that is, regardless of any possibly existing object. But an indexical sign, so far as it is affected by an object, possesses a quality in common with that object and thereby refers to the object in this respect. "[An index is] a sign . . . because it is associated with general characters which that object happens to possess, as because it is in dynamical (including spatial) connection both with the individual object . . . and with the senses or memory of the person for whom it serves as a sign" (PW, 107). An indexical sign is an actual thing and has properties of its own. Take, for example, a weathercock. It is an actual weather vane having the distinctive feature of being in the shape of a rooster, but these features are

not relevant insofar as it is an indexical sign. Because in actual contact
with the wind, the weathercock swivels to indicate the wind's direction, and because in actual contact with the wind, it signifies that
direction to the interpretant in the interpreter's mind. It is only as a
result of the actual contact that the weathercock has this quality
(direction) in common with the wind.

The importance of this type of signification cannot be exaggerated
in the context of contemporary studies of semeiotic. The indexical
component ensures that sign activities, however mediated by higher
forms of abstraction, inevitably include some continuing reference to
the actually existing world. Peirce accepted the fact that all thinking
was in signs; but these signs always refer beyond themselves and
beyond the other signs with which they are connected to a world that
is really external to the activity of signs and therefore external to the
representations of thought. Thought is always *thought of* a reality that
it may more or less and accurately or inaccurately represent. It is
through signs, especially the indexical, that an interpreter is brought
into an existing relation with the real. A sign in the mind, produced
by a sign that is itself in real relation to some aspect of reality (such
as direction of wind) is a sign of that directionality. It indicates a
quality that the real is exhibiting at the moment and is not just in the
interpreter's mind.

Before moving to the third type of signification in this division, I
should point out that it is because of the first two types that Peirce
avoids the problem described earlier as an infinite regress of signification, or the problem of signs interpreting signs without referring to
anything external to signs. The first two kinds of sign, icon and index,
ensure that the interpretation produced in an interpreter's mind at any
point in any given chain of semiosis is brought into real relation with
an object that is in some sense independent of thought. By virtue of
genuine likeness and indexical reference, signs signify not just other
signs, but also the world independent of thought. Even symbolic sign
actions, though in many cases dependent on conventional associations
and rules of interpretation, always include these iconic and indexical
features as part of their triadic makeup; moreover, they also represent,

even in (or because of) their generality, general forms of mediation that are really operative in nature.

Sign action, or development of a chain of semiosis, does not take leave entirely of the reality that gives rise to it. Rather, further signs are not just signs of something else, but of something *more*. They add, qualify, complement, and even compromise earlier representations of that which is supposedly represented. A better picture to have of this activity is not one in which a string of signs disappears over a horizon in search of the original that gave rise to the process of signification, but one in which developing sign processes run alongside the real they represent, continually in contact with a reality that is itself in process of transformation (in part because of this very relationship with semiosis). Abstraction allows for some distance from this reality, but not in the sense that it is ever really severed from it.[4]

As already suggested, the third sort of sign according to Peirce is symbolic. The symbol is often the most important of signs among conscious, enculturated agents and therefore receives the lion's share of attention from semioticians. According to Peirce, "A symbol is a sign which refers to the Object that it denotes by virtue of a law, usually an association of general ideas, which operates to cause the Symbol to be interpreted as referring to that Object" (PW, 102). A law, as previous chapters have suggested, is a habit or tendency. Having its being in the future, it is a form of mediation that determines how things *would be* in the future if the law in question were operative. In this case, the habit is a linguistic one, determining how a general term will be interpreted among members of a given community. The word *stairwell,* for example, is a general term that, whenever a replica of it is encountered by a linguistically competent agent, will be understood as referring to a general sort of thing with some specific kinds of characteristics and not others. Such a term may act thus on the interpreters' minds only through replicas because it is general in nature and thus necessarily of the nature of a legisign. Moreover, because it is general, that to which it refers is also general.

In Peirce's view, symbols refer usually by an association of general ideas. This suggests that for Peirce, no less than for Saussure, symbolic interaction requires a complex set or system of relations in order for signification to occur. As Peirce writes, "All that part of the understanding of the Sign which the Interpreting Mind has needed collateral observation for is outside the Interpretant. I do not mean by 'collateral observation' acquaintance with the system of signs. What is so gathered is *not* COLLATERAL. It is on the contrary the prerequisite for getting any idea of what is signified by the sign. But by collateral observation, I mean previous aquaintance with what the sign denotes" (CP, 8.179, italics his). A given symbol is distinguishable from others because it requires a rule (or habit) for it to be properly understood or interpreted. This proper intepretation may occur only if the symbol participates in a system of signs that is more or less consistently arranged and if this system is already familiar to the interpreting agent. But because the symbol is represented in a replica, it has both indexical and iconic components. As for other generals of all kinds, there must be existent instances upon which the symbol has real effect, and it is through these instances that the symbol retains an indexical character.

Moreover, the symbol itself, in its general character, is affected by these replications. As Peirce writes, "The symbol will indirectly, through the association or other law, be affected by these instances; and thus the Symbol will involve a sort of Index" (PW, 103). Active through its replicas, the symbol also has positive, qualitative features associated with it. The size, shape, or color of the replica indicates to the interpreter what the replica is symbolically connected to and thereby how it is to be interpreted. Thus, although the rule or habit of interpretation predominant in symbolic activity, and although systematic differences are requisite, other qualitative and indexical characters remain and, indeed, are necessary for appropriate or meaningful interpretation.

More important for present purposes is what Peirce includes as symbolic sign activity. Words, sentences, and other sorts of conventional signs are symbols and are widely recognized as such. But Peirce claims that it is an error to restrict symbols to conventional signs, as he himself did in 1867 (CP, 2.2440). In a letter to Lady Victoria Welby, Peirce

wrote that the interpretation of a sign "depends either upon a convention, a habit, or a natural disposition of its interpretant (that of which
the interpretant is a determination)" (CP, 8.335). A symbol may be said
to be interpreted according to convention that is at least in some
respects arbitrary, but it may alternatively be either interpreted by a
natural habit or by some combination of natural and conventional
habits. When, for example, the child interprets the presence of a snake
as a sign of danger and flees, she is not doing it in accord with conventional behavior but is being determined to act according to natural
dispositions or habits.

It should be remembered that in a Peircean framework habits that
are natural may be distinguished from those that are conventional by
way of a distinction of specific difference. In one sense, all habits are
natural. Habit is a pervasive feature displayed by all existing things of
whatsoever kind. Conventional habits differ from natural ones not in
the sense of being "unnatural" but rather in the sense that they are
learned by or imposed on the members of linguistic agents by way of
their participation in culture. Conventional habits are additive, but
also reconstructive. They are forms of mediation that transform the
already existing habits of the organism. This understanding of habit,
along with the broader conception of symbolic interaction, is significant because it allows that much of the symbolic activity experienced
by linguistic agents is not merely conventional but also natural, or at
least mediated in part by natural habits.

Moreover, it also suggests that other organisms, even if not explicitly linguistic, engage in symbolic activities as part of their everyday
existence. The scent given off by the doe, for example, is an index to
the male that she has recently been in some place; but far more important is the natural habit of interpretation that leads him to understand
this smell as an invitation to courtship. Other examples are everywhere,
involving complex organisms and activities all the way down to the
rather rudimentary behavior of the parameicia swimming about in
the stomachs of human organisms.[5] In Peirce's view, it is not just
humans that introduce symbols and bring speech to bear on nature.
Rather, nature is replete with practices of communications in which

we may participate if we develop a sufficiently attuned ear. No more often is it the case that we, as linguistic agents, must *make* sense of the world than it is the case that we must *discover* or interpret the sense and meaning, the messaging, that is already there, already transpiring among other living things.

The third trichotomy introduced by Peirce concerns the relationship of the sign to the intepretant. The first element of this trichotomy, a rheme, considers the sign as a sign of qualitative possibility—that is, a kind of possible object. Present actualities may be regarded as significant of something else, even when the state of this other is not actual. Or rather, a present actuality may be a sign of potentiality, of what could be in the future under appropriate circumstances. This figures heavily in the activity of imagination, in which a situation is modified in thought so as to give rise to some possible and desirable consequence. A dicent sign, the second element, is one that the interpretant takes as a sign of actual and not merely possible existence. A slightly opened door, for example, suggests that someone may have entered the house while I was away, but a moving figure in the kitchen indicates that someone is actually present here and now.

An argument—the third element—is, for its interpretant, a sign of law. The interpretant in this case takes the sign to be a sign of a replica that is itself an instantiation of a general law (PW, 103–4). The sign claims to be really affected by some law operative upon it. This relation is crucial in the context of scientific inquiry, where what is sought through experiment is not how some particular acts on another, but what general laws are at work guiding particular interactions. These laws are general, may equally refer to any number of actual things, and indicate general tendencies to which the future will conform so long as they are operative. Actual things, when they become signs of general law, pave the way to discursive knowledge and more adequate representation. Perhaps more important, they produce symbols that may be then brought into relation to one another, in thought, independently of the existing things that exhibit them. This relationship provides an opportunity for extending knowledge as well as for imagining the probable course of events without pursuing them in fact—just as the epigraph from Santayana given at the outset of this chapter suggests.

In addition to these trichotomies, two further triads are useful for present purposes. One speaks more directly to the nature of the interpretant itself. Interpretants are distinguished by Peirce as emotional, energetic, and logical. An emotional interpretant is a feeling. It may be anger, joy, loneliness, indifference, fear, or any number of other possibilities. When one hears Keith Jarret's Köln concert, for example, a particular feeling is wrought in one's mind, and this is what Peirce is referring to as an instance of an emotional interpretant in the process of semiosis. "Everything in which we take the least interest creates in us its own particular emotion, however slight this may be" (SW, 67). An energetic interpretant is one in which an action is the predominant effect of a sign. A sergeant's command of "Ground Arms!" is an example. It is primarily interpreted not by a feeling (although some semblance of a feeling may be involved), but by a response by the soldiers who hear it. Consider also T. L. Short's example: "A deer hears a noise and flees danger. The deer's movement has as its goal, safety; it is a flight from a supposed predator. Yet this flight is elicited by a noise. Since the deer is fleeing a predator and not a noise, his flight, which was triggered by a noise, in effect interprets that noise as being the sign of a predator" (1981, 208). Here the deer hears a noise and takes it as a sign of an existing object, and so the sign is a dicent. It also interprets the sign as the sign of a predator, not another deer, for instance, so the sign may be said to be a symbol. The natural habit of the deer is to infer an enemy from this sort of sudden sound. It further interprets the sign energetically, through flight. The sound may also produce fear as a component, so there is an emotional aspect, but because the deer does not interpret the sign by feeling alone, insofar as it flees, the sign is primarily an energetic interpretant.

An interpretant may also be a logical one, such as those produced by verbal linguistic signs. This kind of interpretant is a habitual one, one that has been informed, is being informed, or would be informed (Short 1982, 288). The reading of a text, in which words are understood according to linguistic habits, is an example. The words of the text generate ideas in the interpreter's mind according to already formed habits; in other words, to read the text, an interpreter must already have in place a storehouse of meanings. In reading this text now, the interpreter calls forth those concepts to which symbols are attached through the mediation of these habits, and the habits of the self are thereby reinforced or modified by the activity. As reinforced, the interpretant becomes relatively more fixed in meaning and automatic. No one, for example, normally pauses long over words such as *and* because these words so rarely deviate from accepted usage, but a text may also challenge or transform habits of understanding by questioning or recontextualizing a familiar symbolic understanding. A discussion by Heidegger, for example, of the meaning of terms such as *Being* and *technology* may serve to transform the logical interpretant of these terms in insightful, provocative, and even useful ways.

Interpretants may also be distinguished, according to Peirce, into those that are ultimate and those that are nonultimate. The latter occur in the flow of semeiotic activity. They are a succession of feelings, actions, and understandings, each of which in turn becomes interpreted in subsequent sign activity. In principle, this sort of activity is potentially unlimited in its development, but there are also ultimate interpretants. Peirce claims that particular trains of semiosis come to an end. They achieve this definite feeling, prompt that ultimate response, and form or sustain some habit of interaction. Particularly significant in this division is the ultimate form of the logical interpretant. Semiosis begins in connection with real objects (actual or possible), and it properly terminates, in Peirce's view, in the ultimate logical interpretant, which pitches beyond the semiotic process per se in a habit change of the interpreter. He writes, "It can be proved that the only mental effect that can be so produced and that is not a sign but is a general application is a habit-change; meaning by a habit change a modification of a person's tendencies toward action, resulting from previous experiences or from previous exertions of his will or acts, or from a complexus of both kinds of cause" (SW, 277). The proper effect of a signifying chain is a habit change that, because general, will really modify the agent's future encounters. The habit change is of the nature of a third and thereby governs the individual's conduct in her transactions with self, other, and world by really modifying her dispositions to interact and manifest some qualities and not others in the future.

Although this habit change does not signify an absolute break in semiosis altogether, it does ensure that sign activity does terminate in the reality that gave rise to it and with which it has been in at least some sort of contact all along. The ultimate logical interpretant marks the moment when semiosis indexically returns to the real by modifying or reinforcing some habit of action of an existing organism. This means that the problem of an infinite progress, a concern brought to light earlier in this discussion, is not possible. Rather than supposing that every interpretant demands that it become the object of further interpretation in ongoing sign activity if its meaning is to be fully achieved, Peirce eventually claims that meaning is most properly restricted to the ultimate logical interpretant in which semiosis culminates. Referring to James's view of pragmatism, he writes that James's "definition differs from mine only in that he does not restrict the 'meaning,' that is, the ultimate logical interpretant, as I do, to a habit" (CP, 5.494). Peirce may have gone far in the direction of deconstructing the transcendental signified as an immediate presence, but he also secured the real connection of a potentially endless play of signs to an existing world that sustains and in significant ways transforms it.

The last trichotomy to be considered here is that of the immediate, dynamic, and final interpretants. As Short points out, this division has been at times identified with that of the emotional, energetic, and logical. But this identification is a mistake, and keeping the two divisions distinct rewards the reader with further clarification of Peirce's semeiotic (1981, 212). The immediate interpretant is a potential one; it is the condition for a sign's ability to be interpreted as a sign of something. "My Immediate Interpretant is implied in the fact that every Sign must have its peculiar interpretability before it gets an Interpreter. . . . [It] is an abstraction, consisting in a possibility" (SW, 414). The possibility in which it consists may be a possible feeling, act, or thought.

Peirce is here again pressing the point that signs must have some connection (or ground) to their objects, which is prior to—and independent of—their actually being interpreted as signs by some interpreter. A hole in the wall, for example, may give rise to an interpretant that calls to mind the presence of a gun because the sign (the hole) has been in real contact with a bullet, and it is a sign regardless of whether or not interpreted as such. Because of this real connection, the immediate interpretant grasps the real object. As Short writes, "in the immediate interpretant of the sign its immediate object is apprehended or responded to or felt. For the immediate object is the object of the sign as the sign represents it to be (8.314). The immediate object and the immediate interpretant are two sides of one coin, or, rather, of one sign" (1981, 215). The immediate object correlates to what Peirce calls the immediate interpretant. The latter is that which the sign produces in the mind such that the mind apprehends of the object what is represented by the sign. The immediate object is what is captured in the interpretant as an interpretation of the sign when interpreted correctly.

Although the immediate interpretant is merely possible, the dynamical "is that which is experienced in each act of Interpretation and is different in each from that of any other" (SW, 414). Just as, categorically speaking, seconds embody firsts in actual events or occasions of existence, so dynamic interpretants embody immediate interpretants. They are, in short, particular acts of interpretation, which is why each one of them is unique in its occurrence. This does not imply that a dynamical interpretant is primarily energetic; it may as well be emotional or logical and is most likely some combination of all of these. Peirce's point is only to identify particular instances of interpretation as both partial to the whole and different from previous and succeeding acts of interpretation to at least some extent.

A particular dynamical interpretant realizes some aspect or aspects of a real object, an object Peirce calls dynamic. The dynamic object may determine multiple signs, all of which truly pertain to that object in some respect or another. So, although different acts of interpretation may generate quite different dynamic interpretants, each may embody an immediate interpretant that correlates to an immediate object, an immediate object that is some part of the dynamic object that has determined the sign in such a way that the sign may accurately signify it. Also, any given sign may have multiple objects, signifying differently in different contexts (Short 1982, 286). A baseball, for example, may be a sign of a set of rules that constitute a kind of game in which it figures; a sign of the complex industrial and technological practices that conspired to produce it; or a sign of some past experience, recalling a special joy or regret to someone who once played the game. All of these objects may be connected to the sign and, depending on the context, one, another, or several are brought out or signified. In short, there is always more to any object or set of objects than some sign tells of it, and every sign is significant of more objects that it is ever going to be recognized as signifying by any one or number of persons interpreting it.

Rather than representation being unable to represent the fullness of reality, representation always *outruns* any effort to exhaust its capacity for representing the real. This is an extraordinarily robust conception of representation, but, as pointed out in chapter 2, the real is of such a complex and interrelated nature that no less is required of modes of representation if the real is to have any prospect of being adequately represented. Peirce's theory of signs, instead of concluding that the real is simply too much, too variegated (as a nominalistic theory would), shows how such representation is not only possible but really does the work of more or less adequately representing the world.

Which facets of the real are made manifest and which of these facets receive representative attention depend at least in part on the purposes and preferences of the members of a given community (Short 1981, 214). Those elements of the world that are relevant to the well-being of an individual or community, for example, are more likely to be attended to than others. As James points out, "Things reveal themselves soonest to those who most passionately want them, for our need sharpens our wit" (1912, 176). This fact again underscores the partial character of actual representation, but, more important, it indicates that any actual representation of the real reflects not only the nature of that represented, but also the specific purposes of those doing the knowing. Different "knowledges" differ in part as a result of the fact that knowers attend to different features of the real because implicated

in it differently and also because they have different investments guiding
their attention to the specific contours of the real.

Nevertheless, Peirce retains in the midst of this rather complex
account of sign activity a sense of convergence and constraint on representative practices. Multiple dynamic interpretants, each of which is
different, provide "collateral observation" of the dynamic object in
question (Short 1981, 215). The process of inquiry develops more inclusive, corrective knowledge of an object through multiple dynamic
interpretants. It is of course possible to be in error, to misunderstand
the sign or signs interpreted. Not only may one mistake a sign as signifying what it actually does not, but also signs often present *themselves*
as signifying something other than that of which they are truly a sign
(think, for example, of an insect that appears to be another, more
dangerous creature in order to avoid predators).

The task of inquiry is in part to discover the relations between the
way things appear, or signs, and that which they seem to represent. As
inquiry proceeds, a more inclusive and reliable representation of
dynamical objects may be generated (CP, 6.318, 8.178–79). At some
point, a time that Peirce explicitly recognizes as ideal, an interpretant
may be generated that correlates fully, or rather coincides, with its
dynamical object. This is the final interpretant, and it, as an ideal, reg-
ulates communal inquiry. It is that which the community seeks and by
which its actions are constrained.

That the final interpretant is ideal in Peirce's approach means, first,
that any interpretant short of the ideal final interpretant (as all actual
interpretants are) is approximate only. Any interpretant is therefore
fallible, susceptible to correction as part of a more inclusive whole.
Second, inquiry, as inextricably bound up in sign activity, is incapable
of producing apodicticity. It may produce bodies of knowledge that
inform persons of the relations between signs and their objects, but a
given appearance of a sign cannot give certainty in a particular
instance of an extant relation. What is generally a sign of some event—
a local manifestation that is part of a larger whole about which it suggests something—may in any particular instance misrepresent. The
clock face on the wall may indicate that I still have hours to sleep, but

it may also be a very different sign on this particular morning—a sign of the electricity having gone off and my now being two hours late for an important meeting. Fallibilism, in short, systematically pervades Peirce's view of representation.

But Peirce was convinced that, despite this fallibilism, dependable and accurate knowledges were in the process of being created, knowledges that allow persons to know things, in countless instances, as they really exist independently of us. "There is nothing, then, to prevent our knowing outward things as they really are, and it is most likely that we do thus know them in numberless cases, although we can never be absolutely certain of doing so in any special case" (SW, 413). Things are not known immediately or incorrigibly precisely because they are known through the complex mediation of signs; but they are known in a mediated and fallible manner.

Peirce in Contemporary Context: Avoiding Fashionable Alternatives

At this point, it is possible to broaden and develop further Peirce's view by placing it in contrast to other, now prevailing views of representation. Kathy Ferguson, in her book *The Man Question* (1993), identifies two current epistemic models that I employ here. She identifies them as the *interpretivist* and the *genealogical* approach to the relation between reality and representation. The interpretivist claims both that there is a strong distinction between reality and appearance and that persons have the ability to know the real that resides beneath the shift and shimmer of appearance. Interpretivists think that "there is a fit between human desires, human categories of understanding, and the world that humans inhabit" (1993, 11). Assuming that there exists a world independently of human doing and knowing, interpretivists employ an ontology of discovery in order to reveal its features. Beneath the disguises and distortions of reality in the manifold of appearance, bedrock waits to be found. Language provides the medium of discovery, and this approach assumes that the medium is a more or less transparent one: language reveals without distortion of the object represented.

The genealogist is suspicious of the interpretivist because although the interpretivist claims that it is possible to move beyond appearance and the distorting effects of power to reality, the genealogist sees beneath the first layer yet another layer of disguise and deception. Only this time, she thinks she has reached something genuinely independent, not recognizing it as disguise. As Feguson points out, "We make up our claims to truth, Nietzsche argues, then we forget we made them up, then we forget that we forgot" (1993, 11). The discovery to which the interpretivist points as explanation appears to the genealogist as a production that is itself in need of explanation, and the genealogist thinks that the interpretivist is painfully if not dangerously naive for having missed this. The appearance of something stable, unitary, or "originary" makes the genealogist wary because she suspects that it too is a product of our own making. She does not claim that there is no independent world; rather, she asserts only that the world does not appear to us unless transformed by human categories of understanding and human activities of other sorts. As Nietzsche himself argues, the world of subjects, substances, and reason is a fiction we have introduced to regulate unruly realities (1968, 268–75).

Without considering more closely the reasons for accepting either of these approaches or the problems they incur, we can distinguish Peirce's approach from both of them. As a convinced semeiotician, Peirce agrees with the interpretivist's emphasis on appearances. But as chapter 2 on substance argued, he does not have a dualistic ontology in which reality is distinguished and privileged over appearance. On the contrary, Peirce shares the following claim made by Dewey: "The primary, innocent neutral meaning of appearance may best be expressed participially, by the word 'appearing.' The world is so constituted that things appear and disappear; the opposite to appearance is not reality but disappearance" (1931, 57). As phenomenal manifestations, signs are real regardless of what kind they are, for every sign, taken in itself, has a material quality (SW, 390). That which signs signify are also real because they are immediate objects determined in some way by dynamical ones. The question for the semiotician is not to which of two categories does a manifestation belong (appearance or reality), but what kind of relation, if any, the visible holds to the invisible or the not presently manifest.

On this view, every particular occasion is a sign not only of what exists (though at times in nonobvious or misleading ways), but also of the complex regulating relations that make the world what it is at a given time and in any specific place, as well as a sign of possible future actual arrangements and forms of regulation. Dewey's example of the sun is illustrative. The appearance of a disk on the horizon signifies the existence of such an orb (a dicent indexical sinsign) in the heavens. It is also a phasal manifestation of the complex interaction of the laws of gravity and rotation among celestial bodies (a dicent indexical legisign) (Dewey 1931, 57 and 76; PW, 115–16). It is a sign that by knowing it one knows substantially more. Peirce consequently offers a position that neither trades upon an appearance/reality distinction, as the interpetivist does, nor asserts a world of surfaces (or signs) that offers no legible face. He offers a world of real appearances really connected to dynamical objects that are not immediately present but which may be known through the mediation of signs. The real contours of the world may be known—are known in countless instances—through triadic signification.

Peirce's grounds for defending this view are rooted in the semeiotic process of sign activity. His claim that signs are tied to dynamic objects that are independent of what we may think about those signs may under special circumstances be tested. Let the individual disregard or randomly interpret the significance of a number of signs. Suppose that upon crossing Lexington Avenue an individual faces down an oncoming taxi and decides to interpret it in ways other than it recommends itself for interpretation—as an illusion for example—despite furious honking and swerving. The result is real enough. The person is struck by more than just a sign and in ways that suggest that an alternative interpretation would have been a more accurate one. The same shape signified mere seconds earlier is to some degree now physically impressed upon him; the yellow on his belt buckle is the same yellow that is on the cab; and the irate person yelling at him for denting his car is now unmistakably an actual New York taxi driver. More mundane examples that support Peirce's position are everywhere ready to hand. A photograph, for example, is an indexical sign of what it represents. The exposure of film in conjunction with laws regulating the interaction of light and specific chemical reagents creates an image that is for a moment in real connection with the object and forever afterward resembles it as an icon of it. Is it really a sign of some object, accurately representing the object's qualities and thereby bringing an interpretant into relation with the object? A comparison of the photograph with the person would seem persuasive; it reveals the shared qualites—color, shapes, peculiar "imperfections"—that make the photograph an iconic representation of that person and no other. Peirce's claim that generals are real and may be truly represented is similar to this photograph. As indicated in chapter 1, inferences are made constantly and, as predictions of future occurrences, are overwhelmingly verified.

To argue that regulating laws are not at work flies in the face not only of scientific practice but of experience common to everyone. Such generals are not "more real" than the existent objects in the world, but they do mediate interactions in ways that transform the participants. The genealogist's suspicion, although in some ways warranted, is excessive according to Peirce. Surely persons may be misled, but for each of these instances of being misled there are countless instances in which representations of the real, as it is independently of how persons choose to think of it, are borne out. They are verified and supplemented, and, to the extent that they do work, they gain our trust.

Some Plausible Criticism

A significant challenge to my interpretation of Peirce as a realist over against the choice of either genealogy or interpretivism is posed by Joseph Margolis's recent representation of Peirce as a kind of constructivist. In his essay "The Passing of Peirce's Realism" (1993), Margolis suggests that Peirce eventually came to defend a view that I call here *epistemic constructivism*. By this term, I mean those views that claim that human thought constitutes that which it knows in such a

way that inquirers cannot have what I think Peirce stalwartly claimed
to have: access to knowledge of things as they really are, independently
of what we think of them. This definition includes the entire genealogical tradition, as described earlier, but also other traditions, according
to Margolis, such as those headed by Hilary Putnam, Thomas Kuhn,
and practically everyone else in contemporary philosophy (including
Peirce). Margolis says, "The trick is that a plausible theory of science
must effectively reconcile a realism of generals or generality with the
conditions under which human inquiry can claim to be objective *by
generating the predicates it generates.* In our own time, such a linkage
can only be achieved in a constructivist way. . . . Dewey, Dewey's fol-
lowers, nominalists and conceptualists, nearly all contemporary thinkers
restrict thought to human thought" (1993, 304–5, italics his). Margolis's
claim is that although Peirce's attempt to articulate a plausible theory
of science is unsuccessful, Peirce's development of an evolutionary
doctrine in metaphysics is compatible with recent constructivist
views. Moreover, Margolis suggests that Peirce's own linking of evolution to tychism (chance) makes it difficult to see how Peirce himself
avoids the constructivist view if evolution is considered in a global
fashion (1993, 305–6). Defending my interpretation of Peirce against
Margolis is worthwhile, not only because his interpretation is strongly
opposed to mine, but also because a defense helps to clarify further the
sort of distinctive approach to epistemology that I think Peirce offers
in contrast to the alternatives of the interpretivist, the genealogist, or
the constructivism that Margolis has in mind. In this defense, I argue
that Peirce does offer a kind of constructivism, but one significantly
different from that proffered by Margolis.

The difficulty for Peirce, as Margolis sees it, lies in his claims for
thirdness. "The trouble now appears to be that universals are inseparable from thirdness and that thirdness entails the activity of mind or
intelligence in some decisively constitutive sense" (Margolis 1993, 306).
This statement is significant because universals both appear to require
the human mind for their reality and are attributed to nature as explanatory of its processes. Yet they cannot be both. Either one attributes these
mind-dependent universals to nature, which is tantamount to idealism,

or one accepts that these universals do not really refer to anything outside of the human minds that generate them.

Nevertheless, Peirce argues that from within human practices of knowing, persons or communities of persons may know a truly independent reality. This suggests that there is some sort of parallel between human cognition and the nature of the world and that they somehow correspond. Margolis thinks that this is an arbitrary explanation and an implausible one at that: "On the face of it, Peirce's solution is also a *deus ex machina*. It suggests that there is an assured correspondence between science and reality (in the ultimately fated opinion: the 'truth') *because* there is an antecedent and continuous correspondence between the triadicity of the improvised generals human scientists invent and the triadicity inhering (somehow) in cosmic evolution (which therefore harbors real universals)" (1993, 307, italics his). But why should one believe that there is such a correspondence? What grounds are there for supposing, as David Hume did, for example, that there is such a "divine" harmony betwixt the two (Hume 1990, 54)? When we see this assumption to be groundless, Margolis suggests as an alternative that we interpret the triadic structures of intelligible reality differently, in a more "historicist" manner. Rather than appealing always to independently standing reality (which cannot be reached), we should consider these structures "*artifacts of human construction*" that are forged in the ongoing process of human inquiry (1993, 309, italics his).

This position implies that intelligible reality is not entirely independent of human thought because the real (as here defined) would be a product of human thought itself. It would retain something of its objective character in that both structures (that of thought and that of reality), first, would be social constructions. This means that the opinion of the community would not depend on the arbitrary whim of one or some group of individuals but would rather reflect the resulting opinion of the community as guided by agreed upon methods in any particular area of inquiry. It would remain objective, second, because what the resulting opinion of the community ends up being is constrained by the brute oppositions of existing things on the community

(Margolis 1993, 309). Reconstructing Peirce's view of thirdness, Margolis here also underscores the continued role of secondness. He says that this approach "would scuttle 'mind-independence' completely, without denying the objectivity of 'thirds.' . . . It would construe *their* objectivity as a (triadic) artifact posited, from within human inquiry, as holding independently of the mind" (1993, 313, italics his).

Peirce's project of epistemic convergence appears in the main sundered in Margolis's reformulation, although some of his dearest views remain. Constructivism undermines the possibility for which Peirce held out: the ability of the community of inquirers to progress in a fallible way toward ever more adequate representations of the real, as it is, independently of human knowers. In the long run, according to Peirce, the final interpretant would correlate to its dynamical object to the point where community opinion would truly coincide with the real. But under Margolis's constructivist modification, there is no way in which human thought may be said to correspond to an independent reality because this very human mind independence has been "scuttled" and replaced by a formulation in which the real is itself defined by the community of interpreters. The real is that which is *posited* by the communty, not *encountered* by it; triadicity remains real, but as an artifact of inquiry it is not in any ontological sense external to the community. So there is nothing, in Margolis's approach, to which the final interpretant may ultimately correspond. Rather, the triadic structures posited by the community are occasionally shocked or jolted by the brute resistence of existing objects that somehow continue to affect opinion (how this is so remains to me unclear). The advantage that constructivism brings in its wake, however, is according to Margolis well worth the price. It is no longer necessary, he insists, to try making sense of the view that "our thinking only apprehends and does not create thought" (1993, 320).

Margolis's effort is illuminating not only because it provides a novel and provocative approach to Peirce, but also because it suggests precisely the manner in which Peirce *should not* be made into a historicist or a constructivist. First, as Carl Hausman and Douglas Anderson have pointed out in their excellent essay "The Telos of Peirce's Realism"

(1994), Margolis fails to take into account adequately Peirce's semeiotic and doctrine of categories. Although Margolis appears determined to separate the brute opposition that is characteristic of secondness from the feature of intelligibility that is the hallmark of thirdness, Hausman and Anderson observe that "a proper modified constructivism sees the intrusions of secondness as inseparable from the spontaneity of qualitative occasions (firsts) and the growth of generals or of thought—seconds are the constraints that force thought onward" (1994, 829).

Rather than separating secondness, or an externally constraining world, from thirdness, Hausman and Anderson point out that thirdness always includes secondness and firstness as constitutive of its structure. There is no such thing as thirdness without secondness, so the possibility of their being of separate orders is precluded. The thirdness involved in human constructive representations of the world includes external opposition that is genuinely external if it is to be secondness at all. Consequently, Margolis's move is categorially not possible within a Peircean framework.

Moreover, Margolis's apparent reluctance to address Peirce's theory of signs precludes him from seeing the role that the dynamical object plays in Peirce's view. The dynamical object is an explicitly extramental reality that constrains thought precisely through its relationship with the immediate object (Hausman 1991, 485–87). In turning abruptly from Peirce's notion of evolutionism to his view of an intelligent, living cosmos without doing the necessary spadework in terms of semiosis, Margolis misses an important dimension of Peirce's thought (Hausman and Anderson 1994, 828–29). The result is a kind of constructivism that both departs sharply from Peirce's view and fails to develop the tools Peirce provides on behalf of a more plausible view of constructivism.

It seems that Margolis offers his alterative account of representation and his modifications of Peirce's view because he objects to two beliefs that he attributes to Peirce, but that Peirce did not ultimately hold (though he may have held either or both earlier in his development). One belief is that all of nature is intelligent, which may be inferred from the following argument: (1) all thirdness entails the activity of mind or intelligence; (2) thirdness is operative in all of nature; (3) therefore, all of nature involves mind or is in some sense intelligent. But Peirce only claimed that all of nature displays habitual and habit-forming activity, of which one kind is mind. The laws of gravity, for example, are essentially of the nature of thirdness because they mediate the activities of solid bodies upon one another. But this does not mean that mind is present, only that the activity, insofar as it is triadic, is intelligible and may be adequately represented in signs by an interpreting agent.

The point here is only that positing the intelligibility of nature surely does not necessarily entail claiming that nature is itself intelligent. On the contrary, Peirce repeatedly argued that there is a real affinity between the human mind and nature, which would surely suggest that he did not think nature intelligent in the same way the human mind is intelligent. In *The Neglected Argument for the Reality of God,* for example, he writes, "it is the simpler hypothesis in the sense of the more facile and natural, the one that instinct suggests, that must be preferred; for the reason that unless man have a natural bent in accordance with nature's, he has no chance of understanding nature, at all" (EP2, 444, cf. 152). That humans have an affinity with nature does not mean that nature is of the same sort of being as intelligent mind; rather, it means that nature is intelligible and the mind is able to guess at its workings by virtue of its natural affinity with it. In short, although the second premise is correct, the first one is not, which undermines Margolis's conclusion that all of nature is, according to Peirce, intelligent.

Margolis also mistakenly attributes to Peirce the belief that because all thought is in signs, thought is an order separate from nature. He claims that Peirce must somehow get thought and nature together. He concludes that Peirce's solution to this difficulty is a deus ex machina (1993, 307). But this argument arbitrarily separates the interpreter of semiosis—whether human or some other, such as the paramecium—from the process of semiosis. The triadic nature of semiosis involves, by its definition, an interpretant of some sort, and in the case of human semiosis determination of the interpretant occurs in the agent's mind. The sign is a sign of something else that in some way determines the interpretant that is formed. Prior to this, before the interpretant is determined, the sign in nature is but a possibility, unrealized until caught up in the triadic relation of a dynamical interpretant. This does not mean that nature is not itself, independently of being known by human knowers, triadic. It is, because there are real generalities at work in nature at multiple levels of complexity. The extended treatment of substance in chapter 2 surely makes this much clear. What it does mean is that rather than separate orders that must be somehow melded into correspondence with one another, semiosis is the manner in which interpreters *participate* in nature's ordering and come to know its features through inquiry, through actual participation in its living processes.

This issue may be made clearer by looking at the formation of an interpretant in the mind of an interpreter. An interpretant forms a triad that is itself already part of other triadic (or more complex) relations. As was suggested when addressing the problems of an infinite progress and regress in semiosis, every sign, which is itself triadic in structure, is related to antecedent and consequent signs. This is to say that it is part of an ongoing diachronic series. Moreover, at any given moment a sign participates in a vast complex of synchronic relations. The thirdness present in the interpretation of a sign as significant of some possibility, actuality, or law occurs only through relationships with a wide range of codified rules, some of which are culturally produced and others are more appropriately termed natural habits.

When a sign (interpretant) forms in the mind of an interpreter, that sign brings the interpreter into relation with—makes him or her a participant in—all the further reticulations that constitute the formed sign. This means that the representations produced by a community are always already part of or already participants in semiotic activity that is in some respects genuinely external to it. The mistake Margolis makes, it seems, lies in his thinking of semiosis as being of a separate order from other parts of nature rather than as a kind of activity in which anything that is participates. It was this error, of course, that Max Fisch pointed out and corrected. Margolis's failure to see this error generates a problem that is foreign to Peirce's thoughts and prompts solutions that are even more so.

This point brings out a second reason for not following Margolis's push for epistemic constructivism—namely, that it ultimately strips Peirce of his distinctive metal, his realism. Peirce, I suggest, does offer a constructivist approach—but one very different from what Margolis offers, a version that does not compromise his commitment to scholastic realism. It is true that in Peirce's account of the categories and semiosis the real is indeed a product, to some degree, of the complex interactions of agents and communities with the real. As suggested earlier, culture refers to those aspects of the real that depend on interaction with human communities for their existence. So Margolis is correct to point out that Peirce's category of thirdness leans significantly toward constructivism. Thirdness informs us that the specific, dyadic struggles in which agents engage are mediated by real generals. Speaking of the world, these generals are the general laws of nature that regulate the vastly complex affairs of nature. And in terms of agency, thirdness points to the conceptions according to which agents act.

In fact, belief means for Peirce the willingness to act under specific circumstances in ways that will, through dyadic existential relations, bring affairs more into line with those conceptions to which the mind is itself in conformity. In a manuscript from 1903 that addresses Royce's *The World and the Individual,* Peirce writes that

> We are too apt to think that what one *means* to do and the *meaning* of a word are quite unrelated meanings of the word "meaning," or that they are only connected by both referring to some actual operation of the mind. . . . In truth the only difference is that when a person *means* to do anything he is in some state in consequence of which the brute reactions between things will be moulded [in]to conformity to the form to which the man's mind is itself moulded, while the meaning of a word really lies in the way in which it might, in a proper position in a proposition believed, tend to mould the conduct of a person into conformity to that to which it is itself moulded. Not only will meaning always, more or less, in the long run, mould reactions to itself, but it is only in doing so that its own being consists. (PW, 91)

In order to know what something is, one must inquire into the specific regulating generals that have been operative during its particular history of interaction with others. These generals, acting through their replicas, have molded activity in such a way that existents embody some possibilities and not others, some tendencies and not others. What constitutes any particular event depends on the generals at work.

These generals may be generals in nature (such as gravity) or those that emerge from the beliefs informing the conduct of human agents. Some instances are relatively removed from human intervention, whereas others are peculiarly contingent upon it. An example of the former is continental drift or the operation of magnetic forces, and an example of the latter is anything specifically culturally produced, such as an automobile or a computer chip. Most actual things, it may be noted, belong in the latter category; in some ways they are independent of our activities, but in other ways they are dependent. The computer chip, for example, requires not only cultural production but also depends upon relatively independent generals operative in nature (those, for example, regulating the nature of silicon and the ways it may and may not be used in manufacturing).

Discerning the generals at work as well as the *kinds* of generals at work goes toward explanation of what something is. But this explanation is not itself ultimate. All existents, of whatever sort, are contingent; they are products of the history of interactions that manifest them. As such, any existent, however explanatory of subsequent events, is itself liable in turn to explanation in terms of its antecedent history. In other words, the explanation of a contingent event is itself contingent; both events might have been other than they are, and any explanation is susceptible to further supplemental explanation. Like the interpretivist, Peirce may appeal to the nature of things as explanatory, but he does so without positing them as necessary or originary. Like the genealogist, he may assert the contingency of everything that is, but without equating contingency with the merely arbitrary or with falsification of the real in any given representation.

This is the sense in which I think Peirce is best understood as a constructivist. His approach is constructive both because it sees the world of things as the outcome of multiple and varied collaborations and because it recognizes that representations of such things are themselves artifacts. They are fictions in the etymological sense of something made, fashioned, or woven together. This view does not at all render them false—although in some cases they are misleading—but only foregrounds the ineluctable fact that they are produced by members of communities in discourse with one another and in interactions with the environment. As artifacts, they are liable to the same sort of analysis, ontological contingency, and deliberate reconstruction to which other artifacts are heir. Donna Haraway makes a similar point with respect to technoscientific practice. She writes that " 'Reality' is certainly not 'made up' in scientific practices, but it is collectively, materially, and semiotically constructed—that is, put together, made to cohere, worked up for and by us in some ways and not others. This is not a relativist position, if by relativism one means that the facts and models, including mathematical models, of natural scientific accounts of the world are merely matters of desire, opinion, speculation, fantasy, or any other such 'mental' faculty" (1997, 301 n. 12). According to Haraway, "Constructivism . . . is anything but disengaged 'relativism,' with its attenuated and idealist sense of difference. From the standpoint of technoscientific liberty, consequences matter; knowledge is at stake; freedom and agency are in the making; and there is no possible transcendent resolution of questions by appeal to context-independent disembodied entities, whether they be called God, reason, or nature" (1997, 115–16).

More important in the present context, however, is the point that this sort of constructivism need not submit to Margolis's claim that constructivism undermines Peirce's view that in the long run knowledge will converge with the dynamical object. Peirce's approach thoroughly recognizes the ways in which interpreting agents transform the real. As Colapietro points out, Peirce believes that "the pragmaticist 'holds that the Immediate Interpretant of all thought proper is Conduct' " (1996b, 86). Such conduct inevitably transforms the dynamical objects that it interprets, but it does so in accord with meanings with which it itself is already in conformity.

We may therefore claim that there is a a drift toward convergence of the community of inquiry and the independently real (Colapietro 1996b, 86). This is so not only because inquiry is developing more inclusive knowledges of the real, but also because the world is itself being transformed in accord with our complex and increasingly inclusive conceptions. What is most significant to note here is that the assertion of constructivism need in no way violate Peirce's insistence on semeiotic realism. Through the mediation of signs, persons may in any particular circumstance have legitimate access to the real, as it is, independently of individual or communal preference. The dynamical object, whatever its nature and history, may determine signs that in turn generate interpretants—may bring the interpretant (in the mind and thereby in the interpreter) into real relation (although a mediated one) with the determining dynamic object. One can know only through the mediation of signs and so only as these signs are represented; but it is also true that through such mediation one genuinely knows the object that is outside of the mind.

A constructivism that is reconstructed along Peircean lines is realistic because it explicitly denies the controlling metaphor of knowing that is operative in Margolis's account as well as in those accounts he mentions as constructivist (including the genealogical). These views sunder the relation between knower and that which is known by claiming that thought and reality are intrinsically of separate orders. According to them, one can know the world only through the lens of a distorting apparatus, such as categories of thought, language, ideology, and so on. Worse yet, a lense can be exchanged only for another, differently distorting lens or framework of interpretation. Such lenses are historically informed, giving rise to partial, perspectival, and ultimately in some ways false knowledges. A Peircean approach readily agrees that knowledge is situated and partial. As Colapietro writes,

> realism sees experience as a process by which we come into contact with what is actually other than ourselves and sees knowledge as the cumulative result of an ongoing inquiry by which we come to glimpse some aspect of what is really so. Put another way what I am proposing is that the indexical and symbolic functions of symbols

provide the basis for a strongly *historicist* reading of Peirce, a reading in which the norms, aims, and ideals of inquiry and also of other forms of semiosis are seen as woven by the fingers of time into the fabric of these processes. (1996a, 134)

Colapietro claims that the indexical function of signs calls for a view in which what is interpreted in semiosis is rooted to a specific here and now. As such, it is an intrinsically local manifestation and can be only partial to some whole. The object of semiosis and the particular interpretation are historically rooted. In the developmental world Peirce sketches for us, signs also must be partial and changing, in part because their objects are likewise in dynamic development. In other words, the correlation of a dynamic interpretant with a real object, as mediated by the sign's truly representing that object to an interpretant, may itself change over time. A sign may today truly represent some object but at a later date fail to signify that object, or at least fail to signify that object in the same way, perhaps because the object itself has changed during elapsed time.

Colapietro makes a similar claim concerning the symbolic nature and functioning of signs. "In the case of linguistic and many other kinds of symbol, however, the habit constitutive of the symbol is a historically instituted convention. . . . The conventionality of symbols is part and parcel of the actual coming together or convening of some finite community" (1996a, 134). Representation is constituted by symbolic habits of interpretation. An individual, as a member of some given community, inherits these symbols as the habits of action and belief that consitute him or her as a member of that community. Indexically and symbolically rooted in some place and time, the representations generated are inevitably partial. But this does not mean that they are hermetic or distortive. Knowledge of a local situation is constituted by particular existents, specific qualitative features, and real mediation. Because all of these elements are historically rooted and contingent, there is no stepping out of one's particular standpoint.

But there is perspectival knowledge, and this knowledge has *reach*. Locally effective generals are often operative over time and space. This is of course what makes inference possible, even from a local standpoint, with regard to some future. As Clifford Geertz incisively points out, "The locus of study is not the object of study. Anthropologists don't study villages (tribes, towns, neighborhoods . . .); they study *in* villages. You can study different things in different places, and some things—for example, what colonial domination does to established frames of moral expectation—you can best study in confined localities. But that doesn't make the place what it is you are studying" (1973, 22, italics his). The questions that must be asked with regard to partial and local knowledge include: How general is this representation? How far does it reach and over what periods of time? Whom does it affect? Upon what does it depend? How contingent is it?

Answers to these questions come only through further inquiry that generates knowledge that remains partial and contingent, although increasingly inclusive as well as aware of its own limitations. It can be learned, for example, that some of the ways in which practices of colonialism affect local structures are not everywhere similar, whereas others are relatively common across a broad spectrum. The limitations become part of the representation, and in this way fallible claims concerning other times and other places are really possible even though adequate knowledge always begins very close to home. Through an inquiry that demands both particularity and generality, both what is common to many and what is unique to individuals may be discovered.

This sort of inquiry also provides the conditions for the possibility of critique, for discovering the bias or distortion that is operative in a locally developed form of knowledge. Developing inclusive representations—in which the context, values, systems of belief and representation of other persons and other contexts are included, among other things—allows one to criticize one's own situation, values, forms of belief, and going representations. These inclusive representations render visible the actual contingency of one's own historically conditioned view, providing the means for freeing (at least in part) shared representations of misrepresentations and distortions. Without providing an Archimedean point from which to judge, these sorts of inclusive representations make partial critique really possible. In light of those inclusive representations, one's own views may appear insupportable or in need of considerable revision. Rather than multiple and equally distorted points of view, Peirce's approach suggests multiple more or less partial points of view. The difference between the two approaches is that although the former emphasizes that knowledge always obscures that which it represents, the latter, through practices of inclusivity, may increasingly come to know the object as it really is.

This means that partiality does not commit Peirce to the genealogist's insistence of falsification and violence. Trading on something like Heidegger's metaphor of enframing, some have suggested that the positing or revealing of some aspect of the real inevitably occludes, denies, or silences some other aspects. It is important to see not only that Peirce denies this view, but precisely why he does so, given the purposes of this book. So I conclude this chapter with Peirce's argument against this kind of epistemic view.

Peirce's response may be found in a dialogue he constructs between a man and a surveyor. Peirce has the man make claims that resemble remarkably the more recent claims of the genealogist. The man tells the surveyor that the maps he makes are just lines, but the surveyed region is a surface, and no amount of lines can truly represent the surface. Such abstraction denies the real nature of the lay of the land. According to the man, the map *lies*. The surveyor responds by saying that, yes, the lines do not make up the land, and therefore the map is not the land. "But it does not prevent it from truly representing the land, as far as it goes. It cannot, indeed, represent every blade of grass; but it does not represent that there is not a blade of grass where there is. To abstract from a circumstance is not to deny it" (PS, 93).

In other words, it is not the fault of the abstraction or the fault of the partial character of knowledge that the part is taken for the whole or that something is thought not to exist because it does not appear on the map. The map may be *taken* as the whole, but this calls not for a denigration of abstractions or partial constructions (which are both truly representative and useful), but for better understanding of abstraction. We need to understand better the nature of representation, how it works, and what it reflects. It calls also for recognition of and response to the fact that knowledge is itself historically situated.

To be situated means that one is privy to knowledge of the local along with extending radii of ultimately indeterminable and fallible length, a definition that must be kept in view in practices of interpretation. Any given map has its own particular limitations.

Peirce, of course, does not deny that persons falsify or inadvertantly misjudge representative claims. On the contrary, the record is full of such falsifications and misjudgments. Some claims are arbitrarily privileged over others; some voices are silenced intentionally; others are violently marginalized or ignored. That we also remain blind to our own personal and shared forms of blindness, despite our best efforts to free ourselves of misrepresentation, is also no doubt true. But none of these admissions compromises our capacity to know, in varying degrees, the real itself and in increasingly inclusive and extraordinarily complex ways. The amelioration of the difficulties of representation lies ultimately in the hands of members of the community. Only inclusive knowledge claims about the real can forestall or bring to an end the arbitrary substitution of some part for the whole; only earnest search may reveal piecemeal our negligence and missteps; only through a recognition of our historically situated and contingent condition can we begin to criticize our inherited representations and values and protect the fragile and transient—but adored—strands of our community. Toward that end, the next chapter picks up the problem of representation in a different way in order to further this description and to introduce normative constraints that include those imposed on us by the externally real but do not rely on these alone.

FOUR

COMMUNITIES OF INQUIRY

Authority, Constraint, and Inclusivity

There is nothing mysterious or natural about authority. It is formed, irradiated, disseminated; it is instrumental, it is persuasive; it has status, it establishes canons of taste and value; it is virtually indistinguishable from certain ideas it dignifies as true, and from traditions, perceptions and judgments it forms, transmits, reproduces. Above all, authority can, indeed must, be analyzed.

—Edward W. Said, *Orientalism*

In chapter 3, the principal concern was to show how constructive representations really can coincide with the real. It argued that the real not only impinges on representation in a relatively external way, but also informs its content. This chapter focuses on a descriptive account of the conditions under which members of actual communities construct representations and then offers some normative guidelines in order to show how these practices may be improved. Two methodological adjustments are required and should be introduced at once. First, the term *representation* itself changes in significance. Whereas in chapter 3 representation was narrowly construed within the context of a theory of signs, in this one it is more broadly understood as a narrative practice in order to address problems of authority in representation. I call it a practice because it is not this or that representation that is in question, but rather *characteristic ways* in which some portion of reality is represented by particular members of an epistemic community, in some ways and not others, for themselves in particular and for the community in general. Individuals do the representing, but as this chapter makes clear, they belong to one or several "subcommunities" within the community at large and by virtue of this membership have common interests, share forms of life, and enjoy specific kinds of privilege and responsibility within the larger community.

I call the practice narrative because representations of the real are typically a rather large collection of signs, gathered together in a more or less coherent whole, according to some set of operative rules and in light of going interests. These accounts may take many forms— paintings, verbal stories, written texts, museum exhibitions—but they all have one thing in common: they are put together by someone or a group of persons, and once constructed they accumulate some degree of authority over the community in representing the nature of that which they portray. So *authority* throughout the chapter has a double meaning. It is the capacity to construct—which is already a position of relative privilege in a community—as well as the power to constrain others to accept what it produces as veridical.

The second methodological change concerns Peirce's role. The previous three chapters were devoted primarily to explication of Peirce's own views. But Peirce's writings on the nature of epistemic communities and on the role authority plays in the production of representation are, at best, limited. Peirce is quite critical of authority's circulation within the community. He recognizes that some communities have historically relied on some form of authority for disposing of empirical questions, but he thinks this practice anathema to the construction of good representations. To the extent that authority is present, it imports with it bias and arbitrary preference. In his "Questions Concerning Certain Faculties for Man," he claims that

> In the middle ages, reason and external authority were regarded as two coördinate sources of knowledge, just as reason and the authority of intuition are now; only the happy device of considering the enunciations of authority to be essentially indemonstrable had not yet been hit upon. All authorities were not considered as infallible, any more than all reasons; but when Berengarius said that the authoritativeness of any particular authority must rest

upon reason, the proposition was scouted as opinionated, impious, and absurd. Thus, the credibility of authority was regarded by men of that time simply as an ultimate premiss, as a cognition not determined by a previous cognition of the same object, or, in our terms, as an intuition. (CP, 5.215)

The problems Peirce sees in introducing authority into the practices of representation are, first, that it amounts to another form of intuition-ism, but, second and more important, that the normative value of authority lies only in its reasonableness, which is a question not nor-mally addressed when authority is introduced into an account of representation. It is instead an ultimate that grounds other claims in an at least apparently arbitrary manner.

I entirely agree with Peirce's view of authority here as far as it goes, but I differ from Peirce, as I intend to show in this chapter, in that I do not think that authority may or even should be entirely strained out of going practices of representations. I argue that authority, always pre-sent, needs to be analyzed and subjected to more adequate normative constraints so that it may serve the end of producing better representa-tions rather than the isolated preferences of some (powerful) members of the community. The goal, I think, is to render authority more responsible—that is, really more reasonable, just as Peirce's reference to Berengarius suggested that it should be.

One reason why Peirce does not have a more sophisticated analysis of the role of authority in communal representation is, I suggest, that he has a particularly homogeneous understanding of who constitutes members of the community of inquiry. Vincent Colapietro has sug-gested that "the community of inquirers is truly never anything more than a motley association of companionable antagonists" (1995, 43); I understand this statement to mean that members of any given com-munity may vary widely in terms both of the conditions under which they are able to participate in an inquiry and of their interests in so participating.

But this is surely not how Peirce tended to think of communities of inquiry. The "man of science" was (obviously) male, participated in a very specific European tradition tracing to the Greeks, employed some methods while "jeering" at others, and was characteristically interested in problems of nature independently of social or cultural conditions (CP, 1.235 and 6.568). Although this depiction of the traditional community of science may well be descriptively accurate, it is surely reductive in its present normative constraints. The scope of what may be taken as the object of inquiry is surely much larger; the participants are surely not such close ken in terms of shared traits and training; and these differences have been shown to influence commonly the practices of the epistemic community in significant ways. When communities of inquiry are seen not to be peopled by the "men of science" as Peirce pictured them, but as motley associations, then authority's role becomes more complex. On the one hand, communities are shown to harbor forms of distortion and inversion in the production of communal representations that have not been heretofore acknowledged. But on the other, authority is seen to be not only ineluctable, but also crucial to the construction of good representations.

Toward this normative end, I develop in this chapter an account of practices of representation that directly confronts the problems of authority and responsibility that are pervasive in all kinds of representation and provide some normative guidelines for making these practices better. *Authority* here refers to the power that some have in our community, for a range of reasons, to construct representations for the rest of us. Such a representation may be overtly scientific, such as the nature of the quark, but it may be (and is generally more likely to be) about social relations among persons, such as moral dilemmas or the differences between the realities that different persons, differently situated, experience. Responsibility is closely connected to this power, marking the specific ways in which the community (i.e., at least some group of others) succeeds or fails in holding these persons accountable for their actions. By "better" I mean more reliable, more objective, increasingly freed from the bias that always infects (at least to some degree) the production of representative knowledge in any given community.

In this account, science is always regarded as "special": it provides limited methods that are more useful in some contexts than in others, although always useful to some degree in any context. In any description that refers beyond a merely fictional arrangement that someone may have in mind, there are always features that may be subjected to controlled inquiry. Any description of a moral dilemma, for example, may be checked for discrepancies in terms of the objective conditions being described and (at least in limited terms) for ways in which variously proposed solutions will affect those conditions and unnamed others in ways other than advertised. But rather than beginning with science and radiating outward to see how the social affects its representations or trying to justify other sorts of representation by virtue of their "closeness" to good science, I begin with social conditions and show how they constrain and enable the production of more or less reliable representations of the real, whether these representations be scientific or otherwise.

In the first section of the chapter, I offer an account of what communities of inquiry actually look like and of how authority plays a role in their efforts to construct representations, and I discuss ways in which this role introduces arbitrary bias, distortion, and even inversion. I start with a short genealogy of Nancy Hartsock's feminist standpoint theory and the criticism it has suffered. Hartsock's approach is widely recognized as still influential in feminist scholarship but warily regarded as problematic in epistemology. Like Kathleen Jones, Bat-Ami Bar On, and Helen Longino, I too find standpoint theory unpersuasive, but I think that the view that has emerged from critical engagement with standpoint is extraordinarily valuable for further developing plausible conceptions of situated knowledge, representative authority, and communal privileging in the production of knowledge. Nowhere else, to my knowledge, has authority in epistemic practices been both embraced as constitutive (in a positive way) and subjected to regulative constraint.

My thesis in this section is that representations that are produced in and accepted by communities of persons rely at least in part on these practices of accounted privileging for their objective character and that a community takes a representation as objective in part because it understands the representation to have been produced by those properly authorized to make that representation. Thus, a considerable amount of going representations comes not by shared critique (an ideal of science that is often impossible or impractical) but by systems of authorial privileging and accounting. If this practice is a fact, it goes no distance toward telling whether representations in general or this or that representation in particular is either good or bad, reliable or not, objective or biased. These differences depend instead on what sort of practices of accounting are employed and how well they work. Ultimately the question that comes into focus is, When does someone have good reason to think that she is in a good position to represent the real, and once she has produced it, how do others know that that representation is a good one?

Presuming that authority is ineluctable and valuable, what is needed are methods that may constrain undesirable forms of authority—those given to distortion and inversion—and enable other forms that tend toward the production of increasingly better representations. Although Peirce did not understand the community of inquiry as I represent it here in this chapter, I suggest that he provides one approach for making this argument in his discussion of hypothesis formation in scientific inquiry. Whereas in chapter 3, I used Peirce's semeiotic to show how representation of an independent world was genuinely *possible*, here I use Peirce to provide clues for how we should actually go about producing explanations in such a way that the world being represented may inform the way it is depicted. To the extent that these methods are employed, not only is arbitrary bias checked, but the community also has good reason to think that representative authority is being properly allocated.

This approach to handling authority then will be supplemented by a drive toward a kind of explicit inclusivity in representation. Even though a given practice of representation may work or survive external constraint, this does not mean necessarily that this practice is the best or even a good way of representing the real. I suggest here, therefore, that inquiry should be deliberately controlled so as to include in its representations the conditions under which representations are constructed. To the extent that inclusion occurs, practices of representation may be further checked not for how the representation represents the object of inquiry, but for how authority configures specific interests and privileges in the acts of representation. This approach is intended to provide grounds for criticism and to delimit the scope of the representations themselves. After showing how such an approach may be drawn from Peirce, I offer what I take to be an outstanding representative example already available in the ethnographic work of Nancy Scheper-Hughes.

Striated Communities and Situated Knowledges

In her essay "The Feminist Standpoint: Developing the Ground for a Specifically Feminist Historical Materialism," Nancy Hartsock appropriates the methodological base of Marxist theory to develop what she calls a "feminist standpoint." Her purpose is explicitly political: her standpoint is intended to expose the "laws of tendency which constitute the structure of patriarchy over time" and to provide an epistemological tool useful for opposing domination in whatever form it may take (1995, 69). My specific concern here is only the tenability of her epistemological stance and the claims it makes concerning social reality, individual and group representations, and epistemic authority. Hartsock states that "A standpoint . . . carries with it the contention that there are some perspectives on society from which, however well intentioned one may be, the real relations of humans with each other and with the natural world are not visible" (1995, 70–71). She argues that this contention may be sorted into five claims, but only the first two are of primary importance here. "(1) Material life (class position in Marxist theory) not only structures but sets limits on the understanding of social relations. (2) If material life is structured in fundamentally opposing ways for two different groups, one can expect that the vision of each will represent an inversion of the other, and in systems of domination the vision available to the rulers will be both partial and perverse" (1995, 71). As I understand it, the first claim refers to the fact that persons as members of specific groups are differentially located—hierarchically situated—in social reality. People's experiences are structured and limited by their very different material positions. Persons differently situated inhabit and experience different worlds, which is reflected in their representations of that reality. As Charlotte Bunch writes, "Since lesbians are materially oppressed by heterosexuality daily, it is not surprising that we have seen and understood its impact first—not because we are more moral but because our reality is different—and it is a materially different reality" (qtd. in Bar On 1993, 85). This is not a claim to "different worlds" among different and differently situated groups in the sense that has come to be associated with the incommensurability thesis that Kuhn made famous and that was considered in chapter 1. It is rather the claim that events taking place among agents bear multiple and very frequently contradictory meanings because the agents are differently located within the hierarchical arrangements of class and gender.

The same event or object may simultaneously signify for one actor social acceptance, economic advance, and personal freedom, whereas for another it embodies social marginalization, economic exploitation, and personal oppression. The transaction in the marketplace for the capitalist appears to him a freely engaged agreement—and indeed, for him it is; he may go elsewhere or refrain from commitment altogether. But the worker experiences it differently, for he has no choice but to agree and recks the occasion for what it is—inescapable exploitation of his labor by the privileged in his community. As pointed out in the earlier discussion of substance, not only may the same reality be multiple and contradictory, but that reality and others around it may also depend on this fact for their very existence. Moreover, particular forms of constraint that dominate the experience of some—namely, the oppressed—are not known to exist among the privileged because the privileged do not experience them in their daily lives. The lives of lesbians as described by Charlotte Bunch or of women generally as depicted by Sandra Bartky provide ready-to-hand examples (Bartky 1995, 400).

The point—and it should be a familiar one in light of chapters 2 and 3—is that "things" are not self-identical, not objects "in-themselves," but are many things to many people, which depends in part on those persons' social, economic, and historical positioning. Difference in meaning is both semiotic and material. Events bear an unlimited number of meanings, are multifarious signs, because they represent multiple kinds and levels of material reality for different social actors. These levels of material reality are the concrete differences between who benefits from the economic, technological, scientific, and educational resources (to name only a few) that are generated by a community and those who not only do not benefit, but often have to do the work of producing those resources for others' consumption. Hartsock's claim, I take it, recognizes that these differences (at least those of gender and class in her account) limit what is seen and understood. Persons can know only from where they are, and this knowing is quite limited by the social organization of both material and meaning.

Hartsock's second claim draws more directly on Marx's dualistic conceptions of appearance versus essence and the abstract versus the concrete. Marx claims that the material life of the capitalist is structured in fundamentally different and opposed ways to that of the laborer because the former lives in the world of exchange, whereas the latter lives in the world of production. Marx also claims that each will develop a vision that represents an inversion of the other. For example, the epistemology embedded in exchange inverts the evaluative hierarchy of use over exchange (which Marx claims is "natural") and sees exchange as primary (Hartsock 1995, 73). Both representations are partial, but because the dominant view is also freed from the material relations of the dominated, it becomes fundamentally perverse in that it systematically inverts real relations. As Sandra Harding writes, "Men who are relieved of the need to maintain their own bodies and the local places where they exist can now see as real only what corresponds to their abstracted mental world" (1986, 156). This results in men's impaired ability to understand the actual extant relations of those around them. According to Harding, "Women's actual experiences of their own labor [are] incomprehensible and inexpressible within the distorted abstractions of men's conceptual schemes" (1986, 156). Thus, men's conceptions are not merely exaggerated, claiming to be universal what is in reality quite local or partial, but also mystified and mystifying: they systemically preclude good representations of the real.

Marilyn Frye's description of phallocentric reality illustrates particularly well the claim being made here, and her metaphor has become the controlling one in this discourse. She speaks of the activities of men freely interacting with one another as the foreground, whereas the activities of women constitute the background against which men's activities are enacted. It makes for a paradoxical situation in the sense that backstage work is the necessary condition for the possibility of the play, but these efforts cannot figure in the play itself without disrupting it and so are concealed as part of the production. They *must* be somehow invisible if the "worked up" reality is to seem real at all.

> The motions of the actors against the stage settings and backdrop constitute and maintain the existence and identities of the characters in a play. The stage setting, props, lights and so forth are created, provided, maintained and occasionally rearranged (according to the script) by stagehands. The stagehands, their motions and the products of their motions, are neither in nor part of the play, are neither in nor part of the reality of the characters. The reality in the framework of which Hamlet's actions have their meaning would be rent or shattered if anything Hamlet did or thought referred in any way to the stagehands or their activities, or if that background blur of activity were in any other way resolved into attention-catching events. (1983, 168)

The actors on the stage can draw from and refer to only events that occur within the play, which makes their knowledge not only partial but also perverse. Because they cannot know the actual conditions of their own existence, they take their apparent reality as the ultimately real and as representative of reality everywhere. But the epistemic situation of those who occupy the underside of these hierarchical relations is different because they are not able to move and live in the abstract world of the socially privileged. As "stagehands," they understand the support structures that enable and configure the lived reality of those above them. They thereby understand the lives of the socially privileged in ways that the privileged themselves do not.

Moreover, the oppressed are not free to mystify the real relations of their own lives. Their subjection, whatever its form, is a constantly present conditioning factor, one that must be understood and reckoned with in daily transactions with the privileged. Failure to act according to the expectations of the privileged brings swift and violent repercussions. For this reason, Hartsock believes she can make her distinctive claim that those below know *both* their own lives and the lives of others, so their representations are less partial and not perverse.[1] According to her, "Women's lives make available a particular and privileged vantage point on male supremacy, a vantage point which can ground a powerful critique of the phallocratic institutions and ideology which constitute the capitalist form of patriarchy" (1995, 70). Social disadvantage, on this view, is converted to real epistemic privilege. Hartsock claims that women, by virtue of their place, have better access to better representations of the real. They may know what is denied to the socially privileged by virtue of that very privileging.

This descriptive claim is of course prescriptive also. The oppressed, situated as they are, should have more epistemic clout: in the contest of views, representation produced by the socially disadvantaged, or the epistemically privileged, ought to be regarded as authoritative. Theirs is a description of what *really* is happening, and the accounts offered by their oppressors, where divergent, merely reveal the oppressors' own mystification.

Like Bar On, I see Hartsock's claim of epistemic privileging as principally an authority move. An essential part of social marginalization includes the loss of ability to speak for oneself, to be heard, and to criticize dominant forms of understandings and the practices that they underwrite. This fact is well captured by Edward Said in his account of Flaubert's representation of an Oriental woman:

> There is very little consent to be found, for example, in the fact that Flaubert's encounter with an Egyptian courtesan produced a widely influential model of the Oriental woman; she never spoke of herself, she never represented her emotions, presence, or history. *He* spoke for and represented her. He was foreign, comparatively wealthy, male, and these were historical facts of domination that allowed him not only to possess Kuchuk Hamen physically but to speak for

her and tell his readers in what way she was "typically Oriental."
(1978, 6, italics his)

By virtue of social privilege, some gain the capacity to represent others, whereas those others are correspondingly silenced. The result is that the oppressed are placed in the peculiar position of having available to them public descriptions of their own lives only from others, descriptions in which they cannot see themselves.

Persons in central positions represent what they think is others' way of life without realizing that others who supposedly fall under that category do not understand or experience themselves in that way at all—or at least not easily. For example, in the case Said describes, the woman, confronted by Flaubert's description of what is typically Oriental, must choose between accepting that description (however inadequate) and failing to qualify as Oriental in the relevant respects. Epistemic privileging, as Hartsock deploys it, seeks to avoid this dilemma. Bar On writes, "the claim of epistemic privilege in the realm of sociopolitical theory mostly justifies claims for authority, specifically the authority of members of socially marginalized groups to speak for themselves, which is an authority they do not have if everyone is equally capable to know them and their situation" (1993, 94–95). In other words, epistemic privileging reinstates those who have been dropped out of the discussion because of unequal (and often arbitrary) social privileging. The marginalized regain the right to speak, to describe their own lives, to dispute claims made by others about them. More important, this argument, if found persuasive, invests the oppressed with considerable authority *over others* within the community.[2] Whereas disputes over epistemic claims concerning the real nature of social reality were heretofore decided by the theorist, the specialist, the one with community credentials from the socially privileged (e.g., a Ph.D.), they would now be decided by those most materially implicated in these relations: the socially marginal and oppressed. Those who have the experience have the right to tell about it.

Notice, however, what Hartsock does *not* do. Having pointed out ways in which social privileging suffuses the privileged with a kind of epistemic privilege that tends toward not only partiality but also distortion, Hartsock does not try to factor out authority altogether. Rather, she urges us to *allocate it differently.* Eschewing the typical and shopworn response of suggesting methods for removing authority or forms of power in the production of representations, she offers rational grounds for shifting that authority to others differently situated in social reality. In other words, instead of dropping authority, she drops the methodological approach that is characteristic of science in favor an epistemological rule. The rule is that those who are marginalized in a social reality should be compensated with epistemic privilege. Hartsock argues that this compensation will provide representations that, because more adequate and true to the real, will uncover social inequities and so subsequently can become better tools for criticism and ultimately social change.

As I pointed out, standpoint theory has been broadly influential but is also deeply problematic. Seeing more precisely how Hartsock's theory goes awry should further refine our understanding of privilege and of the effects of social categories on epistemic constructions. One difficulty is that Hartsock's position is itself susceptible to the charges of abstraction and mystification that she brings to bear on phallocentric practices of representation. Her first claim, given earlier, identifies two categories, class and gender, and she describes how their specific intersection structures social reality and what can be said about that reality by those who occupy positions in relation to these two forms of oppression. But as writers such as bell hooks (1984), Bat-Ami Bar On (1993), and Gloria Anzaldua (1987) point out, these categories are hardly exhaustive. Individual experience is likewise structured by the group categories of color, sexual orientation, and a range of other practices. All of these categories intersect at sites that are not reducible to other sites constituted by other permutations of these categories or to the categories that comprise them. In other words, one cannot reductively claim that although a site is made up of some number of categories, persons are essentially just one of them. Someone African American, female, and lesbian, for example, cannot be reduced to being *essentially* a woman with other accidental characteristics attached. Each is a distinctive site that individuals participating in those group categories may occupy. The consequence is a fracturing of identities in such a way as to render suspect the applicability of general categories such as color or woman. As Elizabeth Spelman pointedly writes, "unless I know something more about two women than the fact that they are women, I can't say anything about what they might have in common" (1988, 22).

Hartsock's first claim is an abstraction because it factors out a wide range of complicating categories in its construction of a homogeneous category of women, which results in mystification because it makes it appear that the members of a distinctive group of persons, women, share a privileged standpoint on reality. But not all women recognize claims that have been posited as rooted in "women's experience." The standpoint theory, as articulated by Hartsock, much like the patriarchic epistemology it criticizes, thereby renders it impossible for some (such as hooks) to identify themselves in the descriptions made by other (privileged) women.

These considerations of the first claim trouble Hartsock's second claim in at least two ways. Bar On identifies the first way. If we try to identify epistemic privilege within this far more complicated picture, and such privileging becomes a function of distance from the center, then it becomes difficult to assign privilege at all. How do we decide who the most oppressed is? What happens to those somehow less so? Do they lose authority altogether? According to Bar On, "The source of the problem is the existence of multiple socially marginalized groups; is any one of these groups more epistemically privileged than the others, and if that is not so—if they are all equally epistemically privileged— does epistemic privilege matter?" (1993, 89). The assignment of privilege appears to be either hopeless or self-negating because so many different persons—and for different reasons—merit privilege. The task then turns into one of finding the "most" oppressed in order to give those persons power to speak so that they can provide the best representations. Achieving this task is, to say the least, not very promising.

The second problem is that persons do not merely occupy one side of the privilege/oppression opposition (either socially or epistemically).

Much feminist theory has been accused of reflecting its white, middle-class, European background—characteristics that function as social privilege in relation to those occupying other positions, such as mestiza, brown, lower class, Central American. Thus, privilege is not something one simply does or does not have; it comes in kinds and degrees relative to the social positions of multiple others, which implies that no one (unless we somehow find the most oppressed person?) has, in any simple sense, a privileged view on reality as such.

From a different angle, standpoint theory is also problematic with regard to the a priori character of its claims. It appears to claim *(a)* that those below necessarily have better knowledges; *(b)* that those above do not and cannot know what those below know; and *(c)* that epistemic disputes that arise between the marginalized and their oppressors are to be decided strictly in favor of the former.[3] I think there is reason to find each of these claims unconvincing as they stand. First, with respect to *(a)*, it is not necessarily the case that those oppressed have good knowledges even of their own lives, much less of the lives of others. As Margaret Walker points out, though we may be inclined to think persons know their own lives, this assumption is actually unwarranted: "This might seem obvious, for it is *their* life, and we are asking about the standards they follow that given its practical structure, that issue in 'how they live.' Surely, they know how they live? Yet it is not safe to assume that people typically know much of what they are really doing, and it is certainly doubtful that they know what and all that they are collectively doing in reproducing their form of life" (1998, 362).

This lack of knowledge goes for anyone—regardless of what sort of life he or she inhabits (privileged or not). Persons, it turns out, may well understand only some of the characteristics of their lives and the lives of those around them. They may have successful strategies for living with their oppressors without having much idea of why these strategies are successful. That they work and sustain a version of their way of life is enough to maintain them. But the point here is that if we do not have sufficient grounds for thinking that persons have an adequate understanding of their own lives, then we certainly shouldn't presume that they know both theirs and ours (even if, in some cases, they do understand portions of our lives that we do not).

Claim *(b)*—that those above do not know what those below know—seems likewise questionable. Is there good reason to think that those at the center are necessarily afflicted with partial and perverse knowledges? Social and feminist theorists in the twentieth century did much to reveal distortions in our philosophical theorizing. But it seems dangerously mistaken to think that those *in actual power* suffer from systematic epistemic misunderstandings. As Noam Chomsky repeatedly points out in his writings, those actually making decisions in the "New World Order Incorporated" know quite well how things really work. They know what relations are at play, what must be done to preserve interests and order, and who needs to be deceived in order to negotiate the situation successfully.[4] Frye's metaphor of a stage may well be misleading as a representation of what social reality is like and how it gets represented by participants. Rather, those at the center, those actually making decisions, are likewise not in the play. They are puppeteers and taskmasters; they oversee everything—the script, casting, which actors represent what, the stagework, which audience gets to see, and even what interpretations are available—so that everything comes out in the end as planned and to their advantage.[5] Indeed, if one were to claim privileged epistemic access for some group, why wouldn't it be those handful who have the full benefit of capital, science, and media technology? It seems to me that these persons are privy to a vast range of information that many other persons, especially those marginalized by class and gender, have no easy means of obtaining. Moreover, this information often affects in fundamental ways what life opportunities all persons will have.

Claim *(c)*—that epistemic disputes are to be decided in favor of the marginalized—is problematic in that it proves too much. The intent is to invest marginal agents with authority over the descriptions of their own lives in community discourse. But these descriptions take on an unimpugnable, hermetic character. Divergence from descriptions of the marginalized counts not as an objective challenge to the veracity of those descriptions, but as an indication of one's perversion owing to social privileging. Because objections can come only from those "centrist" quarters (as "women's point of view" is treated as a singular perspective), it turns out that there is *no* viable position from which to critique the feminist standpoint. Clearly this position is too strong, too incorrigible, to stand as a viable epistemology.

These considerations and others have dissuaded epistemologists— feminist and otherwise—from embracing standpoint theory. But I think that discussions of Peirce's realism (chapters 1 and 2) and of his semeiotic (chapter 3) give us good reasons to think that Hartsock gets some things right. First, Hartsock's claims (1) and (2), properly modi- fied, stand. The realities of our lives are structured by our being embedded in multiple social categories, and this fact limits and enables our knowledge. It limits our knowledge because knowledge can be only of what is experienced, and this "what" is ineluctably provincial. This "what" is the result of the confluence over time of multiple forms of mediation, some of which may be termed natural, some specifically cultural. We know this because it is not just experi- ence itself that is somehow conditioned by these forms of mediation on a Peircean approach, but also by the things *experienced*. Objects of experience are what they are by virtue of their participation in a range of different sorts of mediation, and they are thereby led to manifest different qualities and tendencies to specific others depending on how those others are situated and what sorts of mediated encounters they have with those others. As products of these multiple ongoing transac- tions, the same "things"—be it a car, a sales contract, a technoscientific product such as Haraway's oncomouse, or a loaf of bread—take on a wide range of meanings to those who encounter them, and these meanings differ greatly (often systematically) depending on the position that is inhabited.

Hartsock is surely correct that the real conditions of one person's life may differ from those of someone else even if that person is very close by. But it is crucial to point out that this fact of positionality also *enables* representation because it is precisely by virtue of somehow being embedded in such realities that persons are capable of repre- senting them. Representation is indexically tied to what it represents, to at least some degree, which means that acts of representing the real are always tied to some place and time and to the forms of mediation that constitute that particular locus. It just turns out that the place and time in question are always far more highly trafficked than epistemologists long thought, for not only are natural laws at work, but also the extraordinarily complex matrix of social forms of mediation. The latter are as efficacious and transformative of the real as are the former, and they must be included if the reality in question is to be adequately represented because such mediation is constitutive of those realities. This inclusion is possible only because persons, as members of communities marked by specific categories, occupy these positions, transact with these realities, and sustain them through their efforts. So far from being an ineluctable fact that inevitably subverts every attempt at representation, positionality ought to be understood as a *conditio sine qua non* of *any* adequate representation of the real *at all*. However partial, distorting, or even perverse representations are liable to be in the sense provided by Hartsock, they may also represent in countless instances the real as it is independently of how we choose to think of it, which is possible only because epistemic agents are embedded, in some way or number of ways, in the realities in question.

More important still, for the purposes of this chapter, is Hartsock's discussion of authority. Different members of our community have different knowledges because they are differently situated; this much should be uncontroversial at this point. We also see that these knowledges are often inclusive.[6] The student, patient, child, acolyte, and ballplayer entrust themselves to the care and instruction of the teacher, doctor, mother, priest, and coach because this inclusive character is broadly recognized. We readily submit to their authority because it is more or less epistemically in the clear that they know something about our situation that we do not and in some way have need of. In other words, there *is* de facto privileging of knowledge. We all recognize others among us as authoritative over us on some issues and not others. But this authority is *not* something that someone (or some group) just has (as Hartsock suggests). It is something that a community invests to those within it or that is forcefully taken by persons in the community.

It is allocated to individuals and groups whose representations are in turn binding on the community to various degrees. This allocation may be done for better or worse reasons and can be held more or less accountable. Many of our privileged relations are enacted precisely because they have broadly accepted narratives of why these relations should hold and because they have known desirable consequences for a way of life of which the community approves. So although the division of authority is in some cases arbitrary, in many cases it is not.

I belabor the point that authority may be reasonable and justified because the recognition of authority in the production of representation is often greeted with such alarm. Authority is seen as something that must somehow be subverted or eliminated because it is inevitably the progenitor of bias and distortion in the account produced under its auspices. As an example of this reaction and of the theoretical projects the reaction provokes, consider briefly James Clifford's account in his essay "On Ethnographic Authority" (in Clifford 1988) of how authority has been handled by twentieth-century anthropologists.[7] Here Clifford discusses four approaches to producing ethnographic studies: the experiential, interpretive, dialogical, and polyphonic. There is of course no room here to explain each approach fully, but they may be sufficiently characterized as follows. The experiential is based on participant observation, and it is by virtue of the participant's participation in the culture that she has the authority to represent it. The participant continually tacks between the "inside" and "outside" of the events, "on one hand grasping the sense of specific occurrences and gestures empathetically, on the other stepping back to situate these meanings in wider contexts" (Clifford 1988, 34). This method initially (beginning in the 1920s) lent credibility to ethnographic work but has come under attack since the 1950s. Those who still back it now think of it not so much as revealing an "other" as forming a "self-fashioning" in relation to an other; supporters of this view think that the product is better understood as a form of (auto)ethnography than as a revelation of others and their cultural specificities.[8]

The interpretive approach highlights the ways in which the anthropologist "constructs" a representation of that which he experiences;

out of a vast amount of material, some of which is quite contradictory, he builds a coherent narrative that in many cases covers over the very fact that an author is constructing the representation. Proponents of this approach focus on how meaning is "made up" by those in the position of authority (the native informer and then the writer) and are uncomfortable about this fact. Some say that these representations may remain realistic *despite* all this construction of meaning, whereas others think that the construction of meaning undermines any claim to objectivity as that has been traditionally conceived.

The third method, the dialogic, seeks to produce texts in which two voices (the ethnographer's and the native's) are involved so that effects of the ethnographer's authority may be minimalized. The native is supposedly able to correct ethnographic distortions and speak for himself and on behalf of his own culture. The polyphonic method, adding to the dialogic model, tries to include a multitude of voices in the account, each representing facets that may or may not cohere with the others. The task in the polyphonic method, it is argued, is to avoid the ethnographer's temptation to reduce or eliminate these differences by producing a coherent account of the whole, an account that clearly depends on her authority to represent even though the representation itself naively purports to reflect the object (which, in this case, is really a complex social reality) (Clifford 1988, 41–52). Rather than producing an instructive narrative, the goal is to locate discontinuities, ruptures in the accounts told by various tellers. So although appropriating the dialogic model, the polyphonic model seeks the opposite goal. Rather than eliminating the bias of authority for objectivity, it seeks a proliferation of forms of bias that undermines any aspiration to objectivity from the outset.

Clifford shows ways in which each of these models is problematic, but the point here is that all of them have something in common that makes the issue a family quarrel. All of them (except for the initial version of the experiential, which, significantly, has been overturned) regard authority as pernicious. Some devise ways to undermine it; others argue that its presence is ineluctable and that realism and objectivity are thus thereby always out of reach. This seems to me to beg an extremely important question: Are there not situations in which someone or some group of persons legitimately has the authority to represent some portion of the real? And is it not by virtue of that authority that he or she is able to produce an objective account for the community? It is of course true that representation is selective and limited in scope, but are there not situations in which this selectivity is not only reasonable but fully justified by the situation in question? Not only do I think that there are such situations in which authority is *needed* for good representation, but I also think that what is being called privilege in this book is regularly given out in epistemic communities and just as regularly held accountable in order to produce good, reliable, objective representations of that which they are entrusted to represent. The problem with the approaches discussed by Clifford is not just that authority is unavoidable (that has been said often enough), but also that those approaches fail to see practices of authority as central to producing good representations. This means that there is a glaring absence in their theoretical description of the situation. More important, the description precludes (by covering over its role) the development of appropriate modes of criticism for improving the ways in which authority is allocated among members of communities by pretending it should not be there at all. As Barthes points out (in the epigraph at the beginning of this chapter), the epistemic agent is supposed to crouch in the shadows, motionless, so that he may spy surreptitiously on a reality undisturbed by the spectator, which means that nothing the agent does and nothing about his relationship to others in the community should impinge on or color what he sees.

But practices of authorizing persons to make representations must be examined, must be brought into the light of epistemic scrutiny and criticism, because who gets to decide who are competent knowledge producers in particular situations is very frequently rigged in favor of the socially privileged. A prime source of distorting and perverse representations is the fact that only a few, and often not those who seem to have any good reason for being listened to, frequently get to make descriptions of other people's lives. One reason I think that

Hartsock's initial investment of authority to the marginalized—her attempt to raise the ground floor—is interesting, even if problematic, is that it tries to subvert this form of rigging. Who gets to speak initially— that is, who gets to contest claims and negotiate for epistemic privilege on some specific issue—is crucial for the outcome of who is counted by a community as competent and in the end is decisive for which representative claims are binding on that community at large. I see Hartsock's argument as a contested claim within a community for suggesting why particular persons—marginalized women, specifically— should be heard and counted as authoritative. Because marginalized persons have perspectives that those in the center do not, ones that can correct ongoing centrist distortions, Hartsock suggests that their claims ought to have more epistemic weight.

Unfortunately, for reasons I have already given, Hartsock's strategy is untenable. Rather than providing a solution, standpoint theory and the criticism it has provoked continue to set specific problems for which there have been no suitable responses. Granting the presence of authority in communal efforts to construct shared representations, we have to ask the question, when *should* authority be approved? By whom, with regard to what specifically, and why do we think so? How is it that this person (or group of persons) has access to knowledge that we (the rest of us) can in principle know but cannot get to from where we are without their help? To whom do we need to speak in order to get a relatively comprehensive, reliable account of the conditions and consequences of our own practices? In the next section, I draw on Peirce to provide some possible responses to these questions.

Accounting for Authority

Before we construct new methods for coping with the problems that authority poses for representation, it is important to consider of what value traditional approaches to producing good representations may be in this new context. Although it should not be presumed that old ways of handling epistemic problems will readily handle these difficulties, it would be not only strange but also unconvincing if one were to presume that traditional procedures were now superfluous. Indeed, to embrace the latter presumption would impose the burden of explaining, perhaps even explaining away, the success of science to date. In this section, I first discuss briefly Peirce's view of science and method, then argue that traditional methods are quite useful, but not in the way that is traditionally understood.

In his 1903 lectures on pragmatism, Peirce identifies three kinds of reasoning: the abductive, the inductive, and the deductive. According to him,

> Deduction is the only necessary reasoning. It is the reasoning of mathematics. It starts from a hypothesis, the truth or falsity of which has nothing to do with the reasoning; and of course its conclusions are equally ideal. . . . Induction is the experimental testing of a theory. The justification of it is that, although the conclusion at any state of the investigation may be more or less erroneous, yet the further application of the same method must correct the error. Abduction consists in studying facts and devising a theory to explain them. Its only justification is that if we are ever to understand things at all, it must be in that way. (EP2, 205)

Abduction is the first stage of inquiry; it provides possible explanations that will subsequently be subjected to empirical testing and expanded through logical deduction. For our purposes, we must focus on abduction alone and explain what Peirce means by it and how he thinks it ought to be deliberately controlled. Abduction begins with observation of facts and a specific kind of orientation. "The act of observation is the deliberate yielding of ourselves to that *force majeure*,—an early surrender at discretion. . . . Now the surrender which we make in retroduction is a surrender to the insistence of an idea. . . . It is irresistible; it is imperative. We must throw open our gates and admit it, at any rate for the time being" (EP2, 47). The experience of facts suggests explanatory hypotheses of those particular occurrences in an instinctive grasp of the order that experienced realities seem to follow. Peirce describes this experience, which is not subject to deliberate production, in much the same way that Kuhn characterizes scientific discovery, as something sudden, perhaps in the dead of night, that strikes without warning. Peirce writes that "The abductive suggestion comes to us like a flash. It is an act of *insight,* although of extremely fallible insight. It is true that the different elements of the hypothesis were in our minds before; but it is the idea of putting together what we had never before dreamed of putting together which flashes the new suggestion before our contemplation" (EP2, 227, italics his). Peirce insists that we have an instinct for forming correct hypotheses, "a certain Insight, not strong enough to be oftener right than wrong, but strong enough not to be overwhelmingly more often wrong than right" (EP2, 217). Long experience teaches us that, given sufficient time, investigators will eventually light on the correct hypothesis; this lesson is well illustrated by the history of science. But such guesses cannot be deliberately controlled; individuals can only submit, for a time, to the compelling ideas that happen to occur to them. This aspect broadly coincides with the view put forth by Hempel, Nagel, Feyerebend, and others that no methods are available in the context of discovery.

This coincidence of Peirce's view and much of contemporary philosophy of science has come under criticism. Nicholas Rescher, an early exponent of Peirce, thinks Peirce's stance too arbitrary to qualify as good science. He writes that the *only* place where he diverges from Peirce is that Peirce "explicitly and deliberately substitute[s] the *methodology* of inquiry and substantiation for his somewhat mysterious capacity of *insight* or *instinct*" (1978, 61, italics his). Also, it appears as if Peirce is operating with an implicit dualism, between the order of nature and the order of ideas, and is claiming that one can somehow instinctively latch onto the other. But as Joseph Margolis argues, if there is such a distinction between orders, then there is little reason to expect that the two orders somehow coincide (1993, 307).

But Peirce's view of semiosis, as discussed in chapter 3, should make it clear that both objections miss. The individual who experiences a complex set of facts is a *participant* in a semeiotic process in which signs outside of the mind create in the interpreter's mind further signs (interpretants) that are capable of bringing the mind into conformity with that to which the objects or realities are themselves conforming.

Signs may be primarily dicent in that they are taken by the interpretant to be signs of actual things, but they may also be primarily of the nature of an argument, in which case the interpretant would take such signs to be signs of laws that are really operative. Peirce's claim to a natural ability (he calls it instinctive, but recall that, for Peirce, *instinctive* is just another word for the embodied habit) to light on these explanations—that is, on laws that are operative and so explain the facts—therefore amounts to nothing more than the claim that persons are capable of this sort of interpretation. There is nothing mystical about it; indeed, it is little more than the sort of interpretive act that occurs constantly throughout the day. The principal difference is that in ordinary circumstances these interpretive acts are habitual inferences that have already been made, whereas in the abductive phase the explanation is guesswork because it has never before been entertained. This is why the observer must be passive, must allow the facts to impress upon him a possible explanation. Mediated by thirdness, the world of things generates signs that include in them, regardless of whether they are discerned are not, signs of these very laws. The task of abduction is, initially, to allow oneself to be molded by what is experienced, and as Aristotle pointed out, the mind is most capable of performing this office.

It should be no less obvious that Peirce is not imposing an implicit dualism in his description. Far from suggesting that the order of ideas is in tune with a world we never made, Peirce gives reason to believe that we are not only participants in the world described, but also its most prolific members. The deliberate construction of representations of the world with which we interact is the attempt to produce symbols that bring the minds of interpreters into conformity with the laws that guide the world. Each of these elements—the laws, the symbols, the habits of interpretation and action—are all of the same order. Each is a manifestation of thirdness in the world. Each element, although embodied differently (in external objects, in words, and in the habits of the human body) work as forms of mediation among existing things in the sense that they guide their activities. There is, in short, no dualism to be found in Peirce's formulation.

Although Peirce insists that the guesswork of hypothesis formation cannot be subjected to method, such guessing is only the *beginning* of the abductive phase, not its entire office. Abduction may provide numerous possible explanations for given phenomena, and these explanations must be sorted out before moving on to deduction and induction. It is here that a method may be employed. Peirce offers a number of rules that he thinks should be considered in choosing among proposed explanations. One rule refers to simplicity. Because he thinks that we have an instinctual ability to guess correctly, he argues that we should go with the hypothesis that seems simplest. He refers not to logical simplicity or to the rule that has been regnant among philosophers of science in the twentieth century, in the sense that the best theory is the one that requires the fewest number of assumptions to sustain it. Simplicity here is that which seems the most natural to the mind. In "The Neglected Argument for the Reality of God," Peirce writes that

> Modern science has been builded after the model of Galileo, who founded it on *il lume naturale*. That truly inspired prophet had said that, of two hypotheses, the *simpler* is to be preferred; but I was formerly one of those who, in our dull self-conceit fancying ourselves more sly than he, twisted the maxim to mean the *logically* simpler, the one that adds the least to what has been observed. . . . It was not until long experience forced me to realize that subsequent discoveries were every time showing that I had been wrong,— while those who understood the maxim as Galileo had done, early unlocked the secret,—that the scales fell from my eyes and my mind awoke to the broad and flaming daylight that it is the simpler hypothesis in the sense of the more facile and natural, the one that instinct suggests, that must be preferred; for the reason that unless man have a natural bent in accordance with nature's, he has no chance of understanding nature, at all. (EP2, 444)

The difference between the two senses of simplicity is significant. Simplicity as a logical method is appropriate when the order of ideas or representation is genuinely thought to be different from that of nature. It is, in such a case, the best that can be done. But Peirce argues that the second sense of simplicity, as that which is more natural, rapidly unlocks the secret precisely because humans *do* have a natural accord with nature; indeed, they are participants in it, regulated by its laws, embodying those laws in their very being as habits and instincts. This is why facility, or ease of mind, is a recommendation for the plausibility of this simplicity. That which is impressed on the mind is more likely to be true than what is produced by it only with difficulty.

A second consideration is that of economy. Experimentation is extremely costly in terms of "money, time, energy, and thought" (EP2, 107). Economy depends on cost of experiment, the value of the knowledge to be gained, and the value of that knowledge for furthering other projects (EP2, 107). These requirements generate a set of rules that C. F. Delaney summarizes well in his outstanding study of Peirce's view of science:

> The first rule is a straightforward application of the general principle: "If any hypothesis can be put to the test of experiment with very little expense of any kind, that should be regarded as a recommendation for giving it precedence" ([CP] 7.220). In the same vein there is the recommendation that that hypothesis should be preferred which "can be the most readily refuted if it is false" ([CP] 1.120). A second rule ... recommends that one hypothesis should be preferred over another if one could not test the latter without doing almost all the work required to test the former but not vice versa ([CP] 7.93). A third rule ... maintains that hypothesis should be preferred which if false would give the best "leave," i.e., whose residuals would be the most instructive with reference to the next move to be explored ([CP] 7.221). . . . A fourth rule enjoins us on the basis of economy to prefer (all else being equal) the broader of two hypotheses on the grounds that the illumination it will shed on the general inquiry will be greater whether it is true or false ([CP] 7.221). (1993, 19)

Because the resources of the community are always limited, the scientist should rank hypotheses that he thinks likely in terms of a cost-benefit analysis. The rules proffered by Peirce are not intended as a calculus; applying them does not determine the one best option to explore, for different options are likely to have different strengths and weaknesses. These criteria merely provide some rules of thumb.

A third kind of consideration, one that Delaney apparently neglects but that significantly constrains the first consideration in terms of what is most natural, is Peirce's suspicion of "likelihood." He argues that ideas that may be refuted are far more important than those that we think are likely to be true. *Likelihood* is not here a synonym for "most natural" but refers to subjective preference. A *likely* hypothesis, according to Peirce, is "one which falls in with our preconceived ideas. But these may be wrong. Their errors are just what the scientific man is out gunning for more particularly" (CP, 1.120). Why are these errors the worst sorts? Peirce writes that "because likelihoods are most merely subjective, and have so little real value, that considering the remarkable opportunities which they will cause us to miss, in the long run attention to them does not pay" (CP, 5.599). He presumes that many of our initial guesses will fall within preconceived ideas of what the world is like and how we would prefer it to be, and these ideas must be sorted out before moving on to deduction and empirical testing.

These sorts of formulas are typically regarded as methods for factoring out the effects of bias on science; in the present context, this would amount to clearing away whatever influence social categories might have on a community's representations of the real. The factoring out is intended to level the epistemic playing field by disregarding the preferences of unequally and differently situated social actors. But this view, I suggest, is entirely misconceived. If it is true that the natures of events and the things of the world are the results of the complex interactions of multiple forms of mediation, as I argued in chapters 2 and 3, then the attempt somehow to factor out some of these categories amounts to deliberately ignoring some of the types of interaction that constitute the event or object. It is nothing less than a paramount example of committing what Alfred Whitehead calls "the fallacy of misplaced concreteness." Whitehead claims that "This fallacy consists in neglecting the degree of abstraction involved when an actual entity is considered merely so far as it exemplifies certain categories of thought. There are aspects of actualities which are simply ignored so long as we restrict thought to these categories. Thus the success of a philosophy is to be measured by its comparative avoidance of this fallacy, when thought is restricted within its categories" (1978, 8–9). When some relevant or even essential categories are avoided, then the object of science, which is supposed to be the external, objective world, becomes itself an abstraction. To paraphrase Sandra Harding, the object then corresponds to preconceptions of what the object should be and not to what it really is. So far from improving the nature of representations, methods such as the one suggested by Peirce, when used toward the end of negating certain categories, systematically undermine the quality of the representations being produced.

But if the end of such methods is not the elimination of the influence of social categories and the disparate authority that influence imports, then what is it? I suggest that authority is useful for improving the quality of our representations *of* those extraordinarily complex sites that persons occupy and through which they engage the world around them. Earlier I pointed out that it is only by virtue of being embedded in a specific reality and in various forms of mediation that an agent is able to represent that reality at all. What is wanted is not an elimination of the specificity but an improved representation of that reality. So the methods offered here are intended to guide this inquiry. A community that recognizes social differences among agents acknowledges that those who occupy different positions will produce complex, conflicting, and sometimes contradictory representations of the world. But the contradictions do not necessarily point to differences that must be somehow smoothed out by consistent representation; rather, they frequently point to inequalities in social reality that must be included in terms of their nature, the conditions of their existence, and their effects. This is a prompt for further inquiry, not a call for a method whereby present representations may be reduced to consistency.

Handling representations in this way not only makes for a more comprehensive narrative (i.e., more "stuff" gets included), but also paves the way for meticulous refinement. Rather than using broad strokes, we start out as pointillists. We mark specific cites, particular nested convergences, because they are the only places from which claims may be made. But those claims are general—they have "reach," as I suggested in the previous chapter—because they are made by and on behalf of members of communities. As Geertz suggests, just because a representation is made in some place, it does not mean that only that place is being represented. Broad, far-reaching tendencies may be detected in a "local neighborhood" of the real. The relevant questions posed by local representations are always, *How general* are these tendencies? What are their specific representative contours? Because no one's claims will map universally or evenly onto our shared pictures of social reality, the task is to delimit and shape our claims, making us aware of the limits of those representations.

More important in the context of this chapter is the point that this approach offers a criterion to the community by which it may discern who is responsibly representing their conditions and who is giving free reign to bias and preference. In other words, it provides a means for determining how epistemic authority *ought* to be allocated: that authority should go to those who use scientific methods precisely because they are most likely to produce good representations. Peirce's methodological approach is able to perform this office for two reasons. First, it imposes a number of values that do not depend on particular forms of social categories; that is, it imposes values (no attempt to be value free is made) that are neutral to the preferences of specific categories such as gender, class, race, and so on. For this reason, they may be shared by everyone equally, which provides a sort of "leveling" without factoring out relevant forms of mediation. Unwanted effects of authority are checked without removing authority altogether. Second, these values are in place because they prompt or encourage the best possible hypotheses for testing. The better testing is, the more adequately and fully the reality that is intended as the represented may impinge upon and inform the nature of the representation. Such testing allows members of the community to see whether an explanation is supported by something that is independent of how the community prefers to think of it and what the scope of the explanation might be. The better this testing is, the better the real may be represented—social or otherwise—and the more often bias, arbitrary authority, or "likelihoods" are eliminated from the community's practices of representation.

Using traditional methods in this way also has a distinct advantage over Hartsock's rule-based model. One is that Peirce's method is not insular in the sense that challenges to representations of any portion of reality may be offered from any position. Even though the representation of a specific site is called for, one does not gain an absolute privilege of representing it only by virtue of occupying that site. Others similarly situated may contest the view, and those situated elsewhere may require testing that supports a local representation by an inhabitant. Members diversely located but still participant in a wider shared community may compare representations not only for partiality and discrepancy but also for scope. The community may begin to discover through discourse how generally representative claims made by its members really are. The price of this kind of methodological approach is fallibilism; a community can never be sure it does not have a biased account because it has no absolute criterion for deciding between accounts. But fallibilism purchases the possibility of ongoing criticism through which accounts may be continually improved. Peirce's methodological approach provides a more adequate medium of discovery, which in the long run improves both the quality of representations produced and the allocation of authority for producing them.

Although scientific method, when properly employed, is useful for addressing the problems of authority and situated knowledge, it is not sufficient. The rules suggested here go only so far because they ultimately rely on external constraints to dispose of proposed representations of the real, and this constraint is limited. It is limited, on one hand, because only certain portions or elements of any theory may be subjected to testing. As Ralph Emerson wrote, "We have such exorbitant eyes, that on seeing the smallest arc, we complete the curve" (1951, 421), and the relatively independent world often has little to say about how or how much it is completed. Peirce himself acknowledged this fact in his 1903 lectures at Harvard. He claimed that the view (attributed to Auguste Comte) that "no hypothesis should be admitted if its truth or falsity is not capable of direct perception is incoherent because this view is *itself* an opinion relating to more than is actually in the field of momentary perception" (EP2, 235–36, italics his). Explanations of fact always go beyond the support of the facts that produce the explanations. Indeed, this is why, when explanations are adequate to the realities represented, they are so useful. They make prediction possible.

On the other hand, the diagnosis of our epistemic situation offered by standpoint theory and its critics provides another reason for finding relatively external constraint insufficient. Hartsock points out that the representations of the socially privileged correspond to the abstract world they inhabit. These representations are sustained by the authority that produces them. Privilege serves to conceal the real material conditions in such a way that only the world of the privileged, as they inhabit it, is experienced. As Frye points out, the actors in the play can refer only to elements within the play, and nothing on the outside, which is hidden from view, intrudes upon it. The problem here is that, from the position of the privileged, there is relatively little constraint available to expose the distortion or inversion that circulates among some privileged members of our community. On the contrary, the world they inhabit actually *encourages* these sorts of distortion and inversion.

For these reasons, Peirce's approach must be supplemented in such a way that these forms of epistemic bias, which are especially evasive owing to the authority that produces them, may be detected. I suggest that a doctrine of inclusivity in representation will perform this function. Earlier I argued that the refusal to include some categories in our representations leads to the fallacy of misplaced concreteness because some of the relevant types of mediation that constitute those objects are ignored. This fallacy exchanges a real object of representation for an ideal one. Here I suggest that the problem of bias, distortion, and inversion that Hartsock identifies stems from mistaking the conditions under which representations are made for the intended object of representation. In other words, distortion and inversion appear when the social privileges that produce a particular kind of reality are mistaken for a reality that is independent of these forms of privilege.

Understood in this way, the inverted representation produced by privileged men, as Hartsock discusses it, is sustained by epistemic agents who mistake the relations produced by privilege for reality that is independent of such privilege. Whereas scientific method was chastised for not including social categories in its discussion of the real even though these categories may be relevant to the nature of the object, here I argue that the categorial conditions of the producers of knowledge must themselves be included so that these covert effects be made apparent and subject to criticism. What is needed is a proliferation not only of accounts from multiple sites, but of accounts that include within them descriptions that specifically locate both agents and their objects in the constructed representation. When this is done, representations may be compared both in terms of how well they account for a relatively external reality and in terms of the conditions that produce them. Representations then provide the means for showing how different locations may themselves, owing to various forms of privileging, influence practices of representation. In this way, the effects of social privilege may be detected, in some cases progressively eliminated, and in others at least circumscribed. To discover a form of social privilege in epistemic construction in many cases does not signify that the representation is of no worth (because biased), but that it represents something other than what the one who constructed it intended it to represent; therefore, when properly interpreted, it still provides valuable information about some portion of the real.

Demanding these sorts of representations allows for a further criterion for the reallocation of authority. Those practices that provide inclusive representations are to be considered more worthy of our trust than those that do not because such inclusive representations struggle to include the forms of privilege that go toward their construction and so leave themselves open to criticism and circumcision. This is a vast improvement over those practices that are not inclusive because the latter not only omit relevant elements but in so passing over them conceal their presence and in some cases surreptitiously replace the advertised object with the distorted or inverted conditions that produced the representation.

At this point, I think it more helpful to turn from what this sort of representation *would* look like hypothetically to an example that I think illustrates the sort of normative constraints I am advocating here. Beyond making the point that such representations are really possible, this example allows us to see more precisely what sort of inclusivity is intended, how it works, and what sort of criticism may then fall back on its heels.

A Paradigmatic Example of Inclusion

Nancy Scheper-Hughes, in her monograph *Death Without Weeping: The Violence of Everyday Life in Brazil* (1992), offers a representation of *carnaval* as she and others have witnessed it in Bom Jesus da Mata, a town located in the northeastern region of Brazil. In the space of twenty-four pages, she constructs an account that does several things. First, it inclusively limits itself. It recognizes that what is represented is local, may or may not accurately describe conditions elsewhere, and certainly does not presume that the way *carnaval* is played out in Bom Jesus is the way it is played out everywhere. Second, it introduces numerous voices into the narrative, including those that do not necessarily lend support for the interpretation that Scheper-Hughes is constructing, in order to tease out the multiple sites that may be occupied and how these sites may genuinely differ and yet depend on one another. And third, it brings this representation to bear on other representations of *carnaval* in order to criticize them.

The result is *not* that these other representations are simply displaced; rather, the result is a more refined, delimited, and inclusive set of representations, all of which in some way represent the real event. Taken from different sites with different portions of the event in view, these representations, despite their differences and even because of them, go toward a more adequate composite. Where these other representations formerly advertised universality in terms of their representing an objective social reality, they now reflect other important factors (their conditions) that went into their construction. They are now seen as produced by a limited segment of the population, one that is constrained and enabled by specific forms of privilege, forms that now become part of the subsequent representation. In other words, the loss of universality is simultaneously the gain of thicker descriptions of the myriad forces that go not only toward constructing or producing the reality but also toward the construction and circulation of representations of that reality.

Before turning to Scheper-Hughes's account, I want to consider first the way in which *carnaval* has been represented by Victor Turner and J. C. Crocker, representations that Scheper-Hughes resists in her own representation. Turner writes:

> Antistructure is represented here by Carnaval, and is defined as a transitional phase in which differences of (pre-Carnaval) status are annulled, with the aim of creating among the participants a relationship of *communitas*. Communitas is the domain of equality, where all are placed without distinction on an identical level of social evaluation, but the equivalence which is established among them has a ritual character. In communitas we find an inversion of the structured situations of everyday reality marked by routinization and the conferment of structural status. (1967, 83)

Turner then cites Maria Goldwasser's (1975) study of *carnaval* in Rio de Janeiro. Goldwasser found that actually a great deal of structure went into producing this "antistructure" that is characteristic of *carnaval,* such as the organization of the Mangueria (a samba school). Samba schools such as this one are governed both by a *carnaval* commission and a directory of the school in its preparation for and participation in *carnaval.* Turner notes this structure but is undaunted in his interpretation:

> It takes an awful lot of order to produce "a sweet disorder," a great deal of structuring to create a sacred play space and time for anti-structure. If "flowing"—and communitas is "shared flow"—notes "the holistic sensation when we act with total involvement," when action and awareness are one, and one ceases to flow if one becomes aware of when one is doing it, then, just as a river needs a bed and banks to flow, so do people need framing and structuring rules to do their kind of flowing. But here the rules crystallize out of the flow rather than being imposed on it from without. William

Blake said a similar thing using the metaphor of heat: "fire finds its own form." This is not dead structure, but living form; Isadora Duncan, not classical ballet. (1967, 83)

Turner insists that despite different forms of complex structuring, *carnaval* really is an example of antistructure in action; it is pure liberation.

This view is echoed, or rather more concisely repeated, by J. C. Crocker in his essay "Ceremonial Masks," which appeared in a collection of essays edited by Turner. Crocker writes that "The masquerade of Saturnalia features not just sexual license but inversion of the usual social hierarchy. In Brazil's carnival, the slum-dwellers traditionally wear the costumes of the eighteenth-century Portuguese court, while the elite appear in such antiestablishment roles as pirates, bandits, Indians, and prostitutes. Such experiences seem to be truly liberating" (1982, 82).[9] This is the way in which *carnaval* is popularly understood, and a view that maintains this form after it finds its way into the texts of at least some anthropologists. Scheper-Hughes offers a brief but vibrant image of this "official" story:

> *Carnaval* players spin on an axis of inversions and reversals of high and low, order and disorder, male and female, inside and outside, public and private, freedom and repression, life and death. *Carnaval* dissolves order and rationality into chaos and nonsense; it tumbles the lofty as it celebrates the humble, absurd, and grotesque. Both the erotic and the maudlin, sexuality and death, are present in *carnaval,* so that destruction and regeneration are merged in the absurd *carnaval* cry, "*Viva a morte!* Long live death!" (1992, 481)

This view has collective approval, both among many of those who participate in the festival and of those who travel to Brazil to watch it and to write later about its nature. It is also the view that Scheper-Hughes contests.

Admitting not only that every *carnaval* does indeed have its mocking voices that invert normal relations by bringing the high down low, but also that, given the nature of *carnaval,* her attempt to criticize it is yet another version of *carnavalesque* in the sense of inverting yet again the going representation, Scheper-Hughes insists that criticism is warranted: "I argue that in Bom Jesus da Mata at least, *carnaval* while containing the lewd and ludic elements of the official description, is something else besides. If Brazilian *carnaval* creates a privileged space of forgetting and a dream world where anything is possible, the marginals' *carnaval* of Bom Jesus also provides a space for *remembering* and is as much a ritual of intensification as a ritual of reversal" (1992, 482). Scheper-Hughes offers several telling descriptions of what she experienced during her time in Bom Jesus. She offers them—in an announcement up front—in order to contest the official representation of *carnaval*:

> What the poor of the Alto do Cruzeiro, women especially, keep most before their eyes during *carnaval* time are scenes of their own exclusion, marginality, sickness, and debt. The opening day of *carnaval* is the Saturday before Ash Wednesday, and Saturday is also *feira*, market day, in Bom Jesus. The *carnaval* image of the abundant, overflowing cornucopia and of the banquet table is mocked by the empty *cesta* basket used for marketing. While cheap bootleg rum from the surrounding sugar mills flows in abundance during *carnaval* time, many among the poor dance on an empty stomach during the four days and five nights of the festival. And so *carnaval* and Ash Wednesday, feasting and fasting, are prematurely joined. . . .
>
> Meanwhile, the *fantasias* (meaning both the masks and costumes *and* the private fantasies) of Alto revelers project images of the fantastically real that emphasize ordinary and everyday social realities. Even while throwing themselves into the spontaneous joy and abandon of the festival, their *carnaval* "play" can also do the dirty work of class, gender, and sexual divisions, which by means of grotesque exaggeration are etched even more deeply into the individual and collective bodies. And here "dirty" takes on more sinister and less playful connotations. . . .
>
> But what I saw that first evening (and for each subsequent evening) after leaving Biu's house and after catching up with the street dancers was a highly segregated and segmented *carnaval* where rich and poor, white and black, male and female, adult and child, loose "street" children and pampered "house" children, knew their "proper" places and kept to them. The wealthy families of the big houses played *carnaval* in the privacy of their vacation homes on the coast or in the elite social clubs in Recife. They never

showed their faces for the duration of the festivities. The middle classes emerged briefly on the street on Friday night, the eve of the official start of the festival. Then they, too, left town.

Organized around the *carnaval bloco* named Grilo (Cricket), the middle-class revelers (middle-aged businessmen, bankers, small landowners, professionals) danced briefly in the town *praça* for the enjoyment of the "little people," the poor and the *mutatos,* of Bom Jesus. And they seized the moment to advance their own class-based agendas. Dressed as the chirping gadfly Jimmy Cricket, the Grilo revelers protested in song and political slogans taped to their backs the old plantation families and the wealth that had dominated local politics and economics since the nineteenth century. Their slogans read "More commerce in Bom Jesus," "We demand better terms of credit," "We need a university in Bom Jesus," and "We want a modern shopping center." . . .

The poor who had descended from their hillside shantytowns danced to the music of the bourgeois Grilo musicians, but they understood little of the protest. The demands of the Grilo were alien to them. "What about clean water?" asked Little Irene, sidling up to me in the crowd. "Are they saying anything about water?" "It doesn't look like it," I replied. . . .

By the next day, Saturday, the real start of the festival, virtually every wealthy and middle-class family had left Bom Jesus da Mata, taking their *frevo* bands, their elaborate *fantasias,* and (as Little Irene wryly put it) "their prestige" with them. The only concession to the poor, who were left behind, was an old, teetering, wooden sugarcane transporting truck that was left out in the main *praça* of town with a single loudspeaker. The mayor agreed to furnish the town with a small *carnaval* band that would play, using the back of the truck for a stage, three hours each evening of *carnaval.* But the town itself was boarded up, as the departing middle-class storeowners made sure to leave their vulnerable storefront windows protected during their absence from the chaotic press of poor revelers. No special lights or festive decorations adorned buildings, lampposts, or Nossa Senhora das Dores Church. The town looked as if it had been quickly abandoned following an emergency. (1992, 482–85)

The ways in which Scheper-Hughes's representation of *carnaval* controverts the official representation and that proffered by Victor Turner is fairly obvious. It is clear that in at least some cases the "flow" of *carnaval* is not "antistructure," that the social categories discussed throughout this chapter are not only *not* inverted or displaced but are in some circumstances poignantly reinscribed. At no time during the year do the poor, the black, the women, and the disabled feel the pressure of these categories more than during *carnaval.*

But the reason for looking at Scheper-Hughes's account, at least in this context, is less that it contests earlier representations, but rather *how* it does so and what results from it. Scheper-Hughes herself insists that

> My point is not that the libertine *carnaval* of Bakhtin and da Matta does not exist in Bom Jesus da Mata, for it does indeed reign as the official public sentiment of the festival. Rather, I wish to explore the more peripheral and marginal expressions of a celebration that is heterogeneous, open, and polysemic, full of ambiguities and contradictions. Real-life *carnavals* can be as egalitarian and eman-cipatory as Bakhtin, da Matta (1979, 1981, 1986), and Davis (1978) wish them to be, as oppressive and hierarchical as the Marxist and clerical critics of *carnaval* play can *only* see them to be, or both simultaneously. (1992, 482)

The account offered by Scheper-Hughes is, in short, an example of specific and yet inclusive inquiry. It is produced in a particular place (a village Geertz might say) and reflects conditions both there and possibly elsewhere. As a limited representation, it does not pretend to be universal, but rather challenges the universality of other going representations that advertise themselves as such. It delimits those others by pointing out that they represent only some of the many forms that *carnaval* can take.

This loss of universality is for the displaced "universal" represen-tation a substantial gain in other terms. For one thing, the official representation, once cut down to size, is freed from distorting bias. Rather than being displaced, it becomes a more adequate representation of a certain portion of reality. *Carnaval* really is, under certain condi-tions, an extraordinary event filled with inversion and liberation. Turner and Crocket were not blind or stupid when they prepared their representations of *carnaval,* but they were unknowingly selective and naively overgeneralized their claims.

Another advantage of this loss is that the reasons for supposing that the former representation was universal can now be explored. What relations of power supported and continually reinscribes this distorted view? Although Scheper-Hughes does not explore these issues—she has others that she prefers to follow out—they may be pursued in subsequent representations of *carnaval.* The forces that not only produce the reality but also sustain it may be better understood, which makes for considerably more inclusive and reflexive representations of the event.

But perhaps most important, the inclusion of these marginal expressions means two things. First, the work that *carnaval* has traditionally done to conceal these features of reality that are constitutive of so many persons' lives is subverted. Once these features are included, *carnaval* can no longer pretend to innocence when it represents itself as a complete inversion and displacement of hierarchical roles. Indeed, it must answer to the ways in which it reproduces precisely these inequities. Second, because formerly concealed features are now revealed, the work of figuring out just when *carnaval* is liberating and when it is repressive may begin. Although the causal conditions may not be difficult to find, it is important not only to cite these facts but to observe them continually so that these representations may facilitate improvements in the lives of people such as the revelers in Bom Jesus da Mata.

As Scheper-Hughes herself points out, this is all very complicated. She is of course right to claim that reality is polysemic and full of contradiction and ambiguity. This means, as Peirce argues, that representations can be only approximations of that which they represent. But they can always be more inclusive, more reflexive about their own limits and extensions. To the extent that this inclusiveness is achieved—and it seems to me that Scheper-Hughes provides a concrete example of what that looks like—better, more reliable, and more responsible representations can be produced. When they are produced, authority to describe, write, represent, and recount is warranted.

FIVE

MEDIATION AND NORMATIVE SCIENCE
Toward an Ethic of Representation

[R]eason, or thought, in its more general sense, has a real, though limited, function, a creative, constructive function. If we form general ideas and if we put them in action, consequences are produced which could not be produced otherwise. Under these conditions the world will be different from what it would have been if thought had not intervened. This consideration confirms the human and moral importance of thought and of its reflective operation in experience.

—John Dewey, *Philosophy and Civilization*

The discussion of a normative account of representative practices so far has remained an abstraction. It has addressed the question of how to produce better forms of representation primarily in terms of adequacy to the object being represented. "Better" means more objective, progressively free from bias and arbitrary preference as well as inclusive of the conditions under which representations are constructed. As I have pointed out in several contexts, however, representation does more than just mirror the real. Its primary function is to mediate our transactions with reality, and the activities in achieving this function have real effects for both us and the objects in question. What we are and the reality we encounter and continually represent are the outcomes of a long history of such interactions.

This means that the way we choose to represent our shared world is of immense consequence for how that world evolves, so not only must representation be adequate to the object, but it also must be cast in light of those possible consequences. As Scheper-Hughes insists, the world is polysemic, contradictory, and full of ambiguity. Producing representation is not just a matter of being inclusive, but of determining which parts of the world are to be privileged, valued, taken up, and considered worthy of preservation. When we choose the forms that our representations *ought* to take, there is, in short, a specifically ethical dimension that is no less important—indeed, I would argue that in many cases it is *far more* important—than adequacy to the reality in question. This is to say that the act of constructing representations is essentially a pragmatic one; what sort of work it does ineluctably turns on how well we go about it in light of the ends that are of most value within the community that engages in it. Seeing how practices of representation may be improved in ethical and not just epistemic terms is thus of paramount importance. This involves nothing less than the development of what John J. McDermott called "moral epistemology," which is rooted not only in classical American philosophy, but also "in Plato and [is] found recurring in the stoics, Augustine, Spinoza, Bergson, [and] Buber" (1986, 105).

In this chapter, I discuss what a pragmatist has to offer on this score. In terms of moral theory generally, pragmatists actually have rather little to say. This is not because writers such as James and Peirce did not think ethics important. Rather, they did not think that ethics as it has been carried out is a plausible project. Professional ethics, as Margaret Walker more recently points out, focuses on a debate about what constitutes the best moral theory. This model understands moral theory "as a *codifiable* (and usually *compact*) set of moral *formulas* (or procedures for selecting formulas) that can be applied by *any* agent to a situation to yield a justified and determinate *action-guiding* judgment" (1992, 27, italics hers). The virtues of various theories are contested in light of how they handle particular moral issues by those who write and talk about professional ethics. A discussion that deviates from this approach may be of interest or indirectly relevant to the discourse, but it is not ethics. Such a discussion comes under the rubric of, for example, anthropology or sociology.

Peirce, conversely, argues that the office of ethics is not to determine whether or not particular moral acts are right or justified. It is rather to determine, more generally, what makes a right right and a wrong wrong. He had his own reasons for saying this, but in light of the discussion in chapter 4 it is easy to see how implausible the contemporary approach is. Given the ways in which social categories striate the community, the very idea that such a compact set of rules (which would guide anyone, however situated) is possible cries out for analysis and criticism. What sorts of relations of power and privilege, for example, must be in place in order for some members of our community to think that this is a plausible representation of what ethics is for us all? Peirce, for his part, suggests that inquiry into the normative science of ethics does provide ideals in terms of which particular evaluations become possible (Potter 1996, 44). But this inquiry only renders decision more intelligent; it does not take the place of decision in particular circumstances, nor does it provide instant justification. So although Peirce accepts the view that there is a normative science of ethics, the way he understood this science is quite different from how it is presently understood in professional ethics. The second section in this chapter further explicates Peirce's view of ethics, especially as it bears on practices of representation.

At this point, however, I think more needs to be said about *how* it is that representation mediates the action of members of the community both with one another and the world at large. This fact is often cited but seldom observed in concrete detail. In the first section, I further develop what I mean by mediation and give some helpful examples, which should provide a backdrop for the subsequent discussion of the normative aspects of representation.

Representations of (and for) a Way of Life

Representation in this context refers to the body of shared understandings that constitute the medium through which individuals engage in transactions with one another, with the world they share, and with themselves.[1] These shared understandings are the inheritance that any agent must competently master if he or she is to participate in the community; they include a body of knowledge, standards of interpretation and criticism, interests in specific problems, and specific problem-solving techniques. By standards of interpretation, I mean assumptions concerning what kinds of experiences count as relevant to the community as well as the meaning of those privileged experiences. Every community makes *some* kind of appeal to experience. The differences lie in which kinds and with what import. To underscore this point, we can compare some examples. Positivist scientists in the nineteenth century drastically attenuated the body of problems capable of discussion by employing highly selective standards of experience: that body constrained itself only to that which is found in immediate sensation. Statements that referred to this kind of experience were meaningful, but anything beyond was disdainfully called "metaphysics" and considered meaningless.[2] Platonic metaphysics, in contrast, tacks in the opposite direction. It denigrates sensible experience as so much mere appearance and looks instead to a realm of fixed Being that, when grasped by thought, provides a complete system of necessary and immutable truth. Here, contemplative experience is privileged, and its object provides the model of intelligibility.[3] Another example, which privileges yet a third kind of experience, may be found in the Calvinist community. Committed to a theology of predestination but uncertain who were the "elect" among them, Calvinists resorted to a doctrine of raised affections for earthly signs of Divine Providence. One sought with the utmost care those special signs that marked the work of the Holy Spirit within one, for, as Jonathan Edwards claimed, "they plainly show the finger of God" (qtd. in Smith 1988, 16). Far from the modern philosopher who treats experience as a veil between the self and the world, the Calvinist knew experience to be sacred, for it was potentially revelatory of a Divine presence, which, once there, was beyond any shadow of turning.

The members of each community share assumptions concerning the value of various kinds of experience. They also share standards for what counts as criticism as well as for acceptable forms for invoking critique. For members of a community to criticize other members, common assumptions must be available; one member must be able to appeal to something that another member holds if his or her criticism is to be persuasive. For example, within a positivist's community one would not appeal to Edwards's religious sensibilities—not just because such a gesture would be ineffective, but also because the gesture would not make *sense,* for the positivist disregards such talk as meaningless. Conversely, one would not appeal to sense experience within Edwards's religious community, for such experience simply does not count in the relevant ways for Calvinist interests. Sense data are meaningful to the Calvinist only when they take on Divine significance.

Criticism must also take the appropriate form for it to receive community approval and to stand any chance of persuading other persons. One does not, for example, hunt down those philosophers with whom one disagrees and change their minds by force. One instead publishes relatively benign essays that employ accepted argument forms in order to persuade them of the shortcomings of their view and the virtues of one's own. One may see also the relevance of common problems and shared problem-solving techniques for the constitution of an epistemic community. Which problems a community engages goes a long way toward determining what counts in their shared representations. A group of persons intent on learning the state of their own salvation will take different objects, consider different questions, and make different assumptions fundamental in contrast to a group intent on developing empirical knowledge of the external world. They will also develop considerably different techniques for solving problems. The articulation of a theory of meaning in relation to practices of verification reflects the particular character of the positivists' problematic, whereas questions of biblical interpretation are paramount for religious communities, driving them toward the articulation of ever more sophisticated hermeneutics.

What is essential to the representations that constitute a form of life is neither the kind of experience privileged nor what specifically counts as criticism nor which problems and problem-solving techniques are engaged. What is essential is that these choices, whatever they are, are shared and that members of the community recognize the values of the community and acknowledge other persons who have them as valid members. These values sustain the group by providing a medium, a form of mediation, through which members may engage their environings. Shared understandings provide a community with a canopy of explanation, the means to interpret ongoing shared experience, and sight lines for future conduct.

It is important to insist upon the fact that *all* representation is social and to lend further support to this claim. In order to be meaningful, both in the sense of significance and of real consequences, a representation must be shared with others. As Lynn Nelson writes, "you or I can only know what we know (or could know), for some 'we'" (1990, 124). No one knows what another in her community *could* not know, even though many others do not actually know what some individuals know. More important, the knowing that is done is possible only through membership in the group. This view clearly controverts the long tradition extant both in philosophy and science that continually reasserts the view that knowing is a solitary affair. Descartes in his den, Newton alone under an apple tree, and the scientist who lights on a solution to a vexing problem "in the dead of night"—all suggest images of knowing by individuals unconnected to any community. But criticism of both discourses shows that this picture is wildly mistaken. Descartes, despite his radical skepticism, doubted not a whit his linguistic community, a community that provided the conditions for the possibility of his meditations. Nor did he doubt either the importance of the problematic or certain philosophical conceptions, such as the scholastic conception of being—both of which he inherited from his epistemic community. Perhaps most important of all, he left unconsidered the social conditions that made possible his withdrawal from the practical world.[4] The historical lesson of Descartes's project is that philosophical practices of representation are irreducibly social constructs sustained by those who participate in that particular shared way of life. A mere glance at present philosophical activities— determined as they are by institutionalized departments of philosophy, conferences, and journal publications for like-minded members of the community—surely reinforces this conclusion.

The view of science as solitary is similarly fated. Sandra Harding has done tremendous spadework to show the social nature of scientific inquiry. In her research, she estimates that of the approximately two million persons involved in contemporary science, only some two to three hundred persons (primarily scientists) are key decision makers in the process that produces scientific knowledge. The rest are technicians, research assistants, data gatherers, computer programmers, and other such personnel (1986, 72). These persons focus on specific details, contributing pieces to an enterprise far larger than themselves. Nor are the top two hundred, the "managers of science," simply autonomous individuals following whatever trail they fancy. Which problems are addressed, what knowledge is produced, and how long valuable resources are allocated to specific projects are all questions decided by economic and political forces relatively external to the scientist. The apt representation for the science worker, Harding suggests, is not the "isolated genius," but the industrial worker. Indeed, few practices so thoroughly reflect the social forces that sustain them as does modern science. The scientific practice of generating representations, like any other practice, is ineluctably social. It is an activity in which multiple members of a community participate in such a way as to produce a particular kind of knowledge product, and this product mediates with extraordinary power and complexity the ways in which members of the entire community live their lives.

One may grant these claims concerning philosophy and science and yet object that certain other forms of knowledge are defined precisely by their solitary quality. After all, is not the mystical experience, in which one gains a kind of knowledge of something "other," essentially individual? On the contrary, I think that examples such as these illustrate better than any other the social nature and consequences of representation. For example, during the 1360s and 1370s Saint Catherine of Siena reported numerous mystical experiences, in particular a mystical union in which she became the bride of Christ. As she told the experience—already a social act—Christ came to her, spoke approvingly of her renunciation of all bodily pleasures, and then drew her toward the wound at his side and bade her drink his blood. Through her extreme worldly abstinence, Catherine became one with her mystical groom. Caroline Bynum writes that "It was identification with

Christ's suffering; it was affective, even erotic, union with Christ's adorable self" (1987, 120). This union between Christ and Catherine was symbolically represented by the ring he gave to her. Hagiographers suggest that this ring was made of silver or gold, but Catherine said otherwise. The ring, according to her, was made of Christ's own foreskin, which was given up to the world in his circumcision. This symbolic choice of materials was far more powerful than rare medals because it represented the worldly suffering and shedding of blood that Christ underwent for the sins of others. In a letter to the queen of Naples, on August 4, 1375, Catherine wrote, "Oh Jesus, gentlest love, as a sign that you had espoused us you gave us the ring of your most holy and tender flesh at the time of your holy circumcision on the eighth day. . . . Notice that the fire of divine charity gave us a ring not of gold but of his own purest flesh" (qtd. in Noffke 1988, 128). Catherine claimed that she could always see the ring of flesh on her finger, and others thought of her as literally taking on the flesh of Christ in her renunciations. But, important enough for our purposes, no one else could actually see the ring she claimed to wear (Bynum 1987, 174–75). Catherine provides an exceptional example of mystical experience because of these latter facts. Not only did she report on experiences that only she had, but she also claimed to see a physical object that no one else could see.

Catherine appears to be quite alone in her experience, but this is not so. She obviously articulated herself within a social medium in which her gestures, her claims, her linguistic habits, and especially her complex symbolism made sense. Others in her community recognized acts such as hers as legitimate expressions of religious belief by a lay person. As a fourteenth-century woman, Catherine inherited a rich narrative that wove together the stories of other holy women. Her marriage to Christ was surely modeled after the life of Catherine of Alexandria, who also had a mystical consummation with Christ. Her choice of the ring was also drawn from extant religious discourses. Medieval theologians and philosophers often discussed the present state of Christ's foreskin as the only piece of flesh he left behind on earth: Had it been taken up in the resurrection, or was it left behind as gift to the faithful? By incorporating the ring of flesh into her own narrative, Catherine availed herself of a symbol already on the minds of many around her, including some very powerfully positioned people. Christ's giving her the ring made sense to them in light of her holy actions and only reinforced their belief that she was on intimate terms with him.

That others could not see the ring did not strike them as suspicious. Other holy persons, beginning with St. Francis of Assisi in the 1220s, had likewise received invisible wounds in the form of stigmata. Such mystical events did not occur every day, but they were common enough to be accepted, celebrated, and relied upon by the community in a period in which lay religious activity was surging. Such behavior was very differently received 250 years later by a religious community whose attitude had considerably changed in its response toward lay religious movements.[5]

Catherine's mystical experience and her representation of that encounter were thoroughly enmeshed in a community of shared understandings. Her experience was privileged, to be sure, but it still falls within Nelson's definition of knowing, as given earlier: "you or I can only know what we know (or could know), for some 'we.'" The fact that others neither saw Catherine's ring nor immediately shared her mystical experiences does not render her way of knowing solitary. Catherine herself, as her missive clearly illustrates, did not think of her relation to Christ as unique. She said that Christ espoused *us* with the ring, and she frequently exhorted other women to be faithful to their common husband (Noffke 1988, 129). Some others did have experiences like Catherine's, and, given appropriate conditions of holy behavior, those persons could also know what she knew, could see what she saw. But because they in fact did not, these persons (the vast majority of the community) relied on Catherine to report experiences for which they themselves longed. That Catherine was able to do so depended on community standards of trust and reliability. So long as she showed the proper signs in terms of holy actions, others were persuaded to give her the authority to make the kind of claims she was making. Far from exceptional, this kind of practice is characteristic of *all* epistemic communities and not just religious ones. As argued in chapter 4, all communities hold certain members responsible for generating representations that all community members consume. Science is an excellent example: certain highly trained members of a subcommunity within our culture are responsible for generating bodies of knowledge, the fruits of which everyone enjoys daily. Rather than problematic exceptions, ostensibly solitary ways of knowing such as Catherine's are in fact paradigmatic instances of the social nature of representation in general.

Social in nature, the various practices of representation extant in a community emerge from given forms of life, reproduce them in some ways, and transform them in others. The example of St. Catherine shows to some extent the manner in which a practice of representation emerges from quite specific conditions. Where but in the matrix of forces constituent of her time, place, and religious climate could her representative claims to a certain type of experience be plausible? Scientific practices likewise reflect the concerns of the body politic that sustains them. Hardly resembling the value-neutral enterprise it is thought to be, science thoroughly reflects the wider social, economic, and political forces that shape it. As Sandra Harding writes,

> it is no accident that in both the natural and social sciences, the objects of inquiry are the very same objects that are manipulated through social policy. It is not that the results of scientific research are misused or misapplied by politicians, as the ideology of pure vs. applied science holds. Rather, social policy agendas and the conceptualization of what is significant among scientific problems are so intertwined from the start that the values and agendas important to social policy pass—unobstructed by any merely methodological controls—right through the scientific process to emerge intact in the results of research as implicit and explicit policy recommendations. (1986, 77)

A form of representation is reproductive in that our shared under-standings give us particular values, specific forms of interaction, and modes of symbolic interpretation—all of which go toward continuing a way of life that the community has embodied for some period of time. Harding's remarks on this point are palpably suspicious and rightfully so; the ideology of science as value neutral clearly serves the interests of some members of the community—namely, those who benefit from present socioeconomic conditions—and not others. But it is a mistake to think that this rather sinister activity is endemic to a representative practice. On the contrary, one should expect a practice of representation to express efforts to reproduce elements of a way of life that members find valuable. After all, a necessary condition for the existence of some particular social formation is that it be able to reproduce essential elements of itself. Better questions concern which elements, for whom, and for what purposes.

But practices of representation are not merely conservative; they are essentially transformative of the social body that sustains them. Those who take science as paradigmatic will have no quarrel with this suggestion. Because present ways of life would be inconceivable without the effects of science and technology on our daily lives, we readily acknowledge the "applied" potential of "pure" sciences like physics and mathematics. But what about other sorts of representation? How might a religious narrative or the choice of one aesthetic over another prove transformative for a particular form of life? Take again the now familiar example of Saint Catherine introduced earlier. In mid-April 1376, she sent a letter to Pope Gregory XI who was then residing in Avignon. She addressed Gregory as *Babbo*—that is, "Dearest Daddy"—and implored him to return from exile to his rightful home in Rome so that the present rebellion against God might be overcome (Noffke 1988, 204–5). Both the terms of intimacy and the presumption of power Catherine expressed are characteristic of her. She frequently wrote to illustrious persons on matters of social import and to substantial effect. As Daniel Bornstein points out, this was an extraordinary feat achieved by female saints during this period. Women in the Middle Ages were heavily burdened by institutional and ideological constraints; they were constrained by numerous legal restrictions, were excluded from institutions of higher education, and were considered physically, intellectually, and morally inferior to men. But through lay religious experiences, of which Catherine is representative, women achieved unprecedented prominence in their culture.

Their relationship with the Catholic Church, which was itself enmeshed in society, endowed them with the power to engage and transform issues of the day (Bornstein 1996, 1–15). Catherine inherited a form of representation, extended it, and through it made significant contributions to the society from which she came. She provides one illustration of how a way of representing experience may be transformative of realities by virtue of its relation to other social practices that sustain it—one that is not properly characterized as "scientific." Her self-representation as the bride of Christ enabled her to transform the world she experienced and not just to represent it.

The aesthetic in representation is perhaps even more to the point. Let me begin with what I take to be the aesthetic dimension of representation (at least in part). The direct experience of sensuous qualities can no doubt be as beautiful in their immediacy, but artistic production involves the reworking of natural and social materials that a person inherits in some meaningful way. The result is that the work takes on a symbolic character; it embodies the ideal transformations of the artist in such a way that it becomes representative of something beyond itself. Embodying a storied past, subsequent experience of the immediacy is enriched. John Dewey writes in *Art as Experience* that "knowledge enters deeply and intimately into the production of a work" and accounts for "the sense of disclosure and of heightened intelligibility of the world" (1989, 294). The world he refers to is the natural, social, and symbolic forces that shape experience and through which we have our enjoyments. Aesthetic enjoyment is spontaneous in its immediacy but does not "bubble up" ex nihilo. Rather, it is funded by past experiences and achieves its "immediate" value through its representation of so much more than itself.

A fine illustration of what is meant here is found in fifteenth-century Italian fresco representations of the Annunciation. These paintings represent the appearance of an angel to the Blessed Virgin, announcing that she is to be the mother of Jesus. Mary characteristically reacts to the astonishing news in one of five ways: disquiet, reflection, inquiry, submission, or merit. Each of these reactions is qualitatively distinct, and each is represented through particular body postures, such as the angle of the neck or the position of the hands in the representation. Members of the community knew intimately the complex symbolic order in which the artists worked and could readily and unreflectively identify these differences. Each possibility was intended to evoke particular responses from the viewer and to provide material on which she or he was to meditate and then imitate in his or her own life (Baxandall 1972, 50–55). As such, a distinctive and extremely powerful aesthetic experience was generated through complex symbolic mediation. It provided resources for meaning, practice, and direct enjoyment for the religious community that produced it. It is in this sense that I regard the aesthetic as an essential component of every representation. Any representation involves a selection of values and a construction of a suitable arrangement in such a way that the representation will meaningfully appeal to others. The choices made— which values and how put together—inform the understandings and the subsequent activities of members of the community. The representation is thus transformative of those realities that it represents.

The transformative role of the aesthetic may be illustrated by reference to Oscar Wilde's *The Decay of Lying*. In this short dialogue, Wilde makes what he regards as a series of paradoxical claims. Contrary to naturalistic theories of art, in which art imitates nature, he suggests that nature imitates art. He astonishes his companion by saying that there were no fogs in London before a certain school of art painted them: "At present, people see fogs, not because there are fogs, but because poets and painters have taught them the mysterious loveliness of such effects" (1995, 48). Social reality, even more than "nature," follows Wilde's description. It is less the case that art imitates persons than that persons imitate artistic creations that they, for whatever reason, find beautiful. He writes,

> life imitates art far more than Art imitates life. We have all seen in our own day in England how a certain curious and fascinating type of beauty, invented and emphasized by two imaginative painters, has so influenced Life that whenever one goes to a private view or to an artistic salon one sees, here the mystic eyes of Rosetti's dream, the long ivory throat, the strange square-cut jaw,

the loosened shadowy hair that he so ardently loved, there the
sweet maidenhood of "The Golden Stair," the blossom-like mouth
and weary loveliness of the "Laus Amoris," the passion-pale face of
Andromeda, the thin hands and lithe beauty of the Vivian in
"Merlin's Dream." And it has always been so. A great artist invents
a type, and Life tries to copy it, to reproduce it in a popular form.
(1995, 38)

Wilde's point in both quotations is less sensational than he lets on. He
is only claiming that artistic production, insofar as it produces specific
attractive forms of representation, transforms our perceptions, modifies our interactions with others, and reconstitutes our experience in
ways different from before their appearance.

The great artist, Wilde asserts, is precisely one who provides a new
type of representation for members of the community. They teach us
how to see, feel, and transact with one another in delightfully novel
ways. London fogs were *there* all along. But persons didn't *see* them,
didn't experience their mysterious loveliness until taught to do so by
artists. They were thereby rendered meaningful and consequential for
the future. My view differs from Wilde's only in that I do not think it
paradoxical. Rather, it is quite reasonable in light of what representation
is like in a pragmatic formulation.

Before turning to questions of ethics, of how representations may
be criticized on grounds other than adequacy to their objects, I should
also point out that persons commonly engage in multiple practices of
representation as members of multiple communities within a shared
way of life. I have argued already that a person knows only as a member of a community. But as Naomi Scheman (1996, 215) and Gloria
Anzaldua (1987, 86) point out, persons participate in multiple communities. The intersection of social categories such as color, race,
gender, and sexual orientation marks various kinds of communities,
each of which determines (constrains and enables) the experience of
those who inhabit them. Again, as argued earlier, because a practice
of representation is enmeshed in other social practices, these practices
condition what reality, form of life, and practice of representation is
generated by a (sub)community. For example, as noted in chapter 4,

Charlotte Bunch writes that for lesbians "reality is different—and it is a materially different reality" because of the differences in social practices between their lesbian community and the heterosexist community that surrounds it (qtd. in Bar On 1993, 84–85). But persons' communities overlap with one another, and individuals must engage in *multiple* forms of understanding. As a woman, for example, one participates in a community of women and has access to shared realities and representations. But as bell hooks makes clear, women participate in subcommunities that differ radically, such as those defined by color and sexual orientation. No woman can speak for the experiences of *all* women because women participate in divergent communities whose experiences and ways of representing them are also discontinuous with one another.

This point may be made in less tangled fashion, I think, by reference to a historical example that shows how persons actually resort to multiple forms of representation in order to render their experience intelligible. In sixteenth-century Europe, persons frequently resorted to beliefs in witchcraft to explain their misfortunes. These explanations involved a complex body of shared understandings concerning the nature of witches, their powers and practices, the signs that revealed their work within one's life, and strategies for resisting their maleficence. But these explanations did not preclude other forms of explanation, such as one we would regard as "scientific." Explanations of this latter sort were insufficient unto the needs of those persons. As Alan Macfarlane writes, "a villager might recognize quite clearly the series of events leading up, on the physical side, to an accident. He might see that a child died 'because' it fell from a chair and broke its neck. 'Because' here meant 'how' it died, the outward, observable, reasons. Explanation was also needed as to 'why' it died. Why *this* child, on *this* day, died. This would explain to an anxious parent why her child, rather than that of a neighbor, had died" (1970, 193, italics his). In this example, a person engaged in two types of representation, one mechanistic or "scientific," the other more teleological or intentional. These ways, Macfarlane points out, were complementary and simultaneously entertained. They were two bodies of shared understandings, both of which were equally applicable to experience under certain conditions. Not mentioned, of course, is a third form of representation, that of the Christian church. The "villager" mentioned no doubt participated in this community as well and shared in its representative forms. Each of these bodies of shared understanding, complementary in some ways and conflicting in others, were sustained by these members of the community and did their work toward constituting a particular form of life. How individuals mediated these conflicts and confluences in their ways of representing the real is in large measure what makes these accounts so very interesting to us. Persons readily shift between these ways of knowing the real; or, rather, they live out the multiple and contradictory commitments that these practices bring with them in everyday life. We "moderns" have perhaps learned to live without this sort of intentional explanatory framework; in its place, however, we have other forms of explanation that similarly mediate communal and individual experience.

I would like to conclude this section by contrasting the view of mediation proffered here and the view suggested by Richard Rorty as a pragmatic "advance." In *Contingency, Irony, and Solidarity*, Rorty argues that the shift to a discussion of language as a medium, when properly carried out, marks a shift from the discussion of language as having something to do with a reality that is "out there" to be discovered and represented to a view that "set[s] aside the idea that both the self and reality have intrinsic natures, natures which are out there waiting to be known" (1989, 11). His understanding of language as a medium drops these assumptions and rewards one with not having to answer questions such as those addressed in the third chapter: "How is it that the conceptual framework constructed in the minds of members of a community of inquiry in any way corresponds to the real?" Rorty writes,

> I can explain what I mean by a medium by noting that the traditional picture of the human situation has been one in which human beings are not simply networks of beliefs and desires but rather beings which *have* those beliefs and desires. The traditional view is that there is a core self which can look at, decide among,

use, and express itself by means of, such beliefs and desires. Further, these beliefs and desires are criticizable not simply by reference to their ability to cohere with one another, but by reference to something exterior to the network within which they are strands. Beliefs are, on this account, criticizable because they fail to correspond. . . . So we have a picture of the essential core of the self on one side of this network of beliefs and desires, and reality on the other side. In this picture, the network is the product of an interaction between the two, alternately expressing the one and representing the other. This is the traditional subject-object picture which idealism tried and failed to replace, and which Nietzsche, Heidegger, Derrida, James, Dewey, Goodman, Sellars, Putnam, Davidson and others have tried to replace without entangling themselves in the idealists' paradoxes. (1989, 10)

Leaving aside his representation of the pragmatic tradition, which others have sufficiently questioned, Rorty here argues that the medium of language dissolves this essentialist way of understanding reality and representation by viewing language neither as a vehicle of expression (by core selves) nor as representation (of an external reality). Correspondence between mind and reality is lost, and truth takes on a significantly different meaning. Truth is now understood as "what comes to be believed in the course of free and open encounters" (Rorty 1989, 68). This argument, of course, bears significant resemblance to the view set forth by Joseph Margolis in his interpretation of Peirce in the article he called "The Passing of Peirce's Realism," with which I took issue in chapter 3.

The point of introducing Rorty here, however, is not so much to argue with him (although it is tempting to ask questions such as, "Free and open encounters *with what?*) as it is to distinguish and further my alternative. As Rorty represents the situation, there is a real dilemma at hand. Either one maintains the traditional view and accepts the fact that it carries in its belly a host of insoluble problems, or one dissolves our cherished ideas of the Self, Reality, and Truth as correspondence. It seems to me, however, that there is a third way to address this problem, one that is offered by Dewey, James, and the semeiotic approach of Peirce. This *media tertia* understands language as a medium *through which* selves interact with other realities. This transaction continually transforms the two *relata* without collapsing them into the medium that sustains them both. So Rorty is right that core selves and inviolable reality must be jettisoned, but this act does not amount to the rejection of selves and reality altogether; rather, it calls for a pragmatic reconstruction of what is meant by these conceptions. The measure of the quality of the reconception is the degree to which it addresses *both* the questions of how reality can be truly represented (in some sense of correspondence) by selves *and* questions of how the medium of language (or rather, semiosis generally) can be constitutive of those realities. That, of course, has been the project of this entire book, and my representation of mediation in this chapter is intended to explain further how mediation does this work. That a pragmatic conception of mediation does not amount to a collapse of selves and mind-independent reality was the task fully shown in chapters 2 and 3.

Criticism: A Pragmatic Criterion

Given the complexity that chapter 4 and this chapter introduce into the discussion of representation, I now turn to specifically ethical considerations. One may genuinely wonder whether or not, supposing what has been said so far is true, there is *anything* useful to be concluded here. When representations that sustain a going form of life come into conflict with other representations—ones that may or may not go toward sustaining that way of life—how does one adjudicate between them? In what sense, for example, can we possibly say that the shared understandings that sustained Catherine are better or worse than those in which we participate? Before addressing this question directly, I introduce some of what the pragmatists thought about ethics generally and then distinguish Peirce from the others.

As noted earlier, James and Dewey both are suspicious of ethics as traditionally conceived. Each takes pains to argue that the relationship between a person and the artificial rules constructed by him or his society to guide his conduct is misunderstood. Dewey insists that theory cannot, by its very nature, provide determinate rules of conduct; rules are guides or principles merely, not assured commands that at any cost ought to be followed (1980, 8 and 136–37). James, in *The Moral Philosopher and the Moral Life*, makes the same point. Citing T. H. Green's *Prolegomena to Ethics*, in which Green states that "Rules are made for man, not man for rules," James claims that rules place demands on persons, but one should understand that persons must also break the rules under particular conditions and that there is no knowing at the outset or by rote when these conditions will occur (James 1977, 624). Rules are, for James no less than for Dewey, tentative guides for conduct. Yet these admonitions prevent neither pragmatist from forging a general criterion for the moral direction of behavior. This rule is to be applied generally, and I argue that it applies in the special case of judging representations. It is also in an important sense *metatheoretical.* By this term, I mean that it is applicable to different forms of life regardless of the shared understandings that sustain it. Whatever conceptual framework is in place, whether sixteenth-century Italy or contemporary south Texas, it may be applied as a tool of critique. I do not mean that this framework is simply supervenient; a pragmatic criticism actually depends on the values operative in the community for the choice that emerges from the critique, which is what distances the pragmatist from his predecessors. Exactly how this is so should soon become clearer.

With regard to a morally problematic situation, James says that the best act is that "which makes for the *best whole,* in the sense of awakening the least sum of dissatisfactions" (1977, 623). Personal conduct should be guided by inclusivity and measured (morally) by its contribution to the growth of values both for the person and the community. Acts that render the social situation more inclusive are to be preferred to those that do not. This view closely coincides with Dewey's criterion for discerning the true from the specious good (and then the Right and Happiness). According to Dewey, distinguishing the two involves an imaginative consideration of potential consequences, and the Good is that which is more inclusive. Acts that contribute to the development or growth of the self and the community are to be considered more worthy of pursuit (1988b, 150). Inclusivity here means promoting those values that not only allow other values, but mesh and reinforce those others in such a way that their existence is rendered more stable and permanent.

This criterion for choosing among alternative courses of conduct is highly general and exceedingly abstract. It does not indicate, for example, *which* integrative values should be chosen or how these values should be *weighted* in relation to one another. Dewey recognizes that a criterion cannot adjudicate such questions from without or in advance. Those answers can come only from individualized personal history, shared experience, and existential choice. The criterion does provide, however, a *practical* guide for the agent. Dewey's argument is that whenever possible the agent should choose according to the rule of inclusivity. He nevertheless fully recognizes that the agent cannot always do so and that he or she frequently has good reasons for not so doing. There are occasions when one value becomes so important that other, more enduring values are understandably sacrificed on its behalf. For this reason, the criterion cannot be a universal rule applied blindly.

Peirce's view is continuous with that of James and Dewey. Peirce claims that "Ethics is the study of what ends of action we are deliberately prepared to adopt. That is a right action which is in conformity to ends which we are prepared deliberately to adopt" (CP, 5.36). The question of which ends are to be preferred is a question for the science of aesthetics as Peirce conceives of it. "The highest of all possible aims," Peirce claims, "is to further concrete reasonableness" (CP, 2.34 n. 2). Concrete reasonableness is, according to Peirce, a doctrine of growth, of evolutionary development, that emphasizes continuity. This means that in the consideration of choice in a particular circumstance, the ultimate good "does not lie in any individual reactions at all, but in the manner in which those reactions contribute to that development" (CP, 5.3). It is not the particular choice that imports moral significance, but the *tendency* of that choice to further reasonableness that marks it as a good. And it becomes reasonable insofar as it is inclusive.

The criterion provided is essentially negative. It does not inform an agent of which value she should choose, what path she should follow, or even how she should go about making those decisions. There is a wide *range* of options available, and nothing may be handed out by philosophical inquiry into the normative science of ethics to determine which of these options is best. Rather, the criterion indicates only what *should not* be done; the agent should not pursue ends that are inconsistent with other ends to which she is committed. This limitation pares away numerous options, to be sure, but it also leaves an indeterminate number from which to choose.

The coincidence of Peirce's view with that of James and Dewey is readily apparent, but there are important differences between them as well. One of these differences may be seen in Peirce's response to Karl Pearson's suggestion that the highest end should be reckoned to be the perpetuation of the biological stock. Peirce asks, "On what principle should it be deemed such a fine thing for this stock to survive—or a fine thing at all[?] Is there nothing in the world or *in posse* that would be admirable per se except copulation and swarming? Is swarming a fine thing at all apart from any results that it may lead to?" (CP, 5.36). This rhetorical question makes several points. One is that an ethical end as Pearson conceives it is *arbitrary*. The highest good is not justified in this conception; it merely accords with human desires and so is intrinsic to the community. But this is not enough in the context of an ethical choice because an ultimate reason for this preference must be forthcoming.

A second point is that this ethical end is in fact *reductive*. It suggests that the highest end of all being coincides with the end (or just the preference) of the human species, which in turn effects an *inversion* of what Peirce thinks is the correct relationship between humankind and the wide universe that sustains it. This inversion takes the latter as a means for the realization of the former when the former should be regarded as a participant in the latter's development of reasonableness in concrete fact. This means that not only are humans not the ultimate end, but also that they may eventually be "cashed out" in the further development of concrete reason (just as so many other species have been).

Each of these criticisms of Pearson may with good reason be turned on James and Dewey. The sort of growth or inclusiveness advocated by each is closely tied to the growth of merely personal and communal satisfaction. Neither writer addresses why these demands should be most highly regarded. Both also may be charged with the reduction and inversion of which Pearson is guilty. Both leave the highest good subject to the community, which is reductive, and thus invert the proper relationship between the community and the wider universe of being. Peirce's point in making these distinctions is twofold. On one hand, it is important that the ideal making criticism possible lies in some respects beyond the actual community in order for the criticism to be real. If it lies within the actual range of preferences of a given community, then it can become, instead of critique, just another form of legitimation for already going forms of practice. The ideal becomes defined as just what the community happens to believe rather than what the community ought to think regardless of how it does actually believe.

On the other hand, Peirce thinks that even if preservation is wanted, then it cannot be achieved by making this more limited goal the end of all inquiry and action. Rather, one must pursue the more inclusive end in order to make possible the actualization of the more limited one. This pursuit, of course, does not guarantee it will be reached, for the growth of reasonableness possibly includes the extinction of humankind, and Peirce did not himself think this the highest end. Other ideals are surely far more worthy of instantiation in the actually existing world than is merely continuing the existence of a mass of people regardless of the actual conditions of their lives. What is wanted are *good* forms of life, ones that are really inclusive and not mere subsistence.

How, then, does inclusivity function as a tool for the criticism of representation? First, as we have seen, representing is a kind of act. It is a constructive effort by some members of the community on behalf of themselves and others to represent some portion of reality in a particular way. Such realities are polysemic, and real choices have to be made as to which elements—which actual facts, what qualities, and what tendencies—are going to be foregrounded in the representation. In chapter 4, I made a bid for inclusivity in the sense of including a great deal in the construction of representations, such as who is doing it, what sorts of limitations it was produced under, and what kind of reach it is expected to have. This inclusivity makes for better and more reflexive depictions of the real. In this context, inclusivity is different. Here it directs agents to privilege those features of the real in their representations that will contribute to what Peirce calls the growth of concrete reasonableness. Conversely, it criticizes those representations that hinder the extension of such inclusion.

Choosing ends in light of concrete reasonableness amounts to choosing those that "*would* be pursued under all possible circumstances" (EP2, 202). This means choosing the end that contributes not only to the growth of the self but also to the growth of those other persons who are affected by one's actions (including the act of representation) because otherwise this end cannot be consistently pursued. If the end were in some respect merely private, then it would eventually come up against others' representations, and a real choice would have to be made. When representations conflict, the one that tends toward better achieving the more inclusive end is the one to be selected, and in the ongoing process of comparing and criticizing representations, inclusivity should really grow. As discussed in chapter 4, in the context of representations of *carnaval,* for example, the "official story" can be accused of being inadequate, overly general, naively one-sided.

Here that same story can be specifically criticized for the ways in which it, through its mediation of persons' actions, reinscribes the inequity experienced by the marginalized of Bom Jesus (especially during the festival). Scheper-Hughes's representation is the better one, not only because it is more reflexive, but also because if persons' actions were to be mediated by her representation rather than by the official one, then those conditions would *tend* to be better addressed. These realities thus would tend to improve for those persons, which would contribute to the growth not only of individuals but also of the community as well. This is, as I understand it, what is meant by the growth of concrete reasonableness. Applied as a criterion, concrete reasonableness seeks out one-sided power relations that arbitrarily privilege the lives of some over others and subverts those relations by offering better representations of the reality in question. In order to have these effects, the representations must be more adequate, more reflexive, but must also be in accord with ethical ends. They must really *seek* inclusion in the future.

In this framework, we do not have to choose, for example, between Catherine's form of representation and the reality it sustains and our own. Every community sustains a history of practices that are truly mixed. Some of these practices may well be deeply worthy of approval, whereas others may deserve our strongest criticism. And the same may be said of individuals. As Cornel West points out, George Washington is *both* deserving of our admiration for continuing the fragile but precious experiment of democracy *and* fit to be criticized as deeply immoral for having been a slave owner. The burden is to recognize both of these views even while, as Fitzgerald writes, retaining the capacity to function. Strands of a tradition, however distant from our own, may be held up as worthy of preservation, of imitation by us, in our efforts to develop a truly more inclusive community, but others can be actively subverted.

We may ask, for example, whether or not Saint Catherine's representation was truly a good representation of the reality in which she participated. Bracketing the question of the adequacy of that representation (i.e., whether or not the event really happened), this query amounts to asking whether or not this way of representing the real contributed to the growth of the community that sustained Saint Catherine. The answer, and this is quite important, depends on the values cherished by the community. Whatever those values were, did this form of representation, by mediating the actions of individual persons, contribute to their growth? Were more members of the community really able to participate in those values? If so, and to whatever degree, then these representation were, on this score, good ones. Beyond this sort of criticism, Peirce's pragmatism has nothing to say about ethics in terms of normative criteria from the outside. Peirce writes that "it appears to me that any aim whatever which can be consistently pursued becomes, as soon as it is unfalteringly adopted, beyond all possible criticism, except the quite impertinent criticism of outsiders" (EP2, 202). So long as the course may be consistently adopted and thereby contributes to the growth of reasonableness, it is beyond criticism; so long as a representation or practice of representation possesses this tendency, it is beyond criticism—at least in ethical terms, anyway.

Nevertheless, I do not think that the significance of this criterion is minor. On the contrary, it provides a tool for criticism that, in the face of an extraordinarily complex reality and widely differing representations of it, allows some basis for choice and action other than adequation. Rather than going relativist or just "punting" on the matter altogether, it directs us toward the construction of more inclusive representations in order to produce really more inclusive realities. This is no small order, and if the criterion really does achieve this goal, then by its own standard it is worthy of our approval. Again, it is useful to contrast this model and Richard Rorty's. In the context of normative considerations concerning a good or true representation, Rorty says the following:

> Is there a way to resolve this standoff between the traditional view that it is always in point to ask "How do you know?" and the view that sometimes all we can ask is ' "Why do you talk that way?" Philosophy, as a discipline, makes itself ridiculous when it steps forward at such junctures and says that it will find neutral ground on which to adjudicate the issue. It is not as if the philosophers had succeeded in finding some neutral ground on which to stand. It would be better for philosophers to admit there is no *one* way to break such standoffs, no single place to which it is appropriate to step back. (1989, 51)

Rorty is surely right to say that there is no neutral ground for making the decisions of which values to hold in what relation from outside of the community. These decisions are specific to the actual historical communities, and it indeed would be foolish—and would lack epistemological tact—to pretend that it were otherwise in order to sustain a philosophical discourse about how to determine the one best way to live.

But once again there seems to be a dilemma in place, one that is not necessary. For Rorty, either one has such a secure place, or there are no criteria available of any sort to adjudicate between representations, to ask intelligibly the question, "How do you know that that is the best possible representation of the situation?" But the view offered here, and I would argue that this view is far closer to that constructed by the classical American pragmatists, is that a general criterion is applicable. Given the values sustained by the community, we may ask which of these values are the more inclusive. Which values bring growth, by which I mean joy in the present and real possibilities for further development in the future, for all the members of the community in question? Those values, I say, are to be privileged above the others.

Of course, there is much more to be said about this view. What has been discussed here, within the narrow confines of this chapter, has been but a single cross-section of what the pragmatists say about ethics. There is more. But what has been said should go some distance toward showing that the situation is not so dire as Rorty would have it; that there are means at hand for intelligent discrimination among competing representations of the real; and that following these guidelines in our everyday conduct will go toward preserving and further cultivating those features of our tradition and the traditions of others that are most worthy of our immediate attention. In short, it will go toward the sacred, ultimate aim not only of the community generally but of those who participate in the tradition of philosophical reflection: amelioration.

Notes

CHAPTER ONE

1. Although the discussion in this chapter focuses on a response to concerns that may emerge from the viewpoint of the philosopher of science, one might also address this issue from a specifically feminist standpoint as well. How, for example, can one reasonably expect someone to view reality independently of the influence of social categories of interpretation and of the authority that comes with occupying any actual social position? To claim that the constraints of class, gender, color, sexual orientation, colonialism, and practices of professionalization (where some gain the "credentials" to speak authoritatively about others) may be somehow "bracketed" seems rather implausible for reasons demonstrated by both feminists and postmodernists. I have chosen to address the philosopher of science because I think that this response may, mutatis mutandis, also satisfy feminist social theorists' concerns as well. It also seems the more inclusive choice because some of the philosophers of science addressed are also feminist and use Kuhn to advance criticism of both the scientific and philosophical communities.

2. For more on Kuhn and science, see, for example, Longino 1990, 26–27, and Harding 1986, 201–10. Longino has showed both that the issue is more complicated than depicted here and that it may be resolvable on its own terms, but the present account suffices for my purposes.

3. This discussion might also be developed in light of current phenomenological or hermeneutic discourses in which, for example, all seeing is a seeing *as*. Kuhn here serves as a representative of this broadly current critique of intuition or immediate experience.

4. One text that might be thought to strain my interpretation of Peirce occurs at CP 5.122. There he says that "Phenomenology treats of the universal Qualities of Phenomena in their immediate phenomenal character, in themselves as phenomena. It, thus, treats of Phenomena in their Firstness." But Peirce's point here is only that the phenomenon is to be considered apart

from any consideration of actuality, which would be a question involving secondness.

5. I refer here to the view James sets forth in "The Knowing of Things Together," where he claims that "To know immediately, then, or intuitively, is for mental content and object to be identical" (1978, 75–76). Dewey, in "The Postulate of Immediate Empiricism," claims that this form of empiricism "postulates that things—anything, everything, in the ordinary or non-technical use of the term 'thing'—are what they are experienced as" (1973, 241). Both introduced this view in order to distinguish the relation of experience from the more specific one of knowledge, which surely tempers their claim to immediacy. The point here is that Peirce never suggested immediacy of any sort except brute resistance, which is itself an abstraction from experience.

6. This fact goes unnoticed. John Boler's (1963) excellent work on Peirce and his relationship to Duns Scotus, for example, does not recognize his early nominalism. Nevertheless, as Fred Michael points out, before 1868 Peirce more resembled Ockham in his position on universals. See W1, 180, and Michael 1988, 317–18. See also Fisch 1986, 184–97, for a full discussion of Peirce's progress from nominalism to realism.

7. Peirce in fact distinguishes two orders of categories, a particular and a universal: "there are at least two distinct orders of categories, which I call the particular and the universal. The particular categories form a series, or set of series, only one of each series being present, or at least predominant, in any one phenomenon. The universal categories, on the other hand, belong to every phenomenon, one being perhaps more prominent in one aspect of that phenomenon than another but all of them belonging to every phenomenon" (CP, 5.43). In this chapter and throughout this book, only the universal categories are treated.

8. This description diverges from Dewey's account of Peirce, but it seems to me that Dewey is mistaken when he claims that "Quality or Firstness *per se* is neither individual nor general" (1960, 202). Peirce claims that it is his admission of qualities as general that separates him from Scotus. Scotus escapes nominalism by only a hair's breadth precisely because he claims that natures in themselves are neither individual nor particular. Peirce is extreme because he claims qualities are real and general, as such both apart from instantiation and as instantiated (CP, 8.11).

9. In his lecture "Philosophy and the Conduct of Life," Peirce is hostile toward Plato with regard to minor issues but claims that no philosopher has ever better articulated what the ultimate purpose and importance of science is; to this claim he adds that Aristotle's criticisms, though warranted, leave

untouched the lodestar of Plato's philosophy. This definitive view, according to Peirce, "results from the correction of that error of Heraclitus which consisted in holding the continuous to be Transitory and also from making the being of the Idea potential" (EP2, 37). It is Plato's insistence on real continuity that Peirce finds so important. There is nothing *purely* individual, so things must be genuinely related, or continuous, with parts of their environings.

10. I think a parallel useful for the reader may be drawn to Whitehead's construction of abstract hierarchies in *Science and the Modern World* (1953, 167–72).

11. This example is taken from Friedman 1995. For this example and others, see especially 382–84.

12. See also "Issues of Pragmaticism" (1905), where Peirce claims, "The Kantist has only to abjure from the bottom of his heart the proposition that a thing-in-itself can, however indirectly, be conceived; and then correct the details of Kant's doctrine accordingly, and he will find himself to have become a Critical Common-sensist" (CP, 5.452).

CHAPTER TWO

1. Andrew Reck introduced this argument in his article "Being and Substance." There he claimed that the metaphysics of process simply cannot match the metaphysics of substance in terms of what it is that must be explained. He wrote, "One of Paul Weiss's most memorable contributions to philosophy is to be found in his early book, *Reality*, where he incisively criticized Whitehead's equation of reality with process [as does Rosenthal]. Weiss said, 'The fundamental temporal fact is not the passage of events, but the occurrence of changes in persistent substantial individuals'" (1978, 546). Reck's point, which is mine as well, is that process, although advertising itself as a more inclusive, richer, "concrete" view of reality, is in fact *reductive*. It equates reality with change and thereby cashes out other (perhaps more) fundamental features of the real.

2. One may also draw on the work of Jacques Derrida, in particular his essay "Structure, Sign, and Play," to make points similar to those James makes in this section. I employ James in this case primarily because Derrida's account would require far more elucidation that can be devoted to it here. See Derrida 1978, 278–82.

3. See *Feminist Epistemologies* (Alcoff and Potter 1993) and *Feminism and Philosophy* (Tuana and Tong 1995) for a range of examples of feminist moral theorists and epistemologists drawing on sex or gender and for a departure from going phallocentric positions.

4. Butler's views are notoriously difficult to understand and represent, and what appears in this chapter necessarily presumes a certain familiarity with her work. For further explication and criticism, see chapter 4 of William Turner's *A Genealogy of Queer Theory* (2000).

CHAPTER THREE

1. For discussion of Peirce's development of a truly general theory of signs and important differences between early and later formulations, see Colapietro 1989 (especially chapter 1) and 1996a, 129–40; Fisch 1986, 321–55; and Short 1981, 197–219.

2. Peirce does not always treat sign and representamen as synonymous. In his writings on speculative grammar, he explains that a "sign is a representamen with a mental interpretant" (CP, 2.274). This means that all signs are representamens, but not vice versa. The idea is that signs must address persons and have mental interpretants, but representamens do not. As Short points out, however, this way of understanding the popular conception of signs is mistaken, and the distinction is not necessary. In any case, Peirce seems to have used it inconsistently and then abandoned it in 1905. Thereafter *sign* itself is more broadly conceived to include both types of occurrence (Short 1986, 98). In this book, sign and representamen are treated as synonyms.

3. See also Barthes, who writes that "nowadays semiology never posits the existence of a definitive signified. Which means that the signifieds are always signifiers for others, and reciprocally. In reality, in any cultural or even psychological context, we find ourselves confronted with infinite chains of metaphors whose signified is always recessive or itself becoming a signifier" (1973, 199).

4. For more on this point, see Eco's distinction between hermetic drift and Peircean unlimited semiosis in *The Limits of Interpretation* (1994, 27–32). He explains Peirce in terms of the earlier formulation of a ground, which was subsequently dropped for the division of icon, index, and symbol, but the point remains unchanged. See also Colapietro 1996a, 131–33.

5. See Deely 1996, 45–67, for a discussion of biosemiosis and physiosemiosis.

CHAPTER FOUR

1. One may object that I have misrepresented Hartsock here, that she says feminists have a knowledge that simply is not partial, is not perverse. I find her text ambiguous on this point, and I withdraw to the more moderate claim, in part to be hermeneutically safe and in part because the stronger form is not necessary for my purposes.

2. Bar On characterizes the position differently. She describes the theory as oppressed persons giving authority to themselves and then criticizes standpoint because it cannot require that anyone listen to claims made by the marginalized. But as I understand it, these claims are being made more broadly; they are intended as challenging and binding on those in the "center" of the community as well.

3. I have some difficulty accepting that feminist standpoint theory, even as Hartsock offers it, makes such strong a priori claims. But the tendency is certainly present, and it is this tendency that makes the theory attractive.

4. See among other works Chomsky's *On Power and Ideology: The Managua Lectures* (1987). An example in this text occurs on pages 30–33.

5. I am not referring here to theory producers. An important achievement in feminist theory has been the recognition of theory making as a kind of privileged and accountable practice. I don't disagree, but there is a drastic difference between these theory producers and those who people the drama of the New World Order—and we must recognize the differences.

6. It might be objected that I have lost the "bite" of Hartsock's claim of inclusivity, which needs the claim that those who do not have inclusivity have perverse knowledges. But I do not think I have. By *inclusivity*, I mean others' having knowledge about us that we do not have and without which our descriptions of ourselves and others may become perverse.

7. Other cases in other disciplines can be cited as easily. For example, see Helen Longino's (1990, 76–82) attempt to provide methodological rules that factor out the distracting bias that is introduced by forms of authority that reinscribe cultural preferences in the representations produced by supposedly "hard" sciences. The point I make here using Clifford might as easily be made by employing these efforts.

8. See Clifford's chapter "On Ethnographic Self-Fashioning," in which he compares Bronislaw Malinowski to Joseph Conrad (1988, 97–112).

9. Obviously not everyone thinks this of *carnaval,* and in fact an earlier generation thought very much the opposite of this ritual. Interestingly, they thought that there was *no* transgressive value whatsoever in *carnaval;* rather, they insisted that it served only to reinforce traditional structures of power already in place (see Gluckman 1963 for this view).

CHAPTER FIVE

1. For more on this last claim, see Colapietro's *Peirce's Approach to the Self.* He quotes Peirce to this effect: " 'Thought, says Plato, is a silent speech of the soul with itself. If this be admitted immense consequences follow, quite

unrecognized, I believe, hitherto'" (1989, 91). This dialogue is a form of participation in the medium here in question.

2. For a brief introduction to logical positivism and its limitations, see Peter Achinstein's *Concepts of Science: A Philosophical Analysis* (1968, 67–91).

3. For a fuller account, see chapter 1, "Escape from Peril," of Dewey's *Quest for Certainty* (1988c).

4. See Jose Ortega y Gasset's *Historical Reason* (1984) for these and other criticisms of Descartes and Cartesian philosophy in general (especially chapters 1 and 3).

5. See, for example, the condemnation of Benedetta Carlini in 1623 as it appears in Judith Brown's *Immodest Acts* (1986). The author interprets the events surrounding Carlini as the manifestation of lesbian sexuality. It is better interpreted as a breakdown in the shared understandings of the community that sustained Carlini and to which she appealed for approval of her actions and representation.

Bibliography

Achinstein, Peter.
    1968 *Concepts of Science: A Philosophical Analysis.* Baltimore: The Johns
           Hopkins Press.
Alcoff, Linda, and Elizabeth Potter, eds.
    1993 *Feminist Epistemologies.* New York: Routledge.
Anzaldua, Gloria.
    1987 *Borderlands/La Frontera.* San Francisco: Aunt Lute Books.
Aristotle.
    1941 *The Basic Works of Aristotle.* Edited by Richard McKeon. New York:
           Random House.
Bar On, Bat-Ami.
    1993 "Marginality and Epistemic Privilege." In *Feminist Epistemologies,*
           edited by Linda Alcoff and Elizabeth Potter, 83–100. New York:
           Routledge.
Barthes, Roland.
    1973 *The Semiotic Challenge.* Translated by Richard Howard. Berkeley:
           University of California Press.
Bartkey, Sandra.
    1995 "Toward a Phenomenology of Feminist Consciousness." In
           Feminism and Philosophy: Essential Readings in Theory,
           Reinterpretation, and Application, edited by Nancy Tuana and
           Rosemarie Tong, 396–406. Boulder: Westview.
Baxandall, Michael.
    1972 *Painting and Experience in Fifteenth Century Italy.* New York:
           Oxford University Press.
Berkeley, George.
    1979 *Three Dialogues Between Hylas and Philonous.* Edited by Robert
           Merrihew Adams. Indianapolis: Hackett.

Bigwood, Carol.

    1991   "Renaturalizing the Body (with the Help of Merleau-Ponty)."
           Hypatia 6, no. 3 (fall): 54–73.

Boler, John.

    1963   *Charles Peirce and Scholastic Realism: A Study of Peirce's Relationship
           to John Duns Scotus.* Seattle: University of Washington Press.

Bornstein, Daniel.

    1996   Introduction to *Women and Religion in Medieval and Renaissance
           Italy,* edited by Daniel Bornstein and Roberto Rusconi, 1–15.
           Chicago: University of Chicago Press.

Brown, Judith C.

    1986   *Immodest Acts: The Life of a Lesbian Nun in Renaissance Italy.* New
           York: Oxford University Press.

Butler, Judith.

    1990   *Gender Trouble: Feminism and the Subversion of Identity.* New York:
           Routledge.

———.

    1993   *Bodies That Matter: On the Discursive Limits of "Sex."* New York:
           Routledge.

Bynum, Caroline Walker.

    1987   *Holy Feast and Holy Fast: The Religious Significance of Food to
           Medieval Women.* Berkeley: University of California Press.

Cassirer, Ernst.

    1951   *The Philosophy of the Enlightenment.* Princeton, N.J.: Princeton
           University Press.

Chomsky, Noam.

    1987   *On Power and Ideology: The Managua Lectures.* Boston: South End.

Clifford, James.

    1988   *The Predicament of Culture: Twentieth-Century Ethnography,
           Literature, and Art.* Cambridge, Mass.: Harvard University Press.

Cohen, Morris Raphael.

    1964   *Reason and Nature: An Essay on the Meaning of Scientific Method.*
           London: Free Press of Glencoe.

Colapietro, Vincent Michael.

    1989   *Peirce's Approach to the Self.* Albany: State University of New York
           Press.

———.

    1995   "Immediacy, Opposition, and Mediation: Peirce on Irreducible
           Aspects of the Communicative Process." In *Recovering*

Pragmatism's Voice: The Classical Tradition, Rorty, and the Philosophy of Communication, edited by Lenore Langsdorf and Andrew Smith, 23–48. Albany: State University of New York Press.

———.

1996a "The Ground of Semiosis: An Implied Theory of Perspectival Realism?" In *Peirce's Doctrine of Signs: Theory, Applications, and Connections,* edited by Vincent Colapietro and Thomas Olshewsky, 129–40. Berlin: Mouton de Gruyter.

———.

1996b "Peirce the Contrite Fallibilist, Convinced Pragmaticist, and Critical Commonsensist." *Semiotica* 111, nos. 1–2: 75–101.

Crocker, J. C.

1982 "Ceremonial Masks." In *Celebration: Studies in Festivity and Ritual,* edited by Victor Turner, 77–88. Washington, D.C.: Smithsonian Institution Press.

Deely, John.

1996 "The Grand Vision." In *Peirce's Doctrine of Signs: Theory, Applications, and Connections,* edited by Vincent Colapietro and Thomas Olshewsky, 45–67. Berlin: Mouton de Gruyter.

Delaney, C. F.

1993 *Science, Knowledge, and Mind: A Study in the Philosophy of C. S. Peirce.* Notre Dame, Ind.: University of Notre Dame Press.

Derrida, Jacques.

1974 *Of Grammatology.* Translated by Gayatri Spivak. Baltimore: Johns Hopkins University Press.

———.

1978 *Writing and Difference.* Translated by Alan Bass. Chicago: University of Chicago Press.

———.

1991 *A Derrida Reader: Between the Blinds.* Edited by Peggy Kamuf. New York: Columbia University Press.

Descartes, René.

1988 *Selected Philosophical Writings.* Cambridge: Cambridge University Press.

Dewey, John. 1931. *Philosophy and Civilization.* New York: Minton, Balch.

———.

1960 *On Experience, Nature, and Freedom.* Edited with an introduction by Richard J. Bernstein. New York: Bobbs-Merrill.

————.

1973   *The Philosophy of John Dewey.* Edited by John J. McDermott. Chicago: University of Chicago Press.

————.

1980   *Theory of the Moral Life.* New York: Irvington.

————.

1988a *Experience and Nature.* Vol. 1 of *The Later Works.* Carbondale: Southern Illinois University Press.

————.

1988b *Human Nature and Conduct.* Vol. 14 of *The Middle Works.* Carbondale: Southern Illinois University Press.

————.

1988c *The Quest for Certainty.* Vol. 4 of *The Later Works.* Carbondale: Southern Illinois University Press.

————.

1989   *Art as Experience.* Vol. 10 of *The Later Works.* Carbondale: Southern Illinois University Press.

————.

1991   *Logic: The Theory of Inquiry.* Vol. 12 of *The Later Works.* Carbondale: Southern Illinois University Press.

Eco, Umberto.

1994   *The Limits of Interpretation.* Bloomington: Indiana University Press.

Emerson, Ralph Waldo.

1951   *Emerson's Essays.* Introduction by Irwin Edman. 1926. Reprint. New York: Harper and Row.

Fausto-Sterling, Anne.

1993   "The Five Sexes: Why Male and Female Are Not Enough." *The Sciences* (March–April): 20–24.

Ferguson, Kathy.

1993   *The Man Question.* Berkeley: University of California Press.

Fisch, Max H.

1986   *Peirce, Semiotic, and Pragmatism.* Bloomington: Indiana University Press.

Foucault, Michel.

1970   *The Order of Things: An Archaeology of the Human Sciences.* New York: Vintage.

————.

1985   *The Use of Pleasure.* Vol. 2 of *The History of Sexuality.* New York: Random House.

———.

1988   *Politics, Philosophy, Culture.* New York: Routledge.

Friedman, Lesley.

1995   "C. S. Peirce's Transcendental and Immanent Realism." *Transactions of the Charles S. Peirce Society* 31, no. 2 (spring): 374–92.

Frye, Marilyn.

1983   *The Politics of Reality: Essays in Feminist Theory.* New York: Crossing.

Geertz, Clifford.

1973   *The Interpretation of Cultures.* New York: Basic.

Gluckman, Max.

1963   *Order and Rebellion in Tribal Africa.* New York: Free Press of Glencoe.

Goldwasser, Maria.

1975   *O Pacio do Samba: Estudo antropologico da Escola de Samba Estacao Primeira da Manguiera.* Rio de Janeiro: Zahar Editores.

Haack, Susan.

1995   *Evidence and Inquiry: Towards Reconstruction in Epistemology.* Cambridge: Blackwell.

Haraway, Donna.

1997   *Modest_Witness@Second_Millennium.Femaleman_Meets_ OncoMouse.* New York: Routledge.

Harding, Sandra.

1986   *The Science Question in Feminism.* Ithaca, N.Y.: Cornell University Press.

Hartsock, Nancy C. M.

1995   "The Feminist Standpoint: Developing the Ground for a Specifically Feminist Historical Materialism." In *Feminism and Philosophy,* edited by Nancy Tuana and Rosemarie Tong, 69–90. Boulder, Colo.: Westview.

Hausman, Carl F. L.

1991   "Peirce's Evolutionary Realism." *Transactions of the Charles S. Peirce Society* 27, no. 4 (fall): 475–500.

Hausman, Carl F. L., and Douglas Anderson.

1994   "The Telos of Peirce's Realism: Some Comments on Margolis's 'The Passing of Peirce's Realism.'" *Transactions of the Charles S. Peirce Society* 30, no. 4 (fall): 825–38.

hooks, bell.

1984   *Feminist Theory: From Margin to Center.* Boston: South End.

Hookway, Christopher.

1985   *Peirce.* New York: Routledge.

Hulswit, Menno.
    1997   *A Semeiotic Account of Causation: The "Cement of the Universe"*
          from a Peircean Perspective. Nijmegen, Netherlands: Katholieke
          Universitet Nijmegen.
Hume, David.
    1989   *A Treatise of Human Nature.* Oxford: Clarendon.
———.

    1990   *Enquiries: Concerning Human Understanding and Concerning the*
          Principles of Morals. Oxford: Clarendon.
James, William.
    1912   *A Pluralistic Universe.* New York: Longmans, Green, and Co.
———.

    1914   *Pragmatism: A New Name for Some Old Ways of Thinking.* New
          York: Longmans, Green, and Co.
———.

    1950   *The Principles of Psychology.* Vol. 1. New York: Dover.
———.

    1975   *Pragmatism and the Meaning of Truth.* Cambridge, Mass.: Harvard
          University Press.
———.

    1977   *The Writings of William James.* Edited by John J. McDermott.
          Chicago: University of Chicago Press.
———.

    1978   *The Works of William James: Essays in Philosophy.* Cambridge,
          Mass.: Harvard University Press.
Kant, Immanuel.
    1965   *Critique of Pure Reason.* Translated by Norman Kemp Smith. New
          York: St. Martin's.
Kuhn, Thomas.
    1974   *The Structure of Scientific Revolutions.* Chicago: University of
          Chicago Press.
Langsdorf, Lenore, and Andrew Smith, eds.
    1995   *Recovering Pragmatism's Voice: The Classical Tradition, Rorty, and*
          the Philosophy of Communication. Albany: State University of New
          York Press.
Lewis, C. I.
    1929   *Mind and the World Order: Outline of a Theory of Knowledge.* New
          York: C. Scribner's Sons.

Locke, John.
  1975   *An Essay Concerning Human Understanding.* Oxford: Clarendon.
Longino, Helen.
  1990   *Science as Social Knowledge.* Princeton, N.J.: Princeton University
         Press.
MacFarlane, Alan.
  1970   *Witchcraft in Tudor and Stuart England.* London: Routledge and
         Kegan Paul.
Margolis, Joseph.
  1993   "The Passing of Peirce's Realism." *Transactions of the Charles S.
         Peirce Society* 29, no. 3 (summer): 293–329.
McDermott, John J.
  1986   *Streams of Experience: Reflections on History and Philosophy of
         American Culture.* Amherst: University of Massachusetts Press.
Michael, Fred.
  1988   "Two Forms of Scholastic Realism in Peirce's Philosophy."
         Transactions of the Charles S. Peirce Society 24, no. 3 (summer):
         317–48.
Nelson, Lynn Hankinson.
  1990   *Who Knows? From Quine to a Feminist Empiricism.* Philadelphia:
         Temple University Press.
Nietzsche, Friedrich.
  1968   *The Portable Nietzsche.* Edited and translated by Walter Kaufinann.
         New York: Penguin.
Noffke, Suzanne, ed.
  1988   *The Letters of Saint Catherine of Siena.* Vol. 1. Binghamton:
         Medieval and Renaissance Texts and Studies.
Norris, Christopher.
  1987   *Derrida.* Cambridge, Mass.: Harvard University Press.
Ortega y Gasset, José.
  1984   *Historical Reason.* New York: W. W. Norton.
Peirce, Charles Sanders Santiago.
  1931   *Collected Papers of Charles Sanders Peirce.* Vols. 1–6. Edited by
         Charles Hartshorne and Paul Weiss. Cambridge, Mass.: Harvard
         University Press.
———.
  1955   *Philosophical Writings of Peirce.* Edited by Justus Buchler. New
         York: Dover.

————.

  1958 *Charles S. Peirce: Selected Writings.* Edited by Philip P. Wiener.
         New York: Dover.

————.

  1984 *Writings of Charles S. Peirce.* Vol. 1. Edited by Edward C. Moore
         and Max H. Fisch. Bloomington: Indiana University Press.

————.

  1991 *Peirce on Signs.* Edited by James Hoopes. Chapel Hill: University
         of North Carolina Press.

————.

  1992 *Selected Philosophical Writings: 1867–93.* Vol. 1 of *The Essential
         Peirce.* Edited by Nathan Houser and Christian Kloesel.
         Bloomington: Indiana University Press.

————.

  1998 *Selected Philosophical Writings: 1893–1913.* Vol. 2 of *The Essential
         Peirce.* Edited by Nathan Houser and Christian Kloesel.
         Bloomington: Indiana University Press.

Popper, Karl.

  1985 *Popper: Selections.* Edited by David Miller. Princeton, N.J.:
         Princeton University Press.

Potter, Vincent G.

  1996 *Peirce's Philosophical Perspectives.* Edited by Vincent Michael
         Colapietro. New York: Fordham University Press.

Proust, Marcel.

  2003 *In Search of Lost Time.* Vol. 1 of *Swann's Way.* Translated by C. K.
         Scott Moncrieff and Terence Kilmartin. New York: Modern Library.

Reck, Andrew.

  1978 "Being and Substance." *Review of Metaphysics* 31, no. 4: 533–54.

Rescher, Nicholas.

  1978 *Peirce's Philosophy of Science: Critical Studies in His Theory of
         Induction and Scientific Method.* Notre Dame, Ind.: University of
         Notre Dame Press.

Rorty, Richard.

  1979 *Philosophy and the Mirror of Nature.* Princeton, N.J.: Princeton
         University Press.

————.

  1982 *Consequences of Pragmatism (Essays: 1972–1980).* Minneapolis:
         University of Minnesota Press.

———.

    1989   *Contingency, Irony, and Solidarity.* Cambridge: Cambridge University Press.

Rosenthal, Sandra B.

    1986   *Speculative Pragmatism.* Amherst: University of Massachusetts Press.

———.

    1994   *Charles Peirce's Pragmatic Pluralism.* Albany: State University of New York Press.

Said, Edward W.

    1978   *Orientalism.* New York: Vintage.

Santayana, George.

    1955   *Scepticism and Animal Faith: Introduction to a System of Philosophy.* New York: Dover.

Saussure, Ferdinand de.

    1972   *Course in General Linguistics.* La Salle: Open Court.

Savan, David.

    1976   *An Introduction to C. S. Peirce's Full System of Semeiotic.* Toronto: Toronto Semeiotic Circle.

Scheman, Naomi.

    1996   "Though This Be Method, Yet There Be Madness in It: Paranoia and Liberal Epistemology." In *Feminism and Science,* edited by Evelyn Fox Keller and Helen Longino, 203–19. Oxford: Oxford University Press.

Scheper-Hughes, Nancy.

    1992   *Death Without Weeping: The Violence of Everyday Life in Brazil.* Berkeley: University of California Press.

Schopenhauer, Arthur.

    1928   "The Philosophy of Schopenhauer." Edited and with an introduction by Irwin Edman. New York: Modern Library.

Seigfried, Charlene Haddock.

    1990   *William James's Radical Reconstruction of Philosophy.* Albany: State University of New York Press.

Short, T. L.

    1981   "Semeiosis and Intentionality." *Transactions of the Charles S. Peirce Society* 17, no. 3 (summer): 197–223.

———.

    1982   "Life among the Legisigns." *Transactions of the Charles S. Peirce Society* 18, no. 4 (fall): 285–319.

———.

1986 "David Savan's Peirce Studies." *Transactions of the Charles S. Peirce Society* 22, no. 2 (spring): 89–124.

Shusterman, Richard.

1992 *Pragmatist Aesthetics: Living Beauty, Rethinking Art.* Oxford: Blackwell.

Smith, John.

1988 "Jonathan Edwards and the Great Awakening." In *Doctrine and Experience: Essays in American Philosophy,* 7–22. New York: Fordham University Press.

Spelman, Elizabeth.

1988 *Inessential Woman: Problems of Exclusion in Feminist Thought.* Boston: Beacon.

Spinoza, Baruch.

1981 *The Ethics.* N.p.: Joseph Simon.

Tuana, Nancy, and Rosemarie Tong, eds.

1995 *Feminism and Philosophy.* Boulder, Colo.: Westview.

Turner, Victor.

1967 "Carnival, Ritual, and Play in Rio de Janeiro." In *Time out of Time: Essays on the Festival,* edited by Alessandro Felassi, 74–90. Albuquerque: University of New Mexico Press.

Turner, William.

2000 *A Genealogy of Queer Theory.* Philadelphia: Temple University Press.

Walker, Margaret Urban.

1992 "Feminism, Ethics, and the Question of Theory." *Hypatia* 7, no. 3 (summer): 23–38.

———.

1998 *Moral Understandings: A Feminist Study in Ethics.* New York: Routledge.

Whitehead, Alfred North.

1953 *Science and the Modern World.* New York: Free Press.

Wilde, Oscar.

1995 *The Decay of Lying.* New York: Penguin.

Wittgenstein, Ludwig.

1996 *Tractatus Logico-Philosophicus.* New York: Routledge.

Index

{ *199* }

AMERICAN PHILOSOPHY SERIES

Douglas R. Anderson and Jude Jones, series editors

1. Kenneth Laine Ketner, ed., *Peirce and Contemporary Thought: Philosophical Inquiries.*
2. Max H. Fisch, ed., *Classic American Philosophers: Peirce, James, Royce, Santayana, Dewey, Whitehead,* second edition. Introduction by Nathan Houser.
3. John E. Smith, *Experience and God,* second edition.
4. Vincent G. Potter, *Peirce's Philosophical Perspectives.* Edited by Vincent Colapietro.
5. Richard E. Hart and Douglas R. Anderson, eds., *Philosophy in Experience: American Philosophy in Transition.*
6. Vincent G. Potter, *Charles S. Pierce: On Norms and Ideals,* second edition. Introduction by Stanley Harrison.
7. Vincent M. Colapietro, ed., *Reason, Experience, and God: John E. Smith in Dialogue.* Introduction by Merold Westphal.
8. Robert J. O'Connell, S.J., *William James on the Courage to Believe,* second edition.
9. Elizabeth M. Kraus, *The Metaphysics of Experience: A Companion to Whitehead's "Process and Reality,"* second edition. Introduction by Robert C. Neville.
10. Kenneth Westphal, ed. *Pragmatism, Reason, and Norms: A Realistic Assessment—Essays in Critical Appreciation of Frederick L. Will.*
11. Beth J. Singer, *Pragmatism, Rights, and Democracy.*
12. Eugene Fontinell, *Self, God, and Immorality: A Jamesian Investigation.*
13. Roger Ward, *Conversion in American Philosophy: Exploring the Practice of Transformation.*
14. Michael Epperson, *Quantum Mechanics and the Philosophy of Alfred North Whitehead.*